.5

Twic

Daughter

Twice a Daughter

A Search for Identity, Family, and Belonging

Julie Ryan McGue

She Writes Press, a BookSparks imprint
A Division of SparkPointStudio, LLC.

Published 2021

Printed in the United States of America

Print ISBN: 978-1-64742-050-5
E-ISBN: 978-1-64742-051-2
Library of Congress Control Number: 2020921439

For information, address:
She Writes Press
1569 Solano Ave #546
Berkeley, CA 94707

She Writes Press is a division of SparkPoint Studio, LLC.

Twice a Daughter is a work of nonfiction. The scenes recreated in this book are based on my own memories, notes, records, correspondence, and journal entries. All the characters in this book are real people and have not been condensed. Some identifying and non-identifying information have been altered to protect the privacy of those involved.

To Steve,
For urging me to take the first step.

To Jenny,
For walking with me, hand in hand,
until we crossed the finish line.

To my children,
By completing my personal story,
you have the beginning of yours.

We dance around in a ring and suppose,
But the secret sits in the middle and knows.
—Robert Frost

Contents

Part Three: FINDING HIM

Part One

FINDING MY WAY

When you stifle curiosity about yourself,
you stifle many other things as well. You shrink your
area of perception. You live in a smaller space.

~ Betty Jean Lifton, *Lost and Found*

1

The Ask

2008

Latching the narrow gray locker, I slip the curly plastic band with its tiny key over my wrist. My hands shake as I retie the over-laundered smock with its opening in the front. In the waiting area, I join several women dressed in matching hospital gowns. They thumb through outdated magazines or stare at the overhead TV. Neither of which I do. Instead of being here, I wish that I were walking along Hinsdale's streets bursting with purple magnolias and dainty redbuds.

Perching on a vinyl chair, I squeeze my eyes shut, not in a light dreamy way, but willfully to stem a spray of tears. I think about my twin sister and wonder why she's escaped the threatening female health issues I face. For the first time in years, I consider my closed adoption and wonder how my biological background factors into the six areas of concern in my right breast. I pick up the chain of prayers that I began after last week's suspicious mammogram.

When I return from Walgreens after the procedure, Steve's sedan occupies the prime spot under the porte cochere by the side door. I park my Buick behind his car and skirt around both, being extra careful not to jostle my right side. The heavy wooden side door complains as I lean into it. Inside, I breathe in the smell of the old house—the lemony scent of furniture polish and the sweet mustiness of the drapes and carpets. It feels so good to be home. Steve calls out to me from the front of the house.

Kicking off my loafers, I avoid the creaky spots in the wood floor as I head toward his office. I expect to find my husband seated behind the antique desk. He'll either be deep in thought, gazing out at the brick street, or sorting and paying bills on his computer. In the doorway, I finger the crinkly prescription bag in my hands.

His high-back desk chair swivels away from the computer screen. "How did it go?"

"Not my best day." Lifting the sleeve of my red sweater, I swipe at a tear.

It's a few seconds before I realize that my husband of twenty-three years is not rising out of his chair to offer me a careful hug. I can't believe this. I need his compassion right now. After all I've been through today, and now this infuriating insensitivity. My anger flares, and I move closer to his desk. Gripping the edge of the big desk, I spare no detail as I fill him in on my breast biopsy.

"It was just me . . . alone . . . with the nurse and doctor in a cold, dark room . . . in the basement of La Grange Hospital. I bled each time the needle pierced my boob. Three tries to get it right." I scowl at him over his computer.

Adrenaline from my rant courses through my system. Still he doesn't get up. I'm shaking with indignation and hurt. I imagine there's spittle forming on my lower lip. One benefit of being a twin is that you know what you look like when you laugh or let hell fly.

As I wind down, my voice whines. "Waiting five days for biopsy results is inhumane."

Steve leans away from the desk, tilting his chair back. I read something in the dark eyebrows that lift into his receding

4

hairline. I'm too spent to wonder about his expression. All I want is sympathy.

"Sounds like I should have gone with you then." His chair twists ever so slightly.

"I should've insisted." I head for the foyer. "I'm getting an ice-pack and going upstairs."

Steve's reply hits my back. "Are you ready to get at your medical history now?"

As I turn to face Steve, the staple on the prescription bag scratches my palm. "What are you saying?"

His eyes meet mine. "It's time, Julie. You've been delaying this for years. Get your adoption records. Access your family medical history. We have four kids to consider."

I blink. His ultimatum whipsaws me. We haven't had a serious conversation about my closed adoption for a very long time. Not since I sent that letter to the adoption agency eighteen years ago. Since then, my "mystery genes" have become an inside joke, a good-natured riddle that has gifted three of our children with the skill to play college sports. I've been fine without knowing where all that talent came from. Well, sort of.

"You really want to talk about locating my birth parents now? After I've had a biopsy? You have terrible timing."

My husband's bent on honesty at all costs, a result of his military background, is a trait I usually respect and appreciate. Not today.

As I storm toward the stairs, a stream of silent, angry excuses ricochet in my head. *I don't need this stress right now. There are loads of people who don't have a family medical history. It's not like I haven't tried to look into my adoption.*

When I was thirty, my twin sister Jenny and I sent a letter to Catholic Charities in Chicago requesting information about our adoption that occurred in 1959. A month later, we received a one-page reply: *Nothing can be shared at this time.* When I wrote that letter back in the 1980s, Illinois adoption statutes favored the rights of birth and adoptive parents over those of adopted children and adults. Powerless to access personal information from my closed adoption file, I moved on. Eighteen years later and halfway through raising a family of four, I've grown content with the course of my life. Why invite uncertainty and trouble to dinner? To be honest, I haven't been that hungry. Besides, I have my people, the ones who wanted me, me and my twin sister both.

I can't recall when I first learned that I'm adopted. I seem always to have known. Yet my adoption wasn't a topic tossed around the dinner table like the White Sox's standings, or Grandma Mimi's health. What I do remember is that on a handful of occasions, my parents pulled my sister and me into the living room for a private talk. By the second or third time this checking-in occurred, Jenny and I guessed what was in the offing. Our parents would sit stiffly next to one another on the sofa, avoiding our eyes and stealing looks at one another. In these chats, Mom and Dad professed their support should we ever want to look into our roots, but I had the sense that they were muttering a script given to them by a social worker.

Jenny and I were happy kids, and we knew we had a good situation. Strict but kind, our folks weren't shy about telling us how much we meant to them. They encouraged us to take on challenges, and often they had to make sacrifices to make opportunities available to us. I can't think of a time when I wasn't praised for an achievement or a good deed. Throughout my forty-eight years, whenever I've contemplated looking into my adoption, the little voice inside has wagged its finger: *You'll be sorry. They'll think they haven't been good parents.*

Trudging into the master bedroom, I avoid Steve's side of the bed and slip under the king-sized comforter. My temples throb from the spat, and the icepack on my chest does little to dull the ache there. Despite my desire to drift off and postpone thinking about all that the day has ushered in, I reach for the phone. When my call goes to voice mail, I figure that my twin sister is caught up with work stuff.

I lie still for several more minutes, debating, and then dial my mother. "Hey, Mom. How's Dad doing today?" I listen to her answer. "I'm glad. He looked better to me the other day. Do you have a second?" I take a big painful breath. "So . . . to solve a disagreement I'm having with Steve. You know how you've always said you'd help Jenny and me if we wanted to look into our adoption. Well, I'd like to get a hold of my medical background. To do that, I need whatever information you and Dad have in your files."

I blurt all this out, hoping I've muted the stuffiness in my voice.

"Oh . . . my." In Mom's two-word reply, I hear a chasm open. The deep crevice that is my adoption splits the common ground on which we've stood for forty-eight years.

Mom clears her throat, but her voice catches. "Of course." Pause. "I'll talk to your dad when he gets back from physical therapy." She swallows hard. "Is everything all right?"

While I may not have my mother's genes, she's schooled me well in the fine art of pretending. Mom doesn't let on that she knows I've been crying or that I've just pulled the proverbial rug out from under her. In turn, I haven't mentioned today's biopsy—something I plan to reveal later on, if necessary. These matters aside, I can no longer pretend that being adopted is no big deal.

"I'm okay. Steve's point is that I'll be fifty in a few years, so I shouldn't delay." The pain in my chest is building, and I can't wait to get off the phone.

Mom's sigh is heavy. "We'll pull out what we have. It's been here for the asking, you know." With these words, I become that shy, anxious-to-please lanky girl who traded looks with her twin through veils of light brown bangs.

"Thanks, Mom. I'll stop by later in the week. Love you." As I hang up, I hope my heartfelt "Love you" is enough to temper the shock of what I've just asked for.

Next to the phone, I grab the prescription bottle and force down a pain pill. As I sink into the pillows, my mother's final comment hits me like a shattering gust of February wind. Damn. My fist slams into the down comforter, sending shock waves of fluff bounding toward my feet. What a setup. By having me ask for my adoption papers, my folks would know exactly when it was I planned to launch an adoption search. Oh, man! Why couldn't they have turned them over to me when I turned twenty-one, or when I got married at twenty-five? I picture my parents later this evening, sharing a glass of wine, disappointment and unrest souring their day. I tell myself, *None of this is your fault.*

The hallway clock strikes three as a welcome lightness descends from the crown of my head and crawls the length of my spine. Two tough conversations have followed a breast biopsy. Even though I'm battling to keep my eyes open, I detect a heavy tread on the stairs. I twist toward the bedroom door that never seems to stay shut. Steve peeks through the crack.

I smile benignly at him. "I'll have the adoption records later this week."

He steps around to my side of the bed. Looking up at him, I reposition the ice pack on my breast and pull the comforter to my chin. "Can you order Chinese for dinner?"

Steve's fingers enveloping mine are a truce. "Sure thing. You'll be glad you did this, you know."

A tear sneaks out from my closed eyes.

The kiss he plants on my brow is gentle, tender. "Get some rest. I got the kids covered. Dinner, too."

Steve retreats around the stubborn bedroom door, and I think about my families. I grew up in a household where pretending was the prevailing wind, yet I married a man whose core has room only for honesty. Pretending as a way of managing life is in sharp contrast with the tone that we foster in our busy household of six. Honesty can be difficult to face, and it's often ill-timed like today. There is one good thing about being candid, though; it doesn't leave any room for second-guessing.

Glancing around the bedroom I love, I take in the ceiling medallion that looks like whipped cream, the egg-and-dart moldings that edge the plaster walls, and the painted pine fireplace surround. This is the second vintage house in the same Chicago suburb that we've renovated and restored. I reflect on my obsession with old homes, their history and furnishings—things that possess a rich provenance. As I lie here, it occurs to me that perhaps my obsession is not simply with old houses, but a subconscious yearning to own things that have a concrete pedigree. Because of my closed adoption, I have no sense of my personal history. For the second time today, anger sparks. Why have I put up with this? Every person deserves to know all they can about who they are.

I toss the lukewarm ice pack to the carpet and squeeze my eyes shut, determined to rest, but my mind snarls with questions. Why did it take a breast biopsy for me to get serious about challenging my adoption, and how will my adoptive parents deal with the search as it rolls out? I wonder too if my husband is right. Will I be glad one day that I set all this in motion?

2

Intertwined

Despite my comfy bed and pain pill, the nap I need is slow in coming. The unanswerable questions ping in my head as Steve pauses on the staircase landing to rewind the grandfather clock. Too numb to call out and complain, I cover my head with a pillow. The clock, a wedding gift from my parents, still keeps perfect time.

The grandfather clock's glass door clicks shut as the phone on my nightstand rings.

"Jules? How did it go?"

At the sound of my twin sister's voice, I snuggle deeper into the down comforter. My sister's mammograms have been normal so far, and she doesn't have a uterine fibroid that is problematic like mine. The reason for our slightly different health situations is anyone's guess, but I have borne four children to her two. Older by twelve minutes, I figure it's my destiny to be the guinea pig for both of us.

"Hey, Jen."

Hearing my sister's voice is like a salve—it soothes the sore spots of my day. From behind my eyelids, we are silly, young girls again, nestled in our matching canopy beds with the white eyelet comforters and dust ruffles, tossing whispered secrets across the green shag rug between us.

"You sound groggy," Jenny says.

When I talk to my sister on the phone, it's as if I'm replaying the voice mail greeting on the message machine in my kitchen. Our speech patterns and word choices are so aligned that we often confound close family members. These days, it's a regular occurrence that my dad slips up: "Jen?" "Nope. Dad, it's Julie." "Oops. Sorry. You sounded like your sister for a second." These blunders don't offend us. As fraternal twins, we're used to it.

From under the comforter, I whisper to Jenny, "I'm in bed. Took some pain meds. Trying to get a nap in before Danny and Kassie get home from school." I flick the messy bangs that distinguish me from my twin out of my eyelashes.

"Oh. Want me to come over? Pick up dinner?"

"That's a lot of questions, Jen." My sigh contains the slightest giggle.

Besides a similar phone voice, Jenny and I share the same laugh. What begins as a short giggle can rumble into a deep chuckle, not a guffaw and not quite a dirty laugh. If the two of us are together relating a funny story, our humor feeds off one another. As teenagers, our contagious laughter often culminated in snorts, hiccups, and an occasional mad dash to the closest bathroom. Friends, and one particular uncle, found it good sport to tickle our funny bones and then howl at our combined antics.

"Thanks, Jen. I don't need anything. Steve's here. Just wish the biopsy results didn't take so long to get." Foggier by the second, my brain pleads with me to give in to sleep.

"Yeah. Waiting stinks." Jenny's voice trails off and the line is still except for our breaths.

Jenny and I don't usually speak every day. If we do, our contact is brief and involves things like planning the menu for a family gathering or offering concern about Dad's latest health issue. Our lack of daily contact has nothing to do with bickering, competing, or desiring space—it's that Jenny and I relate better in person. We've been fine-tuning our own brand of nonverbal communication since the gibberish and gestures we tossed through the rungs of our matching cribs.

An eye roll with an arched eyebrow means something different than a quick, sideways glance. And then, there's the twisted corner on a smile, a chin that juts just so, a thumb that disappears into a fist, and the head that tilts left not right. For my twin sister and me, mannerisms combined with select phrases and just the right dose or lack of inflection convey more meaning than a full conversation. We don't just get one another—it's as if we are in each other's skin.

"Jen, before you go, I have to give you a heads up! Because of this biopsy, Steve insists that I dig into our adoption. You know, get a sense of our medical history? Before you called, I talked with Mom. She promised to pull out the documents they have in their files." Just thinking about the tense conversation with my mother has me snuggling deeper into my warm cocoon.

"Oh, man. How'd that go?"

I fill her in. I imagine Jenny's heavy-lidded eyes fluttering shut just as mine do in the retelling. The weight of what I've done, calling our mom and asking for our adoption papers, is a shocking sequel to a breast biopsy.

"I'm going to head over Thursday to pick up whatever they have." My intonation suggests that I expect Jenny to join me.

"I'm traveling to Minneapolis tomorrow through Friday," she says.

I'm torn. I really want her by my side, but I also want to get the conversation with my folks done and over with.

"Want me to wait?" I ask.

Jenny pauses. I bet she's twisting her hair behind an ear. "Maybe it's better if I have my own conversation with Mom and Dad?"

Now, it's my turn to hesitate. With Jenny's question, she's offered me the reins, told me she's comfortable in the passenger seat. I think about this. Hadn't I already led by phoning Mom? Yet, what would my sister's presence add besides offering me moral support? Through the barely closed bedroom door, the grandfather clock chimes four times. In cahoots with the clock, the voice in my head pounds: You . . . can . . . do . . . this!

I whisper my decision. "All right. We can compare notes afterward."

"Go back to your nap, Jules. Call me later if you need anything." Before she disconnects, Jenny says, "Sorry you're going through this."

I swallow hard. "Me too. Thanks."

After my sister's call, I punch the unwieldy king pillow, flatten a spot for my head, and drift off. In my dreams, I'm ten again. Jenny and I hop aboard our Schwinn two-wheelers. Hers is purple and mine is hot pink, still my favorite color. Our thin, fine braids flap behind us, beating our backs like drums. We lock our bikes at the library in downtown La Grange and return a stack of Nancy Drews, which are strangely overdue—we hated dipping into our allowance for late fees. Popping in at the candy shop on the main street, we count out pennies and nickels for jujubes, lemon drops, and red licorice. We race each other the few blocks back home. Instead of going into the house, we park our bikes across the street at the park. Suddenly, my pink bike morphs into something resembling the biopsy machine, and it won't budge. Entangled in the spokes of the front wheel is a fabric identical to the hospital gown. Once I free the wheel and move to unlock my bike, the key dangling from my curly wristband doesn't fit in the bike lock.

Chimes blast through this wild, nonsensical dream. Westminster chimes. Five of them, followed by a squeaky door hinge and the clattering of the bedroom door hitting the door stop.

"Mommm!" My youngest daughter, Kassie, rockets into the room and hovers at my side of the bed. She takes in the ice pack on the floor, the arm I throw protectively over my chest, and the medicine bottle on the nightstand.

"Dad got Chinese from Jade Dragon. I set the table. He said we're ready to eat. Are you coming down?" The tips of her blond braids are wet from laps in the pool, and her cheeks crinkle from dried chlorine.

"Did you shower at the pool?" I can't help myself. Her golden hair will take on a greenish hue before summer begins.

"No. Dad told me to hurry. I'll do it after dinner. I promise." Giving her a small smile, I reach for her pudgy palm. "Danny's starving. Are you coming?" She holds my hand gently like she's holding a glass too full of milk.

"Yes. Will you take this ice pack down and put it in the freezer for me?" Flipping back the duvet, I sit gingerly on the edge of the warm bed. I shudder, trying to clear my head of drugs and dreams.

Kassie studies me. "Mommy, are you going to be okay?"

I look up into Kassie's eyes, eyes that are not green or brown, but something in between. Flecked with gold around the irises, my youngest daughter's eyes match mine and Jenny's and Danny's, hazel eyes no doubt passed down to us from a birth relative I hope to find. I consider Kassie's question. I have no idea what my husband has said about my breast biopsy to either of the last two kids in our emptying nest.

The answer I offer is not premeditated. "The doctor did a test today. Kind of like a shot. To make sure I don't have poison in my body." Drawing her in close, I pat her damp frizzy braids.

Into her hair, I whisper, "I'll be fine. Let's go eat. I hope Dad got pot stickers." I squeeze her hand and offer a wide smile meant to erase her fears.

My daughter's small fingers lace into mine, and we plod to the stairs. This is when I realize that Steve is right—was right—to insist that I gather more details about my heritage. Avoiding an adoption probe for fear of hurting my adoptive parents isn't valid given my health concerns: suspicious breast tissue and an ornery uterine fibroid. My husband's timing may be poor, but his logic is spot on. I owe this twelve-year-old, my teenage son, and two college-aged daughters every ounce of information that might affect the quality of their lives. That I might have an obligation to myself seems secondary, but the pulse in my right breast suggests otherwise.

As I descend the stairs to the kitchen, something stirs in my belly besides hunger. It's a quickening, a rustling. I test it. It is not anger. No, it's less than that, smaller, more like indignation. Haven't my birth circumstances and family medical history been owed me since the day I was born? I pray that my parents' file addresses some of my questions, and I wish I'd been given the file long before now.

My thoughts go to my sister. Jenny and I have been together since before we were born. That single fact makes being adopted a different equation for us. Like other adoptees, we've always been curious about where we came from and why we were placed for adoption, but it didn't seem to slow us down. By traversing through life with a sibling with whom you're aligned in looks, thoughts, habits, and deeds, you're a little less likely to get hung up on the sharp edges of adoption. We have always belonged to each other. Jenny and I will figure out this adoption search thing, and we'll do it together.

When I enter the kitchen, the large table is set for four. I find my seat at one end and another worry enters my mind: I hope I haven't waited too long.

3

The Paperwork

My heart beats double time as I sign my name in the visitor log and head toward the independent living unit where my parents live. Since Monday's call to my mother, I've been rehearsing the comments I wish to make tonight. I'm uncertain which has preoccupied my thoughts more these past three days: waiting for the biopsy results or gearing up for this event—the handoff of my adoption papers from my aging parents to me. Neither obstacle was on the horizon three months ago when Jenny and I celebrated our forty-eighth birthday together. As I near my parents' apartment, I speculate how many other adult children like me have loitered in this hallway, mustering doorstep courage before discussing vital family matters like wills, powers of attorney, long-term care insurance, and adoption papers.

As I shift from one foot to the other, I consider what awaits me behind the wide door with its centered peephole and brass knocker. Dad might be reading another thriller or blasting the White Sox spring opener, his ill-fitting hearing aids lying somewhere other than in his ears. Mom could be thumbing through the mail-order catalogs stacked on the coffee table. Or together, they might be flipping through the yellowing sheets of my adoption papers, planning what to say to me tonight. By now, they're probably studying their watches, figuring that the evening stream of commuter trains has made me late again.

As I reach for the doorknob, I chastise myself for letting Steve pressure me into tackling this adoption search now, and I wonder if the speech I've prepared is good enough to soothe the hurt and doubt that I suspect my parents are experiencing. I hope my parents are remembering me as the good student that I was throughout my school years—the diligent, reliable, commended leader, rarely in trouble, but who was often a tiny bit sassy. I think of the pride they've expressed in having me as their daughter, but maybe tonight they view me as a malcontent or a troublemaker. Surely, they know my goal is not to recycle them as parents.

"Helloooo. It's Julie. I'm here." My voice sounds too loud, too cheerful.

Alone in the tiny foyer, I glimpse into the entry mirror. I see a pale, nearly middle-aged woman who recently started wearing reading glasses. She looks like she could use a hug. I pinch color into her cheeks, offer her a weak smile, and nod my head in encouragement.

"We're in the sitting room." Mom's tone is distant, crisp.

"Hi, Jules," Dad booms.

I shout out, "Be right there."

Dropping my purse on a chair in the kitchenette, I yank out my water bottle. Dad's hearing aids sit in a saucer by the coffeepot. As I turn toward the den's open door, my heart resumes the gallop that began in the lobby. Before entering the den, I pass the large framed photo of my folks' beloved summer cottage on Lake Michigan. Purchased thirty years ago when I was a teenager, it's our family's collective happy place. I breeze toward it, gulping in the details I know by heart: the deep front deck with its cutout for a stately old oak, aluminum siding the color of buttercream, and shutters Mom

17

stained to mimic the blue that's inside a tumbling wave. My fingers graze the photo's wooden frame, as if touching the likeness of our family icon will grant me luck tonight.

In the sitting room, Mom's gaze is slow to lift from the catalogue on her lap. "Come! Sit down. Would you like a drink?" She means a real one, not the wimpy sparkling water I prefer.

I hold up the plastic water bottle. "Nope. I'm good."

"Huh?" Dad's blue eyes shift from my mother to me.

Mom grimaces. "Where are your hearing aids, dear?"

"They're in the kitchen. I'll get them," I say.

Grateful for something to do, I bring the saucer from the kitchen and hand them to my dad, who's baked into his new specialty recliner. As I fix a light kiss on his forehead, I catch a whiff of the Vicks VapoRub which Mom smears daily onto his back. Rounding the coffee table, I set a matching kiss on the cheek Mom offers me, and then I consider the seating options.

There's ample space on the floral loveseat next to Mom, but sitting there will put my mother between my dad and me, and then I won't have a clear view of either of them. Around the coffee table piled high with magazines, Catholic pamphlets, and catalogues are a pair of upholstered parlor chairs, dainty and uncomfortable. Staying clear of the aging white terrier snoozing under Mom's feet, I slide Dad's chair out from under the pine desk. It's impossible not to scan the papers strewn across the desktop, but I don't see anything resembling adoption papers. This afternoon, Mom assured me Dad had everything ready.

I roll the chair over to complete our family triangle. As many times as I've sat with Dad poring over their bills and finances, it never occurred to me to snoop through his desk. If I were to pull out one of the many deep drawers, perhaps I'd find a file folder for each of my siblings and me. Maybe the folders of the three oldest Ryan children would be thicker than the other three because of our adoption documents. I think about my brother, two years younger than Jenny and me, who is also adopted and an alum of St. Vincent's Orphanage. After tonight, perhaps my folks will turn over his documents to him. Like me, he'd like to have them, but he's been reluctant to ask.

The rattle of the desk chair rouses the whiskered Westie. A paw's length away, her milky eyes are level with my ankles. As I settle into the desk chair, the plastic water bottle in my hand snaps and crackles. The dog's shaggy head pops up and her growl exposes small sharp teeth.

"Enough, Maggie!" Mom scolds. The dog snuggles her head back between her paws, but she narrows her eyes on my water bottle and me.

Dad mumbles. "I think I'll go to the bathroom and put my hearing aids in. Julie, you sit. I'll be just a minute." Dad fumbles for the tripod cane hooked to the arm of his recliner and Mom leaps to her feet, but he waves her off.

With Dad in the washroom, my mom gets up and straightens the framed family photos on the end table by Dad's recliner. When my father flips the switch on his newfangled chair, it launches him to a standing position. In the process, objects rattle and fall to the carpet. This time, it's the preschool headshot of my dead sister. Mom rights Susie's image and then places it back in its spot of honor. I swallow hard.

The three decades since my youngest sister's sudden death have been ripe with family challenges: two divorces, Dad's strokes, job firings, relocations, and much more. Since downsizing my parents from their home into this senior living center unit, there's been a welcome calm, one that my siblings and I are careful not to disrupt. By asking for my adoption papers, I risk plunging my mother into another one of her gloomy spells. None of us wants that. My hand creeps up to my right breast. The pain pill I took this afternoon has worn off, reminding me that I'm not here to stir up trouble. I'm here to ensure my kids and me have our full medical background.

"How's Danny's baseball season shaping up?" Mom asks as she straightens the other photos on the end table.

"He's hitting the ball well. The varsity coach should start him, but he told Steve the other night that this might be his last season. He wants to concentrate on football—thinks he has a shot at playing college ball."

At seventeen, Danny excels at most sports; keeping him focused on schoolwork is why he attends Benet—the same college prep high school that his older sisters, Colleen and Molly, attended.

"Your dad will be thrilled to hear that, honey."

With the table back to normal, my mother reaches for the bottle of Woodbridge chardonnay nestling on a crocheted doily. Mom swirls the goblet and steals a healthy gulp before my dad returns.

I look over at the door as Dad, dubbed "Chief" by one of my brothers when I was in high school, scuffs into the den. Heaving himself into the recliner, he clears his throat and reaches for the manila folder I hadn't noticed wedged into his chair. I peek over at my mother. She sits upright, her back rigid against the loveseat with her fingers curled tight around the throat of the wine goblet. How did we get to this point in our lives, and how will we navigate around the bundle of doubts cluttering the sitting room? Should I begin? I cross my legs and stuff sweaty palms under each thigh. I know I must look like the child I have become inside: shy, fearful of wrongdoing, and always eager to please.

"Julie, this is the file I have on your adoption. I made a separate one for Jenny, who's coming on Sunday. Your mother and I will help in any way we can." Dad's clear blue eyes meet mine. Behind his glasses, tears merge with the dark frames.

"Ah, Dad." I know what's coming.

"Adopting your sister and you was the best thing that ever

happened to your mother and me." Since his stroke, emotion comes easily and often. So does repetition. "While we were stationed in Germany, your mother and I took a side trip to Lourdes, France." His bad hand trembles, and the good one dabs a tissue under his glasses.

Mom nods and sips her wine. "Go on, dear."

"At Lourdes, we joined hundreds at the shrine. Everyone was praying to Our Lady for a miracle. Your mom had experienced several miscarriages by then, so we prayed for a family. When we returned to Chicago, we started the adoption process. I'll never forget the call from Catholic Charities, asking if we'd take twins." Dad's voice catches, so Mom finishes the rehash of the family legend.

"When I asked the social worker what your birthdate was, I knew it was our prayers come to fruition: February eleventh, the Feast Day of Our Lady of Lourdes. You were only three weeks old when we took you home from St. Vincent's."

A shiver runs down my back.

To my parents, the significance of my birthday is not a coincidence. It's proof of the power of prayer. For me, it's less of a divine sign and more of a warning that there's much we don't know about the workings of the universe. My folks' belief in prayer and our inevitable connection fills the cozy den. I'm certain of three things: my parents' love for me, their belief that I was destined to belong to them, and my place in the family they wove together.

As we're reluctant to break the spell, all eyes follow the movements of Maggie, the aging terrier. She swats her paw against my mother's pant leg, and Mom picks her up.

"Mom and Dad. I wanted to make sure . . . that you know . . . that asking for my adoption papers has nothing to do with how I feel about you as parents." My voice breaks a little, and Dad gives me a doting smile. "The purpose of getting into my adoption is to get some medical history." My eyes dart toward Mom, but she's busy situating the dog into the crook of her arm.

In truth, the idea of accessing my biological family's medical history has unearthed more complicated thoughts and emotions. For the past three days, it's as if someone has turned on a spigot in a remote area of my brain. Day and night, my mind races from one "what if" scenario to the next. The desire for medical information involves not just locating my birth parents but also communicating with them, and that realization has led to fantasies about meeting and getting to know them.

Almost like a prayer, my palms meet at my chest. "I promise to let you know how this goes, every step of the way."

I nod at both of them and infuse my smile with as much reassurance as I can muster. I glance at Mom who's gazing at the dog cuddled in her arms like a baby. She strokes Maggie's back, consoling away the canine's irrational fear of loud noises. My mother scratches the dog behind the ears, and I wonder if it's only the dog's insecurities she soothes. Her refusal to make eye contact with me feels like a reprimand.

Ignoring my mother and the dog, I step quickly over to my father's chair, and he hands me the folder. I draw it to my chest. The weight of it is nothing, but the feel of it is everything. I lean over and kiss Dad, and then I massage his shoulder. His dimples deepen, and he reaches up and pats my hand. Ever so slightly, his head nods as if indicating everything is okay and it will be all right going forward. Returning to the wobbly desk chair, I cross my legs and tuck the file under clasped hands.

When it's time for me to go, the three of us circulate around my father's lounge chair. I hover behind Dad, my arm resting along his shoulders. My fingers graze the bare spot in the chair where his head has made an indentation in the fabric.

"Bye, honey. Talk to you tomorrow," Mom says as she leashes the dog.

The pair weaves to the apartment door for Maggie's evening

pee-pee walk. The moody terrier stalls, planting a reluctant hind-quarter onto the welcome mat.

"Come now, Maggie." Mom digs into her pocket for a treat. With Maggie coaxed into cooperating, the door closes behind the old dog and my mother as they leave.

My father's good hand, the one unscathed from the last series of TIAs, reaches to mine.

"Dad, do you really think Mom is all right with my digging into all this?" I wait for his answer, but my mind is more focused on getting inside my parked car and perusing the file.

"She'll be fine. We both knew this day might come. Getting at your medical background is important. We understand that. I'm fine with it." He strokes the back of my hand like it's a silk scarf.

"Thanks, Dad."

As I sandwich his withered hand in mine, I note the age spots and throbbing raised veins. These are the same hands that dragged me to swim lessons, that shared a bag of Twizzlers on the cottage porch, and that adeptly placed winning tiles in family Scrabble games.

"You know your mother," he begins. "She's never gotten over the loss of Susie. Anything that threatens the dynamics of the family knocks her off-kilter. She doesn't want to lose you." His eyes close under the spilled truths.

"Yes. I'm sure you're right, Dad." Lifting my purse to my shoulder, I finger the file. "Shall I put the wine in the fridge on my way out?"

"You better, I think." I lean over for one last hug, hoping that his evening isn't completely spoiled.

"Thanks for this." I lift the prized folder, waving it at him like a winning lottery ticket. "Love you."

"God bless you," he says. His good hand lifts, and the palm is toward me, like a high five or a truce or a blessing. Maybe all of them rolled into one.

When he utters those words, "God bless you," it's as if I've returned to my child-self, the tall, skinny girl with braids whom he tucked into a canopied bed across from my twin sister. Life was simpler when Jenny and I were young. There were no threatening medical concerns. No need to consider a mysterious gene pool, and no tricky adoption search path to navigate.

As I step into the corridor, that nagging inner voice wags its finger at me again: *This is not going to be easy.*

4

What It Isn't

Before the door of my parents' apartment clicks shut, I'm halfway down the hallway with the folder pressed to my chest. The corridor is empty. Even if there were onlookers, I would still bypass the lobby, skip the mandated sign-out procedure, and rush to my car. The anticipation of opening the folder has moved the throbbing in my breast up to my temples. As I head toward the emergency exit door, I send up a quick plea: Please, please let it contain some medical background, so my search can end here.

I barrel through the cumbersome door, and gusts of cool spring air swirl around me. At the far end of the parking lot, where the line of handicapped spots end, sits my Buick. When I climb in that car, I'm going to forget about Dad's fragile health, my mother's moods, and that today is day three in the five-day test result window given me by my surgeon. All I want is to study the folder.

Alongside my car, I fumble with my purse, the folder, and my water bottle as I search for my car fob. Fearing that I left it in my folks' apartment, I have frantic thoughts of a redo—the lobby sign-in process, the long walk to the apartment, and another good-bye. My jaw feels like it's set in a vise.

"You've got to be kidding," I say to myself.

I pat down the pockets of my windbreaker and discover a familiar bulge. In the driver's seat, I breathe. *I'm in. I have the folder.* Using the steering wheel as a desk, I pull out the first document, a single sheet of blue card stock folded in thirds around tissue-thin typed pages. The deeply creased stack looks like it has not been opened in ages. I peek at the white papers, guessing at the page count—a dozen or so. That's all it took to legalize a closed adoption in 1959. I flip up an edge of the blue stock and run a fingertip along the bottom line of the first page. Imbedded in the velum, the black typeface is like braille. As I hold the fragile papers, I hesitate to unwrap the rest for fear of tearing the truths printed here.

When I'm smoothing out the last crease in the blue card stock, my phone rings through the car's speakers. It's Jenny. For a second, I consider letting voice mail claim the call.

"Hey," I say.

"Did you get it?" Jenny asks.

"You sound like you're in a bar or a tunnel."

"At the airport. Meeting's wrapped up. I'm taking an early flight back home from Minneapolis. How did it go?"

"Well . . ." I stare at the pages. I wanted to look at them first. Digest them. Ruminate about what they are or aren't before sharing.

"Are you there? Did I lose you? Julie?" If I disconnect us, Jenny will call back. All I needed was a few minutes alone.

"I'm here. Just got in the car. Fine. It went fine. Mom drank wine. Maggie growled. She'll need to be put down before she nips someone again. Dad did all the talking." I can't help myself. I stall. Didn't I deserve some time with the papers first? Jenny will float in on Sunday, grab her folder from Dad, and all the hard conversations will be over.

"Yes, I got the folder," I say tightly.

"Okayyyy? Anddd?"

The way my twin draws out her words, she conveys her mounting annoyance. Jenny doesn't want to know how my folks acted, or that I twiddled like a moron outside their apartment door before going in. She wants to know what's in my hands. I suck back in another one of those reflexive-sigh things we both do.

"Hold on. Looking through it now . . . There are several things in here. The first one looks like the documents legalizing our adoption, then there's my original birth certificate—you'll get yours on Sunday. It's the redacted birth record, the one with Mom's and Dad's names on it instead of our birth parents. It's dark like they pulled it from a microfiche or something."

"What about health stuff? Anything in there about that?" Jenny asks.

"Looking . . ." My hands sort the papers in a slow, deliberate way, being careful of the fragile condition.

"Julie, I've only got a few minutes. They're calling my flight."

I envision her in the crowded airport terminal, shifting her weight from one professional pump to the other, chin jutting forward, willing me to get on with this. Within her time frame. With each turn of a page, hope slides away. My inner voice murmurs again. Instead of a warning, this time it gloats: *I told you this wouldn't be easy.*

Since our post-biopsy chat on Monday, Jenny and I have strategized and defined our partnership's roles. My sister's full-time job as a director of sales for a major corporation prevents her from being active in the research. We agreed that accessing our medical history and adoption story would become my "job," but I'd consult her at every juncture. Jenny would also share in the costs.

"The last thing in here is that newspaper clipping we found in the 1980s that reads: 'Jeanne and John Ryan adopt baby girls, Ann Marie and Mary Ann Jensen.'" I scan the yellowed newsprint that I had forgotten about.

In 1989, my husband hired a genealogist to build his family tree, and this adoption notice appeared like a forgotten sock. The notice was a matter of public record, a required legal announcement, I suppose. The article surprised us since Mom and Dad had never mentioned our birth names. Jenny and I theorized about why we'd essentially received the same names but in reverse order. I speculated that twins must have surprised our birth mother who had only prepared one set of names. Jenny guessed that the nuns at St. Vincent's orphanage named us after the two most revered women in Catholic theology.

With no one to consult, we tussled over which set of names to claim. Being the oldest by twelve minutes, I argued that it entitled me to first dibs, so I chose Ann Marie. Secretly, I thought it was prettier than Mary Ann. Jenny laughed and said I was ridiculous and that I could have whatever name I wanted since it was a moot point. In the fall of 1959, eight months after our births, the new names chosen by our adoptive parents became our legal identities. Since discovering the clipping, I think of Ann Marie Jensen as my secret identity. It's my link to the person that I might have been and my bond with my birth relatives, people who have become my destiny to seek out.

"We knew about that news clipping. What else?"

Jenny's impatience needles me.

My sister wants me to deliver the punch line, but this isn't a joke I've told before or a book where I can flip to the last chapter. When we discovered that newspaper clipping, we were thirty years old, and it prompted our letter to Catholic Charities to ask for more information about our adoption. The agency's response shoved us back into our tidy, little adoption corner: *No information can be shared at this time.* Not much you can do with that except go on living your life.

"Nothing else here, Jen. Except a letter from Mom, labeled 'Your Story.'" I stifle a giggle. Even though I'm not standing next to my sister, I'm guessing her eyes are bugging out.

"Oh, gawd," Jenny says.

Preempting the "What's that about?" forming on my sister's lips, I tell her, "It's a handwritten note about going to Lourdes, praying for a family, and adopting twins born on the Feast of Our Lady of Lourdes."

The four pages of my mom's neat script detail the story my parents told in their apartment less than an hour ago—a tale about how we came to be our parents' daughters. It contains nothing about our biological beginnings. A sweet dead end.

"So we got nothing. Not one new piece of information?" Jenny says.

The way in which my sister's voice stops on "nothing" and squeaks on "new," her feelings become apparent, and so too are mine. Disappointment, frustration, and indignation descend on us as rapidly as the dusk engulfs my parked car. The reality is that Jenny and I are exactly where we were in 1959 and in 1989. Still together, we are closed off from all knowledge regarding who we are or where we came from, why we were placed for adoption, and whether any concerning health issues exist in our biological families.

I speak as if I'm in church. "Right. Nothing new."

The streetlights are coming on around me. I debate starting the engine, turning on the heat, and buckling up.

"You got a plan?" Jenny asks. I can't help but laugh—I'm in the driver's seat literally and figuratively.

"Well, we could contact Catholic Charities again and see where that leads, or we could hire a private investigator. There are a lot of PIs out there, so we'd need a referral for a good one. Another option is hiring an agency that specializes in adoption searches. We have choices." Choices, as in how to find a birth mother. We had no choice in being placed in a closed adoption.

Jenny jumps in. "I'm not thinking Catholic Charities will be of any more help than they were in 1989. Why don't you look into the costs for the PI and the search firms? Let me know what you find out. Gotta run. Talk to you tomorrow. Good work."

When Jenny hangs up, I sit for a moment staring out the window. Outside my car, a steady stream of pastel-smocked nurses and aides are heading toward parked cars. They're going home, and that's what I need to do. I gather up the documents cluttering the dashboard, my lap, and the passenger seat, and place the papers back into the folder my dad labeled with my name. Clutching the letter from my mom, I scrutinize the section I glossed over with Jenny:

In December of '55, on Christmas Day, we sailed to America to live in our first home in Western Springs, IL. We experienced three more miscarriages and the doctors were not optimistic that we could have any successful pregnancies. We totally agreed to adoption and made an appointment with Catholic Charities.

The first interview, we were told how the adoption process works: an eighteen-month wait with surprise home visits from our assigned caseworker. After this period of time was over, we would expect our "special call" anytime within the next eighteen months.

At the end of this first interview, I said to the caseworker, "If you ever have twins, please consider us." To this day, I think of this comment I made and wonder why I mentioned twins since the thought had never entered my mind. This whole adoption process made us uneasy but we both knew we would do anything to have a baby.

Of course, your Dad was working, and I then decided to use my teaching certificate and took a position at St. Cletus School. Third grade with fifty-four students was a 24/7 job, but I loved it, and it kept my mind busy. With the first eighteen-month period over, we were now in the "active file." That first week, I received a call at school from our caseworker, who said she wanted to clarify our application concerning what appeared to be a last-minute comment since she did not interview us the first time.

"Did you request twins at the end of your interview?" I recall saying "Yes" but feeling extremely disappointed that this wasn't the phone call we'd been waiting for and also upset that she took me from my classroom for a call that could be taken at home.

She said then, "In that case, I must tell you your twin girls are waiting for you!"

I was in a state of shock, and soon the teachers came out of their classrooms with hugs, kisses, and congratulatory comments. I called your dad who was absolutely ecstatic. Our families were notified, and all came the next few days to help us get ready. Such an exciting time!

The next day we were allowed to see you in the nursery, and we both shared tears of joy; you were gorgeous! In a few days we were able to pick you up all dressed in a special outfit. Sister Anthony, the second in command at the Charities brought you out to us. What a fabulous moment!

One thing I do remember at that meeting is saying to Sister, "I am concerned for the birth mother." She replied, "Don't worry about her. She is very close to Our Blessed Mother, and she'll be fine." This I feel, has a great deal to do with your story.

After a while, our life settled down, and one day while you were sleeping, I took out my missal to find what feast day February 11 was. I was touched to find it to be the feast of Our Lady of Lourdes. I often reflect on this and realize that this wasn't a coincidence. Your birth mother and I had a connection through Blessed Mother. If, in the past, I had carried those babies, we wouldn't have you, and I can't imagine life without you.

Enclosed you will see the only information we were given.

We want you to have this in case you are interested in an adoption search. We feel you deserve a link to your biological heritage and possibly have questions regarding genetics, etc. It is extremely important for you to know that you are truly a beautiful gift from Almighty God, and we are your parents forever. We love you more than you can ever imagine. Please know we will give you our full support.

Love, Mom

Through closed eyes, I reflect on my mother's note. She said, "Please know we will give you our full support," yet in the apartment, Mom had not been as overt with her support as she was here in print. She'd sat primly on the loveseat, eyes glued on my father, and swirled her chardonnay. If I were a child or teenager, I would understand my mom's hesitation and fears about another mother entering my life, but at forty-eight, the bond I have with my parents is solid—surely, they know that. I wonder whether Mom will come around, or if this say-one-thing-act-another-way will be an issue going forward.

When I open my eyes, daylight has evaporated and with it my hopes for an easy solution to my lack of medical history. Before the evening began, I envisioned driving home with some of my background to share with Steve. I expected that my parents' file would produce details about my adoption circumstances, and I had counted on my mother being more supportive. I tuck the folder into the passenger seat. Adoption, my forever seatmate. Besides the fact I'm a fraternal twin, adoption defines my existence.

Turning the car on, I blast the heat—suddenly I'm so cold. The car's headlamps improve a portion of the surrounding gloom, but there are pockets of darkness lurking between the cars and at the edges of the parking lot. Pockets of darkness, just like my adoption. Buckling up, I shift into reverse, and check the rearview window.

5

Easter Monday

From where I stand in front of the coffee maker, the pounding on the third floor sounds like an army is deploying. At the turn of the stairs, the stomping gets louder, and when a gear bag lands with a thud outside the kitchen, I jump. My son, Danny, has a double practice for the varsity baseball team today. The racket sets the collies in motion, and they clamor over one another for the best sniff of ripe crew socks and Power Bar wrappers. The clock on the stove reads seven fifteen. Only seventy-five minutes to go until I phone my doctor—I've been waiting nearly a week for a message from his office.

Up nearly an hour ago to let the dogs out into the yard, I'm scrambling eggs and buttering toast as my sleepy seventeen-year-old son careens into the kitchen. The Redwings practice shirt Danny pulled over his muscled torso has a reddish-brown smudge on the sleeve.

"Morning, Big Dan." I slide a generous serving of eggs and toast onto a plate for him.

"Do you need a lunch?" I ask. "You know your T-shirt is dirty, right? Coach won't like that."

My six-foot, two-inch kid who's the size of a full-grown man lands on a counter stool, and I lose him to the eggs. In between huge swallows of food, he mumbles, "I got a clean shirt in my truck." Gulp, chew. "Yeah, I need a lunch," followed by a garbled, "Please."

I study him out of the corner of my eye, concerned that he is about to choke, and then I layer sandwiches, drinks, and snacks into a thermal lunch bag.

Still chewing, Danny snags the lunch. "Thanks, Mom." He gifts me with a one-armed squeeze, which is as much of a hug as a mother of a teenage son can hope for.

"See you after five," I say. The large hand on the clock has barely budged.

Picking up his plate, I move to the sink where I can see him through the window centered there. Danny huddles at the door of his truck. He whips off the stained practice shirt and grabs a "cleaner one" from the floor of his pickup.

Where did he come from?

Out of nowhere, the question presents itself like a call from an old friend. And then a fresh question pops up: Whom do my girls take after? Two six-footers, two dark brunettes, and one strawberry blonde make up my motley crew. Musing about which side of my genetics all that diversity comes from ushers in other questions. Which of my birth parents passed on a competitive, determined nature? Whom can I blame for my chronic sinus infections? Who handed down the freckly fair skin and high cheekbones that two of my children share with Jenny and me? What about my son's ability to grow a full, dark beard that a rabbi would envy? Or my nephew's distinctive bull legs? What about . . . ? What about . . . ?

As Danny's pickup disappears down the driveway, my questions fade. One hour until the doctor's office opens.

Steve's aftershave precedes him into the kitchen. "Looks like everyone's up early." A smooch lands on my cheek as he fills a coffee mug and slides his chair up to the table. "What's up with the kids today?"

"Danny just left for baseball. Kassie's still sleeping." I tighten the belt on my bathrobe.

In a vacant sort of way, I watch Steve dig into his breakfast, and I freshen my own coffee. My eyes popped open at four o'clock and stayed that way until five thirty. During that ninety-minute interval, my mind spiraled: If I have breast cancer, what treatment will be prescribed? Should I cut my shoulder-length hair now and stockpile it for a natural hair wig? What's the right way to let the kids know?

"What have you got going?" Steve's eyes are glued to the front page of the *Chicago Tribune*, the newspaper the dogs and I rescued from the driveway at dawn.

I stare at my husband. I'm jumpy from too much coffee, too little sleep, and the threat of a cancer diagnosis. Has he forgotten? Hours ago, surrounded by our king-sized pillows, Steve wiped away my fearful tears and reasoned with me: If my breast biopsy were bad news, I'd have heard from Dr. Frank by now. He encouraged me to phone the doctor's office first thing in the morning, and then we'd cuddled until sleep came.

Pointing at the clock on the wall, I say, "I'm waiting till eight thirty, and then I'm calling Dr. Frank's office. Remember?" I'm trying to hold it together.

"Right. Of course." Steve's dark eyes flick up from the *Trib*. "I meant the rest of the day."

When I don't answer, he crosses the kitchen and brings me in close. "I have a feeling you're fine," he whispers. "You have good docs. If it's cancer, you'd have heard." I look up into his warm eyes. "I don't have to be at the office till nine. I'll throw this stuff in the dishwasher. You go shower."

At 8:34, I'm stationed at my small desk in the kitchen nook.

Dr. Frank's receptionist transfers me to his nurse, and then I'm put on hold. Classical music spits into the earpiece, and I think about my four children, my health, and the formidable task of digging into my adoption. A stray tear splatters onto the color-coded family calendar that's also a desk blotter.

Finally, a voice replaces the music. "This is Ellen. How can I help you today?"

I explain why I'm calling.

"Oh my! You shouldn't have had to call. I'm so sorry you spent the weekend worrying about this. Let me go to the doctor's desk and pull your file. He won't be in until tomorrow. Do you want to hold, or shall I call you right back?"

"I'll hold." Waiting for a return call is unfathomable.

Steve saunters into the kitchen to refill his coffee. I look over at him. "The nurse is checking for the results."

Three feet apart, we stand staring at one another, two souls sinking in a sea of concern.

By the time nurse Ellen clicks back on the line, it feels like it could be lunchtime. "Mrs. McGue. It's here. Again, I apologize that you had to wait for the results. Someone should have called you before the weekend, but we were closed on Good Friday." My eyelids squeeze shut. *Please God . . .*

"It says here . . . ductile calcifications. Patient to follow up with a repeat mammogram in three to four months."

I'm afraid to open my eyes. "So . . . no cancer?"

I can't look at Steve until I know this is what the report means.

Ellen's voice is gentle. "No cancer. Calcifications and dense breast tissue," she says. *Clogged, perky boobs. No lumpectomy, no chemo, and no natural hair wig.*

When I give my husband the thumbs-up, Steve breaks into a big grin.

"Thanks so much, Ellen."

My thank-you is soft, but in my head the words sing and soar. Fingering my hair, I consider whether to cut it anyway. While I may not need a natural hair wig, somewhere in Chicago there's a woman, a mother like me, who does.

"You'll get follow-up instructions in the mail. Have a blessed week, Mrs. McGue. Go have some Easter chocolate and celebrate," Ellen says. I giggle at the idea of pilfering a sugary Peep from one of my kids' Easter baskets. I just might.

Unlike Steve's hug before my shower, this one is about relief and gratitude. Drained, I linger in his arms.

"I'll take you to dinner tonight to celebrate. You pick the place," he says.

"Sounds wonderful," I say. With a smile and a jangle of keys, my husband is off.

Alone in the kitchen, I'm a hopeless tangle of emotions. While I'm grateful that cancer has passed me over, resentment builds over the unnecessary days of waiting. With my health crisis momentarily resolved, another challenge pops to the top of my to-do list—my adoption search. I can't fathom tackling that today. Today is about being grateful for good health and for the family I love and care for, the family that belongs to me and where I belong.

Punching in Jenny's phone number, I miss the footsteps in the back hall.

"Mom, what's for breakfast?" Cradling the phone, I take in Kassie's messy blond ponytail, rumpled flannels, and middle-school tee.

"What do you feel like, Kass?"

She hitches up her flannels and studies me as if assessing my mood. "Since today is spring break . . . that's like a weekend isn't it?" I sense where this is going. "So can I have Cinnamon Toast Crunch?"

Wearing a mini-version of the smile I wore ten minutes ago

with Nurse Ellen, I say, "Yes, today is like a weekend. Go ahead. Have a bowl of sugared cereal."

Just like that, I've fallen prey to the negotiating skills of a twelve-year-old, and I'm downright thrilled, because today I'm a healthy mom instead of a woman with a compromised body. As I watch my youngest child open the pantry, a series of thoughts flood in. I speculate about that "other mother" of mine, whether she's healthy, and if she ever wonders if Jenny and I are healthy, too. And then, I ponder if the woman who left me at Catholic Charities forty-eight years ago would have made me scrambled eggs and toast for breakfast or opened a box of sugar cereal instead.

6

The First Trace

2010

S teve opens the door to the driveway, and Kassie passes under his outstretched arm with her backpack. The sweet scent of the flowering pear tree in the yard sifts into the foyer—it's another glorious spring day. Still lingering inside the house, Steve bounces a set of car keys in his palm and resumes the debate we began over our first cup of morning coffee.

This past February, Jenny and I turned fifty, and it's been nearly two years since my breast biopsy. Due to managing my kids' busy lives, my father's continued poor health, and grieving a nephew's sudden death, pursuing the details of my closed adoption became less urgent. Colleen, my oldest daughter, moved to Texas for graduate school. The two middle kids, Molly and Danny, are off at college—their collegiate sports schedules have been exciting to be a part of. Molly played women's basketball at Cornell for a while, and Danny's in his second year with Army's football program. Kassie, the last one home, is a freshman at Benet, the same college prep high school her siblings attended. Over the last few months, I underwent a round of high-level mammograms. No biopsy was needed, but that experience combined with troublesome bouts of uterine bleeding has forced my adoption search to take a higher priority now.

I stare at Steve. "Catholic Charities was a dead end twenty years ago. Why would I start with them?"

From the driveway, Kassie shouts, "Hurry up, Dad!" Steve flips me a quick wave and hustles to the car.

Perhaps it's our rushed conversation about Catholic Charities and my adoption search or the dismissive wave, but I pull the door shut with such force that a sharp pain runs up my arm. I slink back to the kitchen, massaging the angry muscle. The remnants of school lunch making and breakfast on the run spew over the countertops. This is where my time goes: family commitments and chores. During all the pressing matters that filled the last two years, the adoption search hovered over me like an unfinished assignment. I suppose I could have fit it in, but I wasn't ready.

Turning my back on the kitchen chaos, I slog upstairs to throw on yesterday's jeans and my favorite red sweatshirt. The floor of my second-floor office looks like a war room. Computer printouts and scribbled yellow tablets disrupt the elegant pattern of the area rug. The desktop overflows with advice from adoption experts: Ann Fessler, Dr. David Brodzinsky, and Betty Jean Lifton. The white envelope from my folks, labeled "Your Story," loiters near my computer keyboard.

The information I've gathered so far has heightened my dilemma: How do I begin the search for my birth parents? I'm inclined to eliminate Catholic Charities from the search because of their response all those years ago. If I do that, then my next step is to either hire a lawyer or private investigator, or to focus on a list of firms called "adoption search angels." Determining which of these options would be most expedient is what I've been working on.

As I wait for my computer to come to life, I look up at the diplomas mounted above my desk. They goad me: You're smart. You can figure this out. I glare back at the credentials as if they're misbehaving kids. Neither the psych degree from Indiana nor the master's from Northwestern have prepared me for an attack on closed adoption. I give myself a pep talk: You did not choose to be adopted; you have every right to know your birth circumstances and family history; and you will figure this out. Just get at it.

Frustrated with the mess around me, I pick up a file from the floor labeled "Adoption Registries." The first page inside is the Soundex confirmation of my entry into their search database. I study their mission, which I pulled from their website:

> *International Soundex Reunion Registry (ISRR) is a nonprofit, humanitarian agency which serves and promotes, through the Reunion Registry, the interests of adults desiring and seeking a reunion with next of kin by birth. The registry serves the needs of birth family members who have been separated by adoption, divorce, foster care, institutional care, or abandonment. ISRR is not affiliated with any registry or other organization. ISRR is the largest free search registry in the world. This registry does not perform a search or provide search advice. Voluntary registration by adults desiring contact or reunion with their next of kin by birth is deemed legal consent for contact.*

Last night before climbing into bed, I plugged my personal data into the Soundex registry. While I slept, I hoped that the registry database would link me to some birth relatives, and that a reunion request would be in my Yahoo inbox this morning. No such luck. I don't know why I keep thinking this adoption search business will be easy.

Stuffing the Soundex details into a desk drawer, I pick up a large file labeled "Adoption Forums." On the forum sites, adoptees discussed search and reunion strategies, but most messages dealt with failure. Failure to locate birth relatives or failure to establish a meaningful relationship once reunion began. Adoptees also ranted about the "primal wound" of their adoption. Feeling more "wronged" by stringent adoption statutes than a "victim" of adoption, I toss the registry details in the desk drawer too. One by one, I lift each piece of research from the floor of my office, study it, and file it away. When the file drawer groans shut, all that remains on my desktop are three pieces of paper: my birth certificate with the real names of my birth parents redacted, a list of adoption search companies, and the phone number of a dear friend who's also an attorney.

I pluck up the redacted birth certificate, flatten out the deep creases, and hold it closer to the desk lamp. How I wish it contained just one identifying detail about my birth parents. It's as if they never existed, and as if I only have one set of parents. Setting down my birth record, I consider the new information I happened upon last night.

In November 2011, eighteen months from now, a change to the Illinois adoption statute could go into effect. This new law would grant me access to my original birth record, the unredacted version, which might contain other important details to aid my search. A year and a half is too long for me to wait—I'm ready now. I snatch up the phone number.

Within minutes, I'm on hold for my friend, the attorney. When her kind voice comes on the line, I relax a little until she quotes the fees for private investigators. I'm stunned. With no cap, just hourly fees, hiring a PI is like spilling my wallet on the ground. I had no idea that my desire for personal history could result in such a pricey battle. In the message I leave for my sister, I recap my latest research. I suspect Jenny's response will be some variation of, "I'll do whatever you think we should do."

Dropping my head into my hands, I consider the responsibility I've taken on for my sister and me. All the registries, forums, and search angel details clump together and settle like a lump of raw cookie dough in my gut. Wasting time or money is not my goal—I want a clear path to answers about who I am, where I came from, and what family medical concerns are lurking there. While the problem is straightforward, the solution is confounding.

I do my best thinking while moving. First, I go to the staircase landing and wind the grandfather clock. Before tidying the kitchen, I release the dogs to harass the squirrels in the yard. Back upstairs, I wander between the bedrooms scooping up stray laundry. Hamper in hand, I pause on the second-floor landing outside the master bedroom. The midday sun has transformed the two-story leaded glass window over the staircase into a myriad of prisms, and every shade of the rainbow flickers on the light-colored carpet.

It's as if I'm gazing into the heart of a fire, and I'm transfixed. For a few seconds, I'm aware of just three things: the primary colors painting the carpet, the breath in my chest that lifts my red sweatshirt, and the grandfather clock clicking in perfect time. I interpret this moment as a cosmic sign, a guidepost for my indecision about what to do next with my adoption search. The hamper thuds on the landing and I march to my office.

The 800 number I dial is answered on the third ring. "Good afternoon, Worldwide Tracers and Adoption Search Bureau. How can I help you today?" The receptionist's slow Texas twang surprises me. Her dialect gives me pause—I'm entrusting a personal crusade to strangers at the opposite end of the country.

"I'd like to begin a search for my birth family. I was adopted through Catholic Charities in Chicago. In February 1959." Getting all this out exhausts me, but I quickly add, "I know my birth name." After I say it, I question if these details are enough to launch a search.

"Perfect. We'll need that information. Can you hold please?" she drawls.

"Sure." A light jazz fills the void between Chicago and Texas.

As I wait for my new search angel to return, my fingers pop around the computer keyboard. The Worldwide Tracers company website shows the stats I've already memorized: a convincing 90 percent success rate in locating birth relatives. The 10 percent sliver of failure is not where I expect our case to settle. The computer cursor glows over Worldwide Tracers' claim of being featured on *Oprah*, not once but several times. This statistic impressed Jenny, too. The $440 fee is hefty, but splitting that cost with my sister makes it manageable. I remind myself that all I want is some medical history and a few facts about my birth circumstances. When the thought of a reunion with either one of my birth parents sneaks in, I shove it away. One thing at a time.

Picking up my redacted birth record again, I wonder how many adopted twins could have been born on February 11, 1959, at Lewis Memorial Maternity Hospital in Chicago. Yesterday, Google Earth and I tracked down the location. The site where Jenny and I were born is now a baseball diamond. She and I chuckled over this since both of our sons played high school baseball. Jenny's son, Stewie, is a college pitcher whom professional baseball scouts are watching.

The receptionist's drawl returns. "I'll connect you to Kurt. He handles all the new adoption searches. One more minute, hon."

"Hello, Julie. This is Kurt. I'm so glad you called us today." A gentle tenor, devoid of dialect, takes the reins for the first stage of the wild ride that becomes our adoption search.

Half an hour later, hundreds of dollars lighter, and our private information divulged, Jenny and I are signed up with Worldwide Tracers. Once we execute the paperwork, Kurt will dig up details on our birth mother. After the call ends, I can't get my feet to move.

To the diplomas above the desk, I whisper, "I'm on it." Then I pick up the phone and schedule another appointment with my gynecologist—it's time to discuss my problematic uterus.

When I return to the landing with its beveled glass windows, lacy clouds mask the afternoon sun. The rainbow that filtered through the glass earlier is a fleeting inspiration. Now, the dappled light showcases an overflowing laundry basket abandoned near the top step. Against my red sweatshirt, the load of the basket is lighter.

7

Interim Weeks

I dose the serving trays from yesterday's Father's Day celebration with an extra splash of Dawn. Hosting my extended family of eighteen, even for an outdoor event with paper and plastic, is a monumental undertaking. It was worth it though to see Dad's face light up as we dished out one of his favorite desserts—French silk pie—with all of the grandkids hovered around him.

From the window over the kitchen sink, I notice that the garbagemen have left the trash cans helter-skelter in front of the garage. When I head outside to move them, I spot the small white van at the end of the block. My hand comes to rest on my pink tee, which does nothing to settle the sudden little skip of my heart.

The mailman is early today.

Six weeks ago, Kurt at Worldwide Tracers (WWT) sent the packet of adoption search paperwork to Jenny and me. From Texas, Kurt directed the filing of several forms with Illinois state agencies. The goal is to access the non-identifying information on our original birth records (OBR) and register with the State of Illinois's Adoption Registry and Medical Information Exchange (IARMIE). My brain is teased by trying to keep up with all these strange new acronyms.

Being listed on the IARMIE sets us up with the state so we can exchange information with members of our birth family, assuming they're registered, too. I fear my entry on the IARMIE will go the way of the other registries and forums I've subscribed to—hours at the computer entering data with no feedback. If my birth mom or biological relatives have ever shown curiosity about Jenny and me, I have yet to see evidence of it.

Once we're officially entered in the IARMIE database, the Illinois Department of Vital Records locates our original birth record. Vital Records sealed this document when the courts finalized our adoption in the fall of 1959—eight months after Mom and Dad scooped us up from St. Vincent's Orphanage in Chicago. I envision the employee at Vital Records, her name badge flapping around as she strips down my OBR and summarizes the non-identifying information to send to me. Worldwide Tracers needs this information to get my adoption search moving, and only then will I have a chance of accessing my biological family's medical background.

For the last forty days, I've staged a three o'clock vigil near the mailbox on the front porch. Sometimes, I sip an iced tea on the porch swing and pretend to admire the peonies and iris below the sugar maple. More often than not, I perch on the edge of one of the wicker rockers, my eyes scanning the neighborhood for the mailman's pushcart or small white van. To the casual onlooker, it may appear that I'm enjoying a few minutes to myself on a pleasant early-summer day, but I'm not relaxing. I'm desperately, anxiously waiting. Waiting for the first set of answers that will help my sister and me fill in the gaping holes of our personal story.

With one hand still resting on the handle of a trash bin, I study the mailman's shape across the street. It's not Dale, our regular carrier. I dismiss the emotional cocktail my body has grown accustomed to at three o'clock. Today can't be the day. I'm certain that Dale, the middle-aged mailman with a gray mullet and ponytail, a man whom I've gotten to know over eight years and whose five children I ask after, is the only emissary who can deliver the precious document I've been waiting weeks to receive.

The young stranger in gray shorts bumbles in his pouch and trudges a route that's the reverse of Dale's trusted pattern. Instead of returning indoors, the dogs and I amble over to the flower beds flanking the front walk. While they sniff in the dirt, I sit on a stone garden bench and eye the mailman. He lingers in the neighbor's walkway, his head in his pouch, sorting and whistling loud, out of tune. The dogs distract me. Our male collie, Emmett, picks up a fallen branch and teases the female, Nellie, into a game of keep-away. As I watch the dogs play, I think about the one-page statement I wrote for the IARMIE weeks ago:

Fifty years ago, my twin sister and I were placed for adoption through Catholic Charities together. We were adopted by a wonderful couple and have had good lives. In the course of the last few years, we have developed medical concerns. We are requesting medical history from our birth parents. . . . It is necessary that we learn from our birth mother whether breast, uterine or ovarian cancer is hereditary. . . . Between us we have six children who we wish to be informed of their medical background.

"Hello. Nice day, isn't it?"

Twisting away from the dogs' antics, I look up at the temporary mail carrier. In his outstretched hand is the day's mail wound with rubber bands. The wad is thick and unruly, and the impatient beast in me wants to rip off the bands and rifle through the pile.

I return the man's friendly smile. "Thank you. It's a beautiful day to be outside. Is Dale sick?"

"No. Just taking some vacation days. I'll be doing his route all week. Have a good one." He waves and saunters back to the pushcart.

I never hear him resume the off-key whistling, nor the slam of the mail truck's door at the end of the block. Nestled between the Valpak coupons and the AT&T bill is an envelope from Illinois Public Health. The white envelope is thin and as light as two sheets of notebook paper. My name appears in bold print across the face of the envelope.

Pressing the letter to my pink shirt, I shout to the dogs. Emmett drops the stick into the flower bed, and both collies fold their tails between their legs. They slink over to where I pace on the front walk and then chase after me through the side door and into the kitchen, their nails clicking like typewriter keys on the wood plank floors. I bribe their silence with a treat and phone my sister. I can't fathom opening the thin white envelope without first learning whether Jenny received hers. Connecting with my twin sister as this big moment unfurls is vital. I want us to cheer or moan together.

"Jen, call me. The letter came. Did you get yours? It's two fifty."

Dropping the envelope, I rummage through the desk drawer for a letter opener. I can't recall ever using one or ever needing to preserve a piece of correspondence before, but it seems like the right idea. Through the neat slit of the envelope, I tug out a single type-written page and settle at the edge of my chair.

I read:

If in the future we receive a similar request from any of your eligible birth family members, we will notify you in writing and exchange information and forms as mutually agreed upon based on the Information Exchange Authorization forms submitted by the registrants.

You have indicated by signing Section D of the IARMIE application form that you wish to have any non-identifying information from the original birth certificate released to you.

The following is that information: the mother's age is listed as 26 at the time of your birth, the birth father's age is listed as 23 at the time of your birth, their races are both listed as white, and the record indicates that no previous children were born to the birth mother. Your date and place of birth are February 11, 1959 at the Lewis Memorial Maternity Hospital in Chicago, Illinois.

If any agency was involved with the adoption, you may wish to contact them with regard to any non-identifying or medical information they may have within their files or any search options they may offer to their clients.

Again, and again, I smooth out the creases of the single type-written page as if this effort alone might explain the facts. For fifty years, I believed my parents to be underage. I'd developed a rich fantasy about them. They were high school sweethearts whose parents refused to let them marry when she became pregnant. He was the captain of the football team. She was popular, perhaps the head cheerleader. They were a much-admired couple whose passion got the better of them at their senior prom—counting back nine months from February puts our probable conception at May 1958. Young with bright futures, they made the understandable choice of placing my sister and me for adoption.

But twenty-six and twenty-three? This isn't what I expected to learn. My biological parents were not only consenting adults, they were well into their twenties when Jenny and I landed in the Chicago orphanage. I find it odd that my birth mom is the older one in the couple by several years. There's more to my adoption story than I imagined, and certainly much more than what is presented on this single page. Squeezing my eyes shut, I will my sister's number to appear on the caller ID.

Emmett nudges me. 1 toss him another treat and hit my husband's office number. I huff when I'm told Steve is on another call.

When I dial Worldwide Tracers, I'm handed off to Kurt's assistant. The combination of these rebuffs along with the letter's bizarre news makes me want to lace up my sneakers and run till my lungs scream.

In her sweet Texas drawl, Kurt's aide says, "This is exactly what we need. It helps us narrow the search. Your birth mother's age at the time of your birth will be helpful if we find other women with the same name."

I borrow her positive outlook. "And how many twins could have been born on February 11, 1959, at that hospital?"

"Another bonus," she affirms and adds that I should fax over the letter. I ask about contacting Catholic Charities for the non-identifying information in their files.

"Anything you can learn will help," she says. "Kurt will be in touch as soon as there's progress to share about your case."

"Okay. I'll send the fax. Thanks."

While waiting for the fax to float over the phone lines from Chicago to Texas, I log on to the computer and locate the address for Catholic Charities Post Adoption Services in Chicago. Again, I dwell on the last time I contacted the adoption agency. Twenty years ago, another typewritten letter, in an envelope similar to the one I received today, scolded me for questioning my closed adoption: *Nothing can be shared at this time.*

Based upon the research I've been stockpiling, I know that in the era of closed adoption, state law protected the rights of adoptive parents and the privacy of birth parents. Lucky for me, adoption law is evolving. An adoptee's "right to know" is at the forefront of a war being waged in half the states of the union. If I request it, I'm due all the non-identifying information in my adoption file. Private adoption agencies like Catholic Charities are not exempt from this ruling.

Beneath the search results for Catholic Charities, several items pop up: the address for St. Vincent's, my orphanage, which closed in 1972, and a book written about its history authored by a trio of alumni staff nurses. I order three copies. One each for Jenny and me, and an extra for my younger brother, Howie, who is also adopted. On my computer screen, the book's black-and-white cover stirs up a few ideas. I wonder if Jenny is up for a field trip.

A few feet from where I sit, the serving trays from yesterday's family barbecue consume the kitchen island. Clean and dry, they're ready to be put away. A half hour ago they represented just another chore. Now they signify something else: family. My adoptive family, the people who raised my sister and me, loved us, cared for us, and gave us a life. A good life.

With the letter from Public Health in my hands, I stare at the trays. Shards of guilt invade the success of the day. My folks don't know that I've hired a search firm to locate my birth parents. There were moments yesterday when I was alone with Mom in the kitchen, but I chose not to bring it up. Why is it that sharing the ins and outs of my adoption search rest on me? It's been two years since my parents handed over my adoption paperwork, and they have yet to ask any questions. None of us want to talk about it—we skirt around it like it's a pit of hot coals. I hate that my quest for my personal story has put a wedge between us.

There's an old adage that midwesterners seem to live by: "If you don't talk about it, it didn't happen." That definitely describes my family, especially as pertains to my adoption search. Perhaps the paperback I ordered about St. Vincent's can serve another purpose outside of appealing to my curiosity. Maybe it can help me create a dialogue with my parents about where my search is headed and what it's like for me.

8

Baptism

Last week, after I faxed the letter from Vital Records over to Worldwide Tracers (WWT), I sent a request to Catholic Charities for the non-identifying information in my adoption file. All my other search efforts are at a standstill. The adoption registries have yet to turn up any connections, and Kurt from WWT hasn't phoned with any news. With nothing but time on my hands, I'm on a mission—a mission to scour our family archives for any documents from my young life that could prove helpful.

Barefoot and cross-legged, I'm on the floor of Steve's office at the front of the house. My search for the childhood scrapbook that my mother made is taking longer than I anticipated. From the bottom shelf, I slide out a stack of family albums. Wiping dust off the top album, I set it aside. I already know what it contains: a collage of photos featuring me as I morphed from a bug-eyed infant into a gangly, knobby-kneed teen. I lift a smaller cloth-covered album into my lap and untie the white satin ribbons that hold the book closed. The spine groans and threatens to split as I open to the first creamy pages of my baby book.

Pasted on the second page is a handmade christening announcement. Written in silver ink by my mother's careful hand, it declares that on February 27, 1959, my sister and I entered the Catholic faith through baptism. Mom's birthday? I didn't realize that my christening overlapped with her birthday. What a strange coincidence—just like my birthdate landing on the Feast of Our Lady of Lourdes, the shrine where my folks had prayed together to start a family. Goosebumps prickle my skin. Centered below our names on the announcement, my mother's neat cursive lists the church where we received our first sacrament: Holy Name Cathedral on State Street in Chicago. Underneath that, my godparents' names are listed, my Aunt Addie and my father's friend, Bob H., a man I don't recall meeting.

Nothing else on the baptismal announcement is new to me. As a previous parishioner, I know that Holy Name Cathedral is the seat of the Archdiocese of Chicago and that only members of the parish can receive sacraments there. A block and a half away from the cathedral, the wrought iron gates of St. Vincent's open onto LaSalle Street. No longer sheltering orphans, it's a Catholic Charities facility that provides relief services to the city's underprivileged. Because my orphanage was within the boundaries of Holy Name's parish, it explains how my sister and I could have received our first sacrament at the cathedral, despite my adoptive parents residing in the western suburbs.

As I study the christening announcement, I consider what the order of things might have been. Did my parents retrieve us from St. Vincent's and meet our godparents at Holy Name for our baptism? Had the sisters at St. Vincent's been instrumental in setting up the christening to coincide with my mother's birthday? I make a mental note to quiz my mom.

The pages following the baptismal notice contain miscellaneous notes made in my mother's perfect penmanship. Perfunctory milestones like I walked at nine months, eyes changed from blue to hazel around four months, and Jenny and I had our own language, which we exchanged through our separate cribs. The book includes a snippet of light brown hair from my first haircut. It tickles me that Mom found the time to assemble all these details and keep them safe.

Flipping past the lock of hair, it occurs to me that I missed the baptismal certificate from Holy Name. I turn back several pages. Nothing. This is when I realize that there are no photographs from my christening either. Thinking this odd but excusing my mom as an overtired first-time mother of two infants, I speculate that the pictures must be in the bulky album I had set aside.

I trudge off to the kitchen, pull open the file drawer, and splay the contents of a folder marked "Important Documents" across my desk. No baptismal certificate there either. I should have it. This bothers me, festers like a splinter, and then an idea forms, coalesces, becomes an urgent question to ask. Now.

After the first ring, I question my resolve and the thought process that sent me punching in digits on the cordless phone. Clutching the "Important Documents," I trudge back to the library with the phone pressed to my ear. I glare at my baby book on the floor.

An older female voice answers after several rings. "Holy Name Cathedral. How can I help you today?"

"I would like to get a copy of my baptismal certificate please." I swallow, banishing the squeak that crept into every word of my request.

"I'll transfer you to Mary. She handles the baptismal records. One moment, please."

"Thank you." Don't disconnect me. I'm not sure I'll call back.

In the late '80s, I christened my two oldest daughters, Colleen and Molly, at Holy Name's marble font on the side altar. Family and godparents fanned around my husband and me as my daughter, draped in a linen and lace gown, received her first sacrament. When cool water washed away her original sin, stunned cries pierced the altar's silence and echoed across the marble tiles. Just like my cry would have done, almost thirty years before, at the same marble basin in the same church with my adoptive parents around me.

I think about the time when sharing a Holy Name baptism with my girls had filled my heart, warmed and enveloped my young family in belonging. Belonging to the church and belonging to one another. As I held each of my daughters over the marble bowl, I imagined my parents mirroring my actions at my baptism in the same space. My parents and me. Me and my daughters. A bonding cycle through Baptism, the sacrament of initiation at Holy Name, the jewel in Chicago's religious crown.

When Mary picks up, I give her my name and the baptismal date from my baby book. "Can you hold while I check the records?" she says.

While I examine the other documents in the "Important Papers" file, I imagine Mary flipping through dusty tomes in the rectory basement to get to February 1959, her eyes scrolling down the names that begin with "R." The longer I hold, I can almost see the line where Julie Anne and Jennifer Anne Ryan pop up beside our baptismal and birthdates and adoptive parents' names. I want Mary to also find, perhaps trailing in parentheses, our birth names and birth parents' identities. I will all this so fiercely that I almost miss the line clicking.

"I've located the records," Mary says. "I'll mail you off a copy of your baptismal certificate in the morning mail." Her brisk efficiency hints at other pending tasks, perhaps other calls blinking on hold.

My "Oh" flutters across the thirteen miles of telephone wire linking Hinsdale to Chicago. I can't release her. There's more I need to ask. Words rush out. "I was adopted. Are my birth parents' names written there?"

"Well . . . we'd never have received that information. This office only certifies baptisms."

While I know what "certifies" means, it's what Mary has not said that sets me in a spin. Another "Oh?" fills the line, but this one is full of disappointment and a question. I suppose that Mary receives this reaction from other adoptees who call in on the same errand as mine.

After a brief pause and a sigh, she continues, "When an infant was adopted from St. Vincent's, the sisters sent the paperwork over to Holy Name. At this office we would have entered the baptismal date, the adoptive parents' names, and the infant's new given name. That's all that's listed here. No birth names. No birth parents' names."

I barrel on like a train through unscheduled stops. "They baptized me on February 27, 1959, at Holy Name, right?"

"The date is correct, but they baptized you at St. Vincent's, not Holy Name."

"Uh . . . I'm sorry? What did you say?" My eyes squeeze, as if this will help the pain budding at my hairline.

"A St. Vincent's baby was baptized in the chapel on the third floor at the orphanage. Nurses acted as stand-in godparents. During that era, it was believed that infants should be christened as soon as possible, so the sisters did not wait for babies to be adopted. Because Holy Name is the seat of the archdiocese, your baptism was certified here. The certificate I'm putting in the mail will say Holy Name with the date of February 27, 1959." Mom's birthday.

Questions pelt my brain, but I remember the manners my mother instilled in me. "Thank you. You've been so helpful."

After hanging up with Holy Name, I glance at but do not see the papers and memories scattered about the floor of Steve's office. Stand-in godparents. Third-floor chapel at St. Vincent's. It's no wonder there are no pictures in the baby book of my godparents and me poised over the baptismal bowl. Why was I given a new set of godparents at all? That's silly. Why perpetuate a farce when the truth will do? While the facts Mary disclosed shock me, it's the realization that I don't share this Holy Name sacrament with my girls that bothers me most.

Glaring at the phone, I vacillate between calling my sister to shock and rant or dialing my mother to accuse. I storm into the kitchen and drop the phone into its charging station. Snatching it up again, I punch in my folks' home number. When I get their answering machine, I try the cottage in Palisades Park. In the summer months, their weekends on Lake Michigan extend from Thursday through Monday evening or sometimes Tuesday morning. As the connection starts into a third ring, I imagine my parents reading on the knotty pine sleeping porch, a breeze scented with seaweed and sunscreen wafting through the screened sliders that open onto the deck.

Out of breath, my mother answers on the fourth ring. "Hello?"

Chagrined, my eyes close. Before this adoption search, my role was perfect daughter, but my new role is definitely "disturber of the peace."

"Hi, Mom. Listen, I'm sorting through my desk, pulling out documents." I suspect she knows where this is going. We will have to talk about "it"—"it" being my adoption. I nibble at my lip. "I couldn't find my baptismal certificate. I called Holy Name."

"Yes." Mom sounds willing and patient, oblivious to the five-decade lie I'm about to expose.

"The woman at the rectory . . ." My speech rushes into the holes of my breath. "I wasn't baptized at Holy Name. They baptized me at St. Vincent's. In the chapel. On the third floor."

"Oh, for heaven's sake!" Her indignation sounds genuine.

"You didn't know this?"

"When your dad and I picked up your sister and you at St.

Vincent's, your baptismal certificates were in an envelope along with the other adoption paperwork. We were told you'd been christened already. The documents said, 'certified at Holy Name,' no mention of St. Vincent's." She sounds sad, as if acknowledging the doubt my questions have tossed in the summer's humid air.

"Why do you think the certificate didn't say St. Vincent's? Because it was an orphanage?" Saying that word, "orphanage," is sticky on my tongue.

Growing up, my folks never linked "orphanage" with any mention of St. Vincent's. For the longest time, I thought St. Vincent's was the name of the hospital where I was born. Until I began this adoption search, I'd not thought of my sister and me as orphans. It's not a label I plan to dwell upon.

"I suppose so. . . ." Mom's voice trails off as if she's looking for a chair to sink into.

We both know an adoption in the late 1950s meant something had gone wrong for the baby's parents: poverty, unwed mother, or an improper union based on religion, ethnicity, or social status. Things that shouldn't be mentioned. Mom has often said that she wished that there weren't another mother before her, that she considers us "hers." But there is another mother to whom I belonged before her, and now I want that woman's medical history.

Mom's breath is thick, drawn out like a puff from a stolen cigarette. "I was afraid of Sr. Mary Alice, the prioress. I tried. I attempted to ask questions."

Oh, God, if she cries, I may cry too. "Mom . . ." I'm willing to end this assault right now. "You don't need to—"

"Let me finish, please." The sizzle in my mother's quick words silences me.

"When Dad and I sat in Sr. Mary Alice's office, before they took us to the nursery to get you, I asked, with a big smile on my face, 'Can you tell me a little about the background of the girls?'

Sister leaned forward across the desk with her winged headdress flapping at your dad and me and said, 'Do you want these children or not?' I said, 'Oh yes, Sister. I do. I desperately want these girls.' Sr. Mary Alice said, 'Then there will be no more questions.' That was it. I just listened from then on."

"I understand, Mom. I do." Having spent years in Catholic schools, I know that when the nuns cast their edicts, you bow and obey, or else.

After I hang up with my mother, I return to the library and sink to the floor. Shame pricks my cheeks like a sunburn. My mother hadn't failed me; she hadn't perpetuated a mistruth on purpose. If something so inconsequential as a christening form could be the source of such deep controversy and potential hurt, what else is ahead? Will all the edges of my adoption search be sharp and painful? And how many more absent truths, misperceptions, or lies am I about to uncover?

9

Catholic Charities
and the History Cop

Sunflowers and hydrangeas stole the garden glory from the peonies and irises weeks ago, and I've stopped meeting the mail carrier on the front walk. While I enjoy mailman Dale's anecdotes about his kids, August's ninety-degree temps have me shuttling to the local pool with Kassie and her pals instead. When the non-identifying information from Catholic Charities slid into the mailbox today, there was no welcome party.

Standing over the kitchen island in a damp bathing suit and cover-up, I discover the cream envelope emblazoned with the organization's fiery red logo. Tucked behind my fall bulb catalogues, it's as if a bee from my well-tended garden has stung me. I drop the letter and run warm palms along the length of my goose-pimpled arms. When I came in a few minutes ago, I had just two thoughts: ridding my skin of chlorine and sunscreen and deciding between leftovers or takeout for dinner. The air-conditioning and the letter from Catholic Charities have frozen me to the kitchen floorboards.

I pick up the cream envelope and gingerly pass it from one palm to the other. It's heftier than the one from Vital Records that jolted my system four weeks ago. Reaching for the letter opener, I slide the blade under the flap. My insides dissolve into chaos. Excitement and anxiety, relief and dread enter the front door of my heart and thrum to my belly. I grab the back of the chair and lower myself into the seat at the desk.

A month ago, when Vital Records forwarded the details from my original birth record, it set off an onslaught of fantasies that pepper me now, day and night. In that hazy lull before sleep comes, I have visions of my twenty-six-year-old pregnant mother laboring alone in a maternity hospital, and I wonder if she was forbidden or unwilling to see my twin sister and me in the nursery. After that reverie, another scene appears: I travel alone to an unfamiliar place and find myself on a front stoop, ringing a doorbell. An older woman cracks open the door. Below her chin, a security chain dangles. Bespectacled eyes squint at me with distrust and lack of recognition. As I'm speaking to the woman, she slams the door.

When I was a young girl, I lay in bed at night much as I do now, considering my adoption. Back then, my musings centered on why I'd been placed for adoption, what my biological parents looked like, and whether I resembled them. I also puzzled whether my first set of parents thought about me, considered coming back for me, and what I'd do if they did.

Now as I stare at the Catholic Charities envelope, I consider the story Jenny and I made up about our birth parents having been teenaged sweethearts. As I slice through the envelope, I question whether its content will support five decades of speculation or if my world is about to be rocked.

I want to yank the pages loose from the envelope, but the dogs scratch and yelp at the back door, and I can't ignore them. Taking them a fresh bowl of water, I rest on the painted wooden steps for a minute. Even though the cream envelope is pulling me back indoors, my mind skips to my attempt weeks ago to tour St. Vincent's, the orphanage where Jenny and I spent the first three weeks of our lives.

When I received the black-and-white paperback, *St. Vincent's: An Orphanage That Shined*, I devoured it and crafted a plan. Not only did I want color photos of the stately red brick building, I wanted to get inside. Following another downtown appointment, I dodged the homeless people loitering outside the center's gates and stepped into the vestibule.

I offered the security guard a shy smile. "I'm an alum of St. Vincent's. From the 1950s. Can I get a tour?"

He shook his head and looked down at the visitor log. "You need someone from Catholic Charities to set that up."

"But—" I started to say. On the last page of the paperback was an invitation, a permission slip to tour the orphanage-turned-relief services center at any time.

Interrupting me, the guard gestured past my shoulder. "The best I can do is let you look at the photos there." He pointed across the lobby toward a dim hallway.

I turned, grateful for a moment to squelch the tears that lately seemed ready and eager to spill. For the next fifteen minutes, I absorbed a dozen black-and-white framed photographs. In them were nuns in full habits and young, uniformed nurses cuddling infants or tending to small children. None of the pictures revealed bug-eyed fraternal twin girls with wispy swirls of light brown hair. I left the city, deflated. A theme was clear. Whenever I challenged my closed adoption, it dealt me deferral, dismissal, or outright rejection. The process was wearing on me.

On the back steps, sweating in the dreadful heat, I'm anxious over what I'm about to learn from Catholic Charities and how it's going to make me feel. Emmett, the male collie, nudges my knee with his long snout. His labored panting pastes his mouth into a grin. Or is it a sneer to mirror my tenuous mood? Inside the cool house, I give each dog a vigorous belly rub. As I pull three sheets of stationery from the envelope, a thought pops into my head. The Catholic Charities staff person who issued this letter could be the perfect person to set up a tour of my orphanage.

When I'm on the phone a few hours later, Jenny asks, "Where do we stand with Worldwide Tracers?"

I imagine my sister sitting like I do with her feet up on a kitchen chair, her lanky legs crossed at the ankles, a glass of wine swirling in her right hand as the dishwasher hums. As I sit alone in the back of the house, the faint sound of Steve winding the grandfather clock makes its way into the kitchen.

"I called them right after I read the Catholic Charities letter," I say. "I talked to Kurt's assistant. He wasn't in the office today. I told her that the Catholic Charities letter revealed that our birth mother used an alias—a common practice that was both encouraged and considered legal. She said she'd relay the information to Kurt." Ever since speaking to Kurt's aide, the worry box in my brain has been rattling.

"Did she say why there aren't any new developments in our case?" Jenny's raised voice sounds accusatory.

Reason tells me Jenny's frustration is with our ineffective search agency and not me, but because I selected and hired WWT, I'm defensive. The four hundred dollars we forked over is steep considering what they've delivered so far. How Worldwide Tracers plans to leapfrog over my birth mom's false identity is a question I want Kurt to answer.

"Kurt's aide suggested that the trouble they've had in locating our birth mom is probably due to the alias." Two towns over from where I live, Jenny sips her chardonnay while I lift my glass of cabernet.

To steer us away from WWT's failures, I flip through the typewritten pages from our adoption agency. This report, which cost yet another fee, reveals all the non-identifying information from our closed adoption file. Current Illinois law doesn't compel Catholic Charities, a private adoption agency, to release our birth mother's real name or where she was from.

"Jen, what surprises you most? The three-year difference in their ages, that they were not teenagers like we thought, or that our birth mom was Catholic and dated a Protestant?"

"I guess the last one. This letter makes it seem that religion was the reason they didn't marry. Back in those days, it was a big deal to date a man who wasn't Catholic. If he didn't convert, they couldn't marry in a Catholic church."

I mimic Jenny's sigh and turn to the second page of the document, running my finger down until I find the paragraph about education. "I was glad to read that both of them went to college. It says here our birth dad was taking graduate courses in psychology." My mind's eye whips to the framed diploma in psychology hanging above my desk.

Jenny pounces on this. "Yeah, it's cool you have that in common with him. I'll tell you what else makes me happy. Our parents were teachers in the same elementary school. They knew one another and were in a relationship."

I'd had the same reaction as Jenny when I read that. I skip down to the paragraph Jenny referred to. There it is in black and white. Tracing over it with the tip of a finger, I whisk it off to the pleasure center in my brain. Our parents were in a relationship— they had meant something to one another.

Jenny and I move to the section where our birth father is described. It explains Kassie's strawberry blond hair, Danny's thick, muscular build, and the blue eyes Molly inherited. Taking the wonder out of where our family's physical attributes came from is marvelous fun and sharing it with my twin sister like this is not just pleasing, it's gratifying.

It doesn't surprise Jenny or me that the main thing that drove us to this moment is missing. In the intake interview with our birth mom fifty years ago, the Catholic Charities staff person posed only basic health questions like "Are you in good health and do you wear glasses?" In our packet, there are no detailed family health questionnaires, nor any addendum from either birth parent alerting the agency about family medical issues that developed since our adoption.

"Besides the lack of medical details, I'm disappointed to find out we aren't one bit Irish." I've been grappling with this all afternoon and want Jenny's take on it.

Our freckled pale complexions have led strangers and family to believe that Jenny and I have plenty of Irish blood flowing through us. As legal members of the Ryan clan, we assimilated our adoptive family's Irish traditions. We donned green on St. Patrick's Day, headed to the city for the parade and the annual dyeing of the Chicago River green. At sixteen, I made it onto Chicago's St. Patrick's Queen Court. On March 17, 1975, I garnered an excused absence from my high school to ride atop a convertible and wave crazily at crowds of kids and drunks on State Street. Since then, I've made several trips to Ireland. Changing my heritage at fifty isn't what I expected to tackle on a Wednesday. I'm not just disappointed, I feel the loss in my core.

"Agreed. Look at the bright side. At least we finally know we have a French, German, and Norwegian heritage." Jenny's being positive, but I detect a letdown in her voice.

She charges on. "How about our birth mom being one of twelve? With that many siblings, I bet they have huge family reunions in whatever midwestern state they live in."

The report didn't divulge what state our birth mom originated from, only that she'd come to Chicago and met with an adoption social worker at Catholic Charities. It's anyone's guess whether she still lives locally or has returned to wherever home was.

"Yeah," I say. "Twelve. What a strange coincidence since Mom is the youngest of twelve."

The similarities between our adoptive and birth moms are uncanny. Our mothers were elementary school teachers, came from large families with a German heritage, and as young women had brown hair and dark eyes. Our fathers have blue eyes and glasses in common. Back in the '50s and '60s, Catholic Charities followed a strict policy whereby they matched adoptees to families with similar physical traits. This practice made it less obvious that a child was not a biological offspring, and it hid the onerous illegitimate/bastard label from a very judgmental society.

"Not much about our birth father in this letter. It doesn't sound like he played a role in the adoption process. I feel sorry for her, don't you?" Jenny's compassion hits a chord with me.

"Yep. She had a lot to deal with. I admire her for figuring it out. We wouldn't be here if she'd chosen abortion." We're both silent for a minute. "Hope she's okay." My voice grows soft and imbedded in it is a wish, a prayer that we will find her healthy and well.

Jenny switches gears. "WWT is a dud. Let's hire someone new. What do you think about moving forward with Catholic Charities as our next search agency? I really don't want to wait for the Illinois laws to change next year."

I consider my sister's statement. Fifteen months is a long time to wait for our original birth record, one that might list our birth mother's alias instead of her true identity. One of the caveats in the proposed change to Illinois's adoption statute concerns me. If our birth mom wanted to block our efforts in attaining the unredacted OBR, the statute provides for it. Would she know to do this? Would she want to keep us from finding her? The thought of her blocking my efforts gives me a sick feeling.

"Jen, I agree with you. Spending more search dollars seems inevitable. Last night, I discovered a feature on Ancestry.com called

Ask the Expert. There's a local guy I want to contact. He calls himself 'the History Cop.'" Perhaps it's the wine, but suddenly I feel like I could nod off in the kitchen chair.

"Okay. Go for it. We may learn something," Jenny says.

"Done. I'll call Ray, 'the History Cop,' and find out what Catholic Charities charges for a search. Let's talk tomorrow." I circle the social worker's name at the bottom of the document. Besides search fees, I plan to quiz her about touring St. Vincent's.

After Jenny disconnects, I pull out the journal I'd scribbled in after receiving Catholic Charities' note this afternoon. Phrases jump out at me: *little knowledge gained compared to time and dollars spent; closed adoption has far too many gatekeepers, too many rules, too many unknowns; birth mother alias could be a huge problem.*

Flipping pages, I reread an older entry about my desire to know what happened with my birth mother in the days following my birth.

Birth Mother,

> *The day after our birth, you were given the relinquishment papers to sign. As wards of the state, our transfer arrangements were finalized. Two winged-hat nuns from St. Vincent's Orphanage would come for us. We were going on to the next stage of our adoption journey.*

> *Without you.*

> *The duty nurse at the women's hospital knew we were not supposed to be with you. A mother herself, the burly matron assessed the cruelty of the impending surrender. She knew your heartache might never loosen its vise-like grip, and so she took it upon herself to deliver us mewing like baby kittens to your room.*

> *You heard us.*

> *The cacophony of two rolling bassinets pushed and pulled down the length of a sparkling linoleum floor from the forbidden area of the nursery echoed toward your room. The curtain*

separating you from the other young women was yanked back, and the matron slid our carts into your antiseptic-scented cubicle. Her glare fell on you, and you assembled your weakened body. Acknowledging you with a stiff nod, she retreated down that long, glistening hallway back to the nurses' station.

You knew.

This moment was a gift from your god, the one you prayed to every day of your unplanned pregnancy. Your god who had forgiven your sins and who delivered to you twin girls—healthy and beautiful and perfect. Fair-skinned and light-haired daughters henceforth gifted to another mother to raise as her own.

You stared at us.

One more baby than you'd expected to emerge from your heavy, young womb. Two sets of fists pummeling air. Two tiny chests heaving in tight pink swaddles. Children of the short spark of passion, the result of a relationship gone awry.

You had only this moment.

The white-uniformed nurse, the one who dropped us on your doorstep unannounced, the one with a maternal bent, would retrieve us imminently. She had broken stringent rules with this defiantly charitable act of presenting us to you.

You leaned over.

Lifting one of us, you brought a day-old daughter up to your breast. The other one of us knew her twin had captured you, so she stirred. You managed somehow to lift the other and position her so that both of us felt your heartbeat leaping like a fire on a windless beach. A chance caress with which to draw strength and love to last a lifetime.

You heeded footsteps.

As you kissed the velvet sweet spot on our virgin brows, we luxuriated in the scent of you on one another. Facing each other in the cradles, you said: you will need one another, stay strong, and someday, God willing, we will meet again.

You blessed us.

You made the sign of the cross on the door of our minds, over our hungry mouths, and upon our yearning hearts. Just as you do in Mass before taking the Lord into your thoughts, into your words, and into your life. After you crossed yourself, your palms met. You pleaded with Him to bless us all the days of our lives.

And He did.

10

Aurelia and the CI

I n August, when Catholic Charities confirmed that our birth
mother used an alias, Worldwide Tracers stopped returning my
phone calls. The four-hundred-dollar fee I paid in the spring produced just two things: the non-identifying information from our
birth record and a listing on the state adoption registry. I know
now that I could have secured that information on my own for free.
Jenny and I are no closer to finding our birth mother than we were
before hiring WWT.

I can't help but wonder what Kurt did with the pink phone slips
requesting he return my call and provide a search update. Did he
slide them into the trash bin under his desk, or had the receptionist
deposited them in hers first? When I'm feeling generous, I think
that some high-profile person jumped ahead of Jenny and me in
the WWT queue, and I half believe that any day now, Kurt will
phone with a breakthrough. I suspect our case landed in a stockpile of unsolved searches, labeled "lost causes." The experience with
Worldwide Tracers and Kurt has left me feeling used and frustrated,
vulnerable and stupid.

The adoption registries and forums with which I registered earlier in the summer have produced the same results as the search agency: no feedback, no links, no clues, and no paths to follow. Catholic Charities Post Adoption Services has become our only option. Whether it's because of the dismissive note from them twenty years ago or the experience with WWT, Jenny and I have been slow to commit.

The reality of our situation concerns me. WWT led us on from April through September, and Catholic Charities has a six- to eight-month waiting list. At this rate, trading out search angels means a year will pass before we track down our birth mom, who is now almost seventy-seven years old. When my name makes it to the top of the Catholic Charities waiting list, I can only pray that she's still alive and of sound mind. The biggest unknown is whether the agency's adoption file contains her true identity. Dollars and months could evaporate before learning a search is not viable.

Before committing to Catholic Charities, I send a message to Ask the Expert on Ancestry.com. Within hours, Ray, a local detective calling himself "the History Cop," agrees to meet with Jenny and me. He promises that no money needs to change hands until he is certain he can help us. This resonates with us.

Jenny and I meet Ray on a chilly Sunday afternoon at Caribou Coffee in La Grange. One block to the north, my folks' senior living complex is visible. The brilliant fall foliage surrounding the senior living center blocks all views of the coffee shop, but it feels as if our parents are watching us plot the next attack on our closed adoption. As we enter the bustling coffee spot, I half expect my mother to burst in, the disdain for our task clear in the way she refuses to meet our surprised looks.

Perhaps the negative karma I imagined did follow Jenny and me in from the parking lot, because when we lay out our search history, Ray shakes his head. He can't help us. Our birth mother's alias is the problem. We need her real name to proceed. If only WWT had been as forthcoming and honest as Ray, "the History

Cop." Before we bundle up in coats and set aside our coffee mugs, Ray offers us fresh advice.

Since Catholic Charities has such a long wait, Ray recommends we look into the Confidential Intermediary Service of Illinois (CISI). The program is new, and it comes with a fee for service. The first step is to contact the Midwest Adoption Center (MAC) in Des Plaines that issues the paperwork to have a confidential intermediary (CI) assigned by the Circuit Court. Ray explains that a supervising judge allows the intermediary's access to the adoption file, and over the course of one year, the intermediary is required to provide updates to the court.

Ray believes that the CISI backlog is shorter than the one at Catholic Charities. I look over at my sister, but Jenny studies the lukewarm tea in her mug. Her half-lidded eyes and pursed lips mean she's thinking. When her eyes open and catch mine, her look says, *Why wait for Catholic Charities. We're ready now. Let's go with CISI.* I nod. The check to the intermediary service will bring the cost of our adoption search over the thousand-dollar mark.

"Hi, Dad, what are you up to today?" I shout into my cell phone.

"Just reading the paper, honey." I picture him sinking into his specialty recliner, fingering the collar of his shirt as is his habit.

As I talk with my dad, I'm rushing along the main street of Hinsdale, my black pumps avoiding the sidewalk cracks. Where the road meets the railroad tracks, I pause outside Corner Bakery and switch my cell phone to the other ear. It's a spectacular November morning, sunny with only a hint of coolness, a day for gloves and hats to remain in the hall closet.

"How's Mom?" I ask, more out of habit than anything else.

Setting my briefcase down, I scan the tracks. No trains in sight. Plenty of time to grab something hot to drink before the forty-minute ride into the city. Across the street where the residential quarter begins, political banners and yard posters spill from brown lawns into the parkway. Election Day. I hope the midterm elections don't foul up my plans to enter the courthouse. My shin presses into the briefcase at my feet—I don't want it too far from reach. The legal paperwork that lines the inside compartment is replaceable but losing it will ruin my day.

Dad clears his throat. "Your mom is lying down, saying her novena."

I know what that scene looks like. Mom lies on their big bed, the one with the headboard hand-painted in verses of love. Her eyes are closed and her lips twitch in prayer.

A thought comes bounding in. I'm an idiot. "Dad, is she low again?"

"Yes, Jules. It's that time of year. Susie will be dead thirty-five years later this week." I picture my dad, his fingers toying with the religious medals layered below his shirt.

"Oh . . ." I catch my breath. I'm so focused on my adoption search that I almost slipped up on an important date.

"Is she taking her meds? Make sure she drinks enough water and gets out for a walk."

"I'm doing my best," Dad says.

I wish I could run the few blocks home, grab the Buick, rush over to the apartment, and wrap my arms around my father. He always does his best. His best is managing life through corny jokes and a lighthearted view toward the world.

"Sorry, Dad." I can't think of anything else to say.

"Where are you off to today?"

I consider all that he's managing and debate whether to tell him about my errand. An inner warning light flashes: Don't be sneaky. In the long run, it's best to be honest.

"I'm going downtown, Dad. I'm filing the paperwork to get a court-appointed intermediary to relaunch the search for my birth mother. I want background information. I mentioned this last week when I brought over the little book about St. Vincent's Orphanage. Remember?"

"Yes, I remember. It'll work out, Julie. Once you decide to do something, there's no stopping you. God bless you." My father is so nice, and I'm a forgetful, self-involved daughter determined to jostle my parents' world with my nosy pokes into an adoption that lit up their world fifty years ago.

"My train will be here soon, Dad. I'll call you later. Say hi to Mom for me."

"Will do."

Before he hangs up, I whisper, "I hope the day is okay for you, Dad. Love you."

Hot tea scalds my hands, and I curse myself for not grabbing a cardboard sleeve. I nestle the steaming cup between my black pumps and tug up the knee-highs that have inched down my calves. I sympathize with my twin sister for dealing with these corporate dress issues on top of lugging a purse and briefcase. My reflection in the train's plate glass window confirms that I resemble Jenny, my twin the corporate sales manager. As the train leaves Hinsdale's depot, I wish that Jenny's work schedule had allowed her to be with me today.

When the eastbound train slows to a stop at La Grange Road, I gaze out the window north of the tracks toward the coffee shop where I met Ray, "the History Cop," three weeks ago. Through the trees that are more than ready for winter, I also see the red brick building where my parents live. I think about the call with my dad, the upcoming anniversary of my sister's death, and the round of tests my doctor recently ordered: another mammogram and a uterine biopsy. I wish that those concerns did not cloud today's task. Today is about putting life back into the lagging search for our birth mom. Reaching into my briefcase, I pull out the intermediary paperwork to check over once more.

On the chilly, overcast Monday morning after our coffee with Ray, I phoned the Midwest Adoption Center. The intake coordinator, Shanika, went over details I'd scanned on their website:

Any adult adopted person, adoptive parent of a minor, and birth parent touched by an adoption that was legally completed in Illinois can request the court appoint a Confidential Intermediary to conduct a search for a biological relative. . . . When appointed by the court, the CI will attempt to locate the sought-after individual, explain who is making the outreach and what options are available, and facilitate exchange of information. The confidentiality of all parties is protected, and no identifying information is released without written consent.

Shanika's voice was full of practiced patience as she explained the process to me. "I'll put the forms in the mail to you today. Once they're complete, mail them to one of the county circuit courts mentioned on the information sheet. You'll receive a callback from our office once a judge has assigned you an intermediary."

"Will I need to attend a hearing?" I asked.

"Sometimes the judge will have questions for a petitioner. While that's a possibility, it doesn't happen often. May I put you on hold for a minute?"

When Shanika returned to the line, I asked a critical question. One that would determine to whom Jenny and I would write our next adoption search check. "Is there a waiting list?"

"We have a short backlog. An intermediary should be available to work on your case around the first of the year."

With one obstacle cleared, I tackled the second one. "Is it a problem that my birth mother used an alias?"

Shanika didn't hesitate. "Your CI will requisition your adoption agency for the records. With any luck, your birth mother's real name is captured in their files." I did the math. If Jenny and I went with CISI, in two months we'd know if our search had a chance. If we hung in with Catholic Charities Post Adoption Services, it might be spring before we learned the same thing.

As the train pulls into Union Station, the overhead lights flicker, and my knees won't stay still. Today is such a big step. I return the CISI paperwork to my briefcase, but the energy pulsing in my legs continues. The reality of entering the courthouse, clearing security, and finding the proper floor to file the forms heightens my anxiety in an already pressure-filled day. One more time, I look at the empty seat across from me and wish that my twin were with me.

Even though Shanika from the Midwest Adoption Center assured me that mailing in the completed paperwork was sufficient, the possibility of a hearing influenced my decision to come into Chicago with the paperwork. So did my birth mother's advancing age and my experience with turnaround time from government agencies. Neither Jenny nor I want any more roadblocks or delays. By filing the CISI paperwork at the courthouse in person, I ensure two things: that my request for an intermediary is processed in the shortest amount of time; and if a hearing is necessary, I'll be present.

Emerging into the throng of passengers at Union Station, I contemplate an appearance before a judge. In college, I was a witness to a traffic accident. The pressure of speaking before an open courtroom drained me. Besides the sweat leaking from every pore, my muscles ached from sitting like a mannequin in the witness box during interrogation. If there is a hearing today, my aim is to be prepared. As I walk the fifteen minutes from the train station to the courthouse, I rehearse my comments. At the forefront of my argument are two issues: I have a personal right to any information that concerns me; and my precarious health demands it.

Julie Ryan McGue

At the Daley Center, I sail through security. Election Day is a blessing. The usual crowds have either taken the day off or are lining up at voting booths. Picking up my briefcase and purse on the other side of the metal detectors, I think about my birth mother and adoptive parents. If either party appeared for my adoption hearing in Family Court in 1959, they were probably not wanded, scanned, and patted down like I am today. A security guard points to the building directory and elevator bank. In the back of the crowded elevator, I release my trapped breath as quietly as I can.

The elevator deposits me outside a large office suite where records and petitions are processed. At the far end of the room, three government workers cluster behind a long counter. Stanchions direct petitioners into an orderly lane that snakes around the anteroom. A young couple and I wait for the workers to finish up their pre-lunch conversation before being motioned forward.

The young clerk who waves me over has never handled a CI petition in person before. Most people mail them in, she says. She dates and time stamps my paperwork and writes a case number underneath. Just in case, I scribble it on my copy, and then I ask about a hearing. She looks at me with a blank expression, ambles over to her coworker, and then directs me up to the Family Court floor. In the elevator, I have that sensation one does before something important is about to happen—expectancy boosts stomach juices and uncertainty riles the bowels.

The layout of the Family Court floor confuses me. Over one shoulder are the judicial offices, and over the other is a maze of courtrooms, conference rooms, and waiting rooms. I enter the judicial section and stop at the receptionist's desk.

"Hi. I filed my petition downstairs for a confidential intermediary. When I asked about a hearing for my case, the clerk directed me up here. Do you know where I should be?"

"I'm not sure either. Hold on, let me ask Judge Norton." Lifting the receiver, she punches an extension button on her phone. A moment later, she looks up at me with a pleased grin. "We're not very busy today on account of Election Day. The judge will be right with you."

Out of the corner of my eye, a man about my age exits an office down the long hallway to my right. He greets me in the reception area and invites me back to his office. As I follow, my briefcase taps my thigh in rhythm with my heart. This is all happening so fast. In his office, Judge Norton takes a seat behind a desk mounded with files, and I explain about filing the CI paperwork and the possibility of a hearing.

"The person who handles those hearings is not in today, but Judge Aurelia Pucinski is. Let me give her a quick call." When Judge Norton reaches for his phone, I sit deeper into my chair and release my briefcase to the floor.

"Aurelia? It's Bob. Listen, I have an adult petitioner, an adoptee, sitting in my office. She just filed the CI paperwork and is wondering about a hearing. Nancy is not in today."

He doodles on his notepad for a second and then drops the pen. "Okay. Thanks. I'll bring her to your office. Hey! Good luck today. I know you're up for retention. See you in a bit."

Judge Norton smiles and stands. "You're in luck. Judge Pucinski not only oversees the CI program, she was instrumental in seeing it put in place. I'll take you to her."

Feeling blessed by good fortune, I follow Judge Norton around a corner, and we weave past darkened courtrooms and small conference rooms. One room has a sign next to the door, which reads: ADOPTIVE FAMILY WAITING ROOM. As we pass it, I wonder if my parents may have sat in there in the fall of 1959 while the judge signed our adoption decree. My thoughts run all over the place. How easy this has been! I've only been in the building twenty minutes and now I'm to see a judge. Judge Aurelia Pucinski. I've been messing around for months figuring out how to get my adoption search up and running, and then snap, it's done. I didn't expect any of this. Election Day luck!

At the door of her office, Judge Norton introduces me to Judge Pucinski, and then he shakes my hand. "You're in good hands. Best of luck to you going forward."

"Please sit. May I call you Julie?" Judge Pucinski asks.

The chair she directs me to is identical to the one in Judge Norton's office. Standard government issue, I guess.

"Yes! Julie is fine. Thank you for taking the time to see me today, Judge."

"My pleasure. It's not often that I get to talk with an adoptee who will directly benefit from our confidential intermediary program. Tell me more about yourself and your case."

Leaning forward, I fill her in about being a fraternal twin and our adoption through Catholic Charities. I share my recent bout of health issues and my fervent desire for some medical background. Judge Pucinski's eyes never leave my face. She nods at me as I speak. It's as if I'm sharing my story not with a stranger but with an interested advisor.

"I'm curious. How did you learn of the CI program?" I explain about Worldwide Tracers, the Catholic Charities wait list, and the private detective, Ray.

She chuckles. "My, oh my! You sure have been through a lot. I'm certain you have landed on the right track with CISI. Do you know your case number?" She picks up a pen and I pull out my copy of the petition and read off the numbers I scribbled downstairs. "Please spell your last name for me." Judge Pucinski writes my full name under my case number.

When she looks up at me from her notepad, I ask, "Judge, will I need to come back for a hearing?"

Her smile is warm. "No need. Let's consider this conversation your hearing, shall we?"

I lower my eyes, willing tears back in. "That's wonderful. Thank you."

Judge Pucinski stands. "You should receive notice within a week, or so, about the CI assigned to your case. I hope this all works out for you, Julie. I'm happy the State of Illinois could help you."

"Thanks, Judge. Good luck with your reelection."

"Don't forget to vote!"

In the elevator down to the lobby, I reflect upon what happened over the last hour. I walked into the courthouse awash in vulnerability and loneliness, and upon my departure, I'm buoyed by not just one advocate but by an entire cheering section of judges. In the taxi back to the train station, I try to put a more definitive label on my state of mind. Yes, I'm surprised by the sequence of events, but I had low expectations from the start. It's as if an unseen force shepherded me from the unknown toward safety. I catch a glimpse of my face reflected in the taxi's window—I'm glowing. I know what's causing it. Hope.

The conductor announces that the 2:34 westbound Metra is leaving Union Station. Before the lights dim and the train lurches onto the tracks, I pocket my cell phone and rest my head against the seatback. What an incredible day! I review all that happened: no crowds at the courthouse, record time in filing my petition, the serendipitous meetings with Judge Norton and Judge Pucinski. Seven months have passed between hiring Worldwide Tracers and applying for a confidential intermediary. In Judge Pucinski, I sense an advocate who will monitor my case, which is a huge relief given the debacle with WWT. The train is almost to the La Grange depot when I think to pull out my phone.

A voice mail. From my doctor's office. When the train screeches to a halt, it feels like my heart has stopped, too.

Bolting upright, I wonder if I have enough service to access it.

It takes two tries before I get the phone to cooperate. Dr. Frank's nurse relays two crucial messages: last week's mammogram was normal, and so was the uterine biopsy. I concentrate on slowing my exhale. What else will this day bring? The nurse continues. If I experience any more breakthrough bleeding, I'm to call the doctor immediately. In six months, I'm scheduled for another pelvic exam, and if the fibroid continues to enlarge, Dr. Frank will explore surgical options with me.

The train's horn blasts, and we gather speed. Two more stations and then a short walk home. As the landscape blurs past, it occurs to me that my lingering health issues run parallel with the drama to locate my birth mother. If one comes to a successful conclusion, perhaps the other one will too.

Part Two

FINDING HER

It is good to have an end to journey toward;
but it is the journey that matters, in the end.

~ Ursula K. Le Guin

11

Linda from MAC

W hen my cell phone buzzes, I'm in the dining room pulling out tablecloths and napkins to prep for the two dozen guests I expect for Thanksgiving. Carrying a Chicago-area prefix, the number on the phone isn't one I recognize. Two weeks ago, I received a letter from the Circuit Court of Chicago informing me that a confidential intermediary had been assigned to my adoption search case, and that I would hear from someone soon. Since then, I'm never far from a phone.

As I pick up my cell, the hammering of my heart is so fierce that I feel it in my ears.

"Julie? I'm Linda Fiore from the Midwest Adoption Center. Judge Aurelia Pucinski appointed me as your confidential intermediary. Is now a good time to talk?"

The young woman's voice is so soft and smooth that I'd like to slip into one of the cushy dining room chairs, but instead I run to the kitchen for a pen and paper.

For the next twenty minutes, Linda and I discuss my case. I elaborate on the reasons for my search, my recent health issues, and I mention that I'm a fraternal twin. Because of all the service fees, I explain that Jenny and I decided I should be "the searcher." While her office has handled other cases involving twins, Linda tells me that we would be her first.

"What happens next?" I underline Linda's name on my notepad.

"I've sent you a packet. It contains a contract for the CI service and a questionnaire. Complete the questionnaire and forward any paperwork you have related to your adoption. Once I receive those, I'll start requesting files and documents from government and private agencies, and then I'll complete your Search Assessment. The Search Assessment will show the relatives about whom I've received information and the probability that I can locate them. This usually takes ten to twelve weeks, but it could take longer if files or documents are difficult to obtain. On the Search Assessment, you'll be given the choice of selecting the relative you want to find. If you want to search for more than one, there's another fee."

I stop scribbling on my notepad and voice my biggest concern. "Linda, we know from Catholic Charities that our birth mother used an alias."

Linda doesn't hesitate. "That was a common practice in the era when you were adopted. The adoption file should disclose the birth parents' real names. I'll give you an idea how likely it is that I can find them in the Search Assessment. Some people are located in a few weeks while other searches continue for many months. I promise to provide you with updates as often as possible. Any other questions?"

My head is spinning. "I can't think of any right now."

Linda's voice grows soft again. "I understand that waiting for news of progress will be difficult. I urge you to talk with a trusted friend or relative about your feelings. In addition, you'll have the opportunity to talk with me about issues that may come up during the process."

"I'd like that." From just one conversation, I can tell that Linda is a good listener.

After I hang up with my new CI, I sit at the kitchen desk looking over my notes. Linda's last words tickled an idea I've been mulling over. When I last spoke with Lisa, the social worker at Catholic Charities, she mentioned a quarterly post-adoption support group comprised of birth mothers, adoptees, and adoptive parents. When I brought the support group idea up to Jenny, she didn't think her schedule could handle one more meeting. The chance to talk openly with other adoptees who are also going through search and reunion is compelling to me.

There's another reason to become involved with Catholic Charities—getting on the list for a tour of St. Vincent's, the orphanage where Jenny and I lived before our adoption. Ever since learning that I'd been baptized at the orphanage and not at Holy Name Cathedral, I can't get the chapel out of my mind. Reconnecting with the earliest moments of my life is something I'm eager to do.

Celebrating the holidays with my family in Montana every year is like living in a Hallmark movie. Nestled into a steep ridge of lodgepole pines, our log home borders a ski resort. My family and I arrived the weekend before Christmas, and already the snow is piled as high as I am tall. The nights in Big Sky have been frigid but deliciously jammed with constellations. The crisp, bluebird days are so sunny that atop Pioneer Mountain, Wyoming and Idaho are visible in the distance. The best part of escaping to the mountains at such a hectic time of year is surrounding myself with my four children, and that they invite close friends to join us only exaggerates the fun.

Yesterday, I spent the day skiing with the kids and their buddies. We charged down corduroy ski runs and took breaks at the main lodge for marshmallow-topped hot cocoa and snacks. Last night, dressed in sweats and slippers, our group sprawled in front of a roaring fire. We toasted Danny and his Army football teammates who are headed to Dallas to play in the Armed Forces Bowl this weekend.

After the boys went up to bed, Steve and I sat up with our daughters, Colleen, Molly, and Kassie. JT, Molly's best friend since high school, was with us too. Much like a daughter, JT's been tagging along with our family to Montana for as long as I can remember. JT's warm brown eyes and gentle nature endear her to everyone. Not just an old high school friend, Molly trusts JT with her deepest secrets.

The six of us talked until the second bottle of cabernet was empty. There was so much to catch up on. With only six months left in her graduate program in city planning at UT-Austin, Colleen, twenty-four, filled us in on her career opportunities. Fluent in Spanish and Portuguese, she wants to focus on transportation planning in a culturally diverse city. A recent graduate of Cornell, Molly, who is almost twenty-three, told stories about her projects for a NY-based pharmaceutical consulting firm. She had us laughing at things that happened as she traveled coast-to-coast with her job. Having forgotten her sneakers on one work trip, she went to the gym in her socks. JT shared the details of her impending mission trip to South Africa, and we all wished we could fit in a trip to visit her.

Eager to tell stories, the girls begged us not to call it a night, so Steve threw another log on the fire. While he got the fire roaring again, Kassie pestered her sisters and JT with worries about her first round of high school semester exams, which would follow Christmas break. Colleen and Molly convinced Kassie that there was no need to fret since she was a good student. JT's advice: spend a few hours each day reviewing for the hardest courses. We all laughed when Kassie rolled her eyes at the idea of studying during a ski vacation. And as always seems to happen these days, we discussed my ongoing search for birth relatives.

"I expect to hear from Linda, my intermediary, anytime in the next month or so. She's requisitioning documents like my sealed adoption records, and then she'll give me an idea how hard it will be to find my birth parents." To the group, I sounded more positive than I felt.

Molly put her arm around my shoulders. "I hope this works out for you, Mom. I don't want to see you get hurt."

I squeezed her back. "I've got a good feeling about this, honey. I've waited a long time to get at this." I looked into her concerned blue eyes. "Aren't you ready for some clues about your 'mystery genes'?"

Everyone chuckled at the mention of the "mystery genes," and each offered their idea as to who and what I'd find on the other side of *this*. Colleen wished that my "other mother" was still alive so that she could provide the health information I wanted. Kassie said she hoped I heard from the intermediary by my birthday in February, because *that* would be an amazing present. Molly, who played college basketball, bet all of us in the room that one of my birth parents was a college athlete, too. JT thought it would be amazing if I found other siblings.

Steve yawned. "I think all of you will be right. Let's call it a night."

The next morning, tired from getting up before sunrise to see Danny and his buddies off to the airport, I decide to take the day off from skiing. As I gather coffee cups and breakfast plates from around the kitchen, the four girls cluster outside in their ski gear. Colleen's brown eyes and short brown hair are hardly recognizable in her helmet and goggles. Next to her, JT tucks her dark ponytail into her neck warmer and then clips into skis. She kids Kassie about something that has them doubled up with laughter. Kassie's blond braids flop around as she bends to tighten her bindings. In her purple ski coat, Molly is the last one to trudge out of the ski room. Someone says something, and she laughs too, her cheeks red in the cold mountain air. Before the girls head over to the ski trail, I grab my cell phone so I can capture this moment for our scrapbook.

The phone buzzes in my palm. When I see the number, my heart takes an extra beat.

I don't wait for Linda's greeting. "Hi, Linda! I didn't expect to hear from you so soon. I hope you're calling with good news?" *Please say you have her real name. Please, please, please.*

Linda is all business. "As a matter of fact, I do have some news. I haven't completed the Search Assessment yet, but I wanted to give you a quick update. The adoption agency provided the two names that your birth mother used at the time of your birth. It's believed that one of these names is an alias, and one is her legal name. One was used in both the court file and on the original birth certificate. I checked the death index and this woman is still alive."

I sink into a kitchen chair. "Thank God." *We're going to be able to look for her.*

Processing Linda's message, I ask, "So is it her alias that's on the OBR and in the court records?"

If this is true, then next year's proposed change in Illinois's adoption law—one that provides adoptees born after 1946 with a copy of their original birth record—won't help me at all.

"I'm sorry, Julie, I can't reveal which name is on what document." I swallow hard. The CI program has so many restrictions, all due to the protection of rights and privacy.

What about my right to know?

"Do you . . . can you tell me how likely it is that you'll be able to find her?"

"As you know, I can't reveal anything about the second name, but what I can say is this: the name is not a common one. I've been able to locate a birthdate, a place of birth, and a marriage certificate. Based on our experience with other searches, the amount of information we've received is average, but we're often successful in locating a birth relative using this kind of information. While I don't know yet if the marriage record pertains to your birth mother,

I believe it's a possibility. The maiden name and the age of the woman whose record I located matches the information I know about your birth mother."

Linda is excruciatingly careful with her wording. She provides information without committing to it, and this frustrates me. "What about my birth dad? Did anything show up for him?"

"I'm sorry to say that I haven't received any information on him. The original birth certificate provided only the age of your birth father at the time of your birth. Should I learn of identifying information pertaining to him, a search for him may be possible."

"Are you saying that his name is not on my OBR or in the adoption file?"

Linda sighs. "That's correct."

"That was legal?"

"Yes, in those times a birth father's name was often absent from the documents."

My mind clicks over to a new set of worries. "So, in order to locate my birth father, we have to find my birth mom first." *There always seems to be one more step.* "This means that only my birth mom knows his name, doesn't it? She'd have to provide it in order for us to find him." I press a palm to my forehead. So many *ifs*.

"Yes."

Linda's reply is so soft that I move the phone tight to my ear. Perhaps I'm imagining it, but it feels as if Linda absorbs some of my disappointment. The thought of this, that another person besides Jenny and Steve and my family might share in my frustration with this impossible situation, makes me feel less bereft.

A fresh question pops out. "You said you found a marriage record. Could she have married my birth father? How long after Jenny and I were born did she get married?"

"I'm sorry. The CISI program does not allow me to be definitive. I can say she got married in the state in which she originated from."

So my birth mother went back home after she left Jenny and me in Chicago. Just like the many women profiled in Ann Fessler's book, *The Girls That Went Away*. My birth mom was one of those unwed mothers who left town and returned without her child. Instead of being irritated with her for using an alias and staying hidden all these years, I feel compassion for my twenty-six-year-old mother who had to make all those decisions.

I can't let go of the marriage detail though. "If you can't be specific, can you at least give me a range? Was it less than five years after I was born? Ten years? Twenty?"

If Linda is put off by my pestering, she doesn't let on. "I suppose I can provide the range." Her sigh is barely audible. "If this is the right woman, she married more than twenty years after your birth."

"Oh, my goodness." I pause to process this new fact. "She probably didn't marry my birth father then." Linda doesn't answer so I press on. "This means she was in her late forties when she married for the first time. I probably don't have any siblings then, do I?" *My birth mother was almost a spinster.* Now I feel bad for both of us.

Linda pauses. "At this point, I can't confirm whether you have siblings or not." If Jenny and I are my birth mother's only children, surely, she'll want us back in her life. Won't she?

As my back finds the sweet spot of the kitchen chair, I look out at the idyllic setting—the steep snowbanks, the cloudless skies, the bundled skiers enjoying their holiday. I'm so glad that I was home to take this call.

"Linda, can you guide me through what happens from here?"

"Yes. I'll formalize my findings in a written Search Assessment, which you should receive in a week. Once you read that over, you need to decide whether to move forward with your search. If you wish to do so, complete the confirmation form, and return it with the three-hundred-dollar service fee."

My head hurts thinking of all the checks I will write to CISI in the coming weeks: contract fee, service fee, and yet more fees if I look for my birth father. "How quickly will the search progress after that?"

"Many searches are completed quickly, and others may be difficult and lengthy. There's no way to predict."

I stifle a huge sigh. "You've given me a lot to think about. I'm so relieved that you found a second name for my birth mom and that she's alive. It's a wonderful Christmas gift. Count on us moving forward."

"I'll be happy to help you." Linda's voice grows serious again. "There's one more thing that you may want to start thinking about."

"Yes?"

"If I'm able to locate a current address for the woman I believe to be your birth mother, a letter will go out to her in January. In it, you can include a short message to her. Something short, two or three sentences, like: 'I'm in good health; I've had a good life; I'd like to fill in the missing pieces of my history.' Those are common themes that other searchers have put in their outreach letters."

The idea of communicating with my birth mom, even in this small way, excites me. "Wonderful. Jenny and I will collaborate. Should I just email the message to you?"

"That's fine. I'll be back to you as soon as I can confirm I have an address. Call me if you have any more questions."

After I hang up with Linda, my forearms fold onto the kitchen table, and I rest my head on top. With so much to emotionally navigate, the Catholic Charities adoption support group is sounding better and better to me.

Knowing that Jenny is in Colorado visiting with her husband's family, I send her an email summarizing the conversation with Linda. I hit the highlights: the CI found two names for our birth mom, she's alive, and she married later in life.

I also tell her:

The CI will send an outreach letter to our birth mother soon. It can contain a message from us, but not a letter or photos. Here's what I came up with:

> My twin sister and I want you to know that we're happy, in good health, and have had good lives. Please know that we've always wondered about you and have tried to locate you several times. It's not our intent to intrude on your privacy or disrupt your life. We wish to make contact with you and fill in the many missing pieces to our medical and family history.

The outreach letter will say that Linda is a court appointed official and has been asked by a woman born on Feb. 11, 1959 in Chicago to find her birth relatives, and that she should respond to Linda by letter or phone.

Linda will make two additional follow-ups one by certified mail to make sure the outreach letter was received. Sometimes there's an immediate response, but sometimes it takes time for all this to settle in before Linda will hear anything. Once Linda hears from our birth mom, she sets up contact between us—by mail or phone.

Our birth mother also has the right to deny contact, but this has only happened ONCE in all Linda's dealings.

SO HERE WE GO . . . every step of this has been worthwhile and surprising, and I'm ready for however it turns out!!! XO Julie

Once the email is sent, I tidy up the log home's kitchen and reflect on all the search efforts I made in 2010. First, I found Worldwide Tracers. They turned us on to the Department of Vital Records, which released facts from the original birth record. Still annoyed with WWT for wasting my time, I credit them for suggesting something I wouldn't have known to do: asking Catholic Charities for the non-identifying information in our agency's file. Even though there was no health history in the adoption file, Jenny and I learned valuable details about our birth parents and their circumstances. Then there was the private investigator, Ray, "the History Cop," who turned us on to the Midwest Adoption Center and the confidential intermediary program. Now we have Linda advocating for us. While not linear, each attempt led to another viable option. Yes, there always seems to be a next step, but our case is alive!

The new year, 2011, will start off exactly as I dreamed it would. We're on track to find our birth mom!

12

Denial of Contact

2011

A normal Tuesday in February would find me hustling around with errands and prepping for the eighth grade religious education class I teach after school on Wednesdays. The blizzard heaping the Midwest with more than six inches of heavy, wet snow has changed all of that. Schools and businesses are closing early, roads are becoming slippery and impassable, and every street corner resonates with the raucous scraping of snow shovels.

The snow has always been magical to me. Autumn's debris, shredded leaves and brown winter grass, vanishes. The transformation of the sepia landscape into something pure and pristine casts me in its spell—I just want to sit quietly and watch it accumulate. The white outdoor blanket is also an equalizer. It offers hope, a feeling that has been absent for days. Besides today being Colleen's twenty-fifth birthday, the day overflows with waiting. Waiting for news about JT, Molly's friend, who's in surgery now at a South African hospital. Waiting for news from my confidential intermediary about the outreach letter she sent to my birth mother. Waiting for the snow to stop so life can return to normal.

It's been three weeks since Linda, the intermediary assigned to me by the Circuit Court, located an address and mailed a letter to the woman she believes to be my birth mom. The rules of engagement are strict: I'm not allowed to know my birth mother's true identity until she grants permission. If my birth mom doesn't respond by the end of this week, Linda will try to reach her by phone. Assuming we have the correct person and she received the correspondence, the time she's taken to reply troubles me. Most days, the fear that my "stranger mother" will shove my twin and me back into obscurity keeps me awake for hours in the middle of the night.

Three days from now, Jenny and I will celebrate our fifty-first birthdays. The day is both a beacon and a deadline. Will our birth mom respond before the day she gave birth over five decades ago, or will she let it pass as if it's just any other day? My moods are like a roller coaster. One minute I'm soaring with optimism, and then I plunge into negativity. I can't wait to get off this wild ride.

Since Sunday, my search saga has taken a back seat to a life-threatening situation concerning Molly's friend, JT, who spent some of the recent holidays with us. She's fighting for her life. I can hardly believe that the young woman I have known for years, who sat with Steve and me before a blazing fire after Christmas, and who raced with my three girls down the ski slopes, is in a cardiac care hospital. Two weeks ago, JT left for her mission trip to South Africa. From the second she walked down the jet bridge, she experienced breathing problems. Initially thought to be allergies, her symptoms worsened. Molly phoned this morning to say JT had gone into surgery to remove multiple blood clots in her lungs and heart. Since that call, JT is never out of my thoughts.

As the white stuff mounds and the wind howls, I pray like a maniac for JT and for her parents. As a mother of four, it's not hard for me to imagine what JT's mother is going through. I remember all too well my own family's grief when my youngest sister died.

I think of my three girls—Colleen and Molly and Kassie—and the thought of losing one of them is unbearable. How not having them in my life compares to losing two daughters to adoption also plays in the back of my mind. I fear for JT's chances and that fear is juxtaposed against my worry about what my birth mom will decide to do. Mothers and daughters and the potential loss of that special relationship is the theme threading through these last few days. How both of these scenarios will play out feels like a game of roulette. Spin once for JT's chances to live, spin a second time for my chances of getting to know my "other mother."

As I snuggle under a nubby afghan, my home's sunroom has become both a lookout and my refuge for the afternoon. Next to the front porch, it's our family's favorite spot for sipping a cup of coffee or lounging with a book. It's not a place frequented by bad news. I find myself believing that my afternoon hours here will ward off any negativity that might arise.

When the landline rings, the effect is so jarring that both of the dozing collies leap into a barking frenzy. I shush the pair and shut them out of the sunroom.

"Julie?"

I'm expecting an update on JT, so the voice of Linda, my intermediary, startles me.

"Is this a good time?" Linda's voice is smooth like velvet. It tempts me into relaxing, but there's no way.

I exhale. "Sure."

"The center received a note from your birth mother today."

Everything stalls: my brain, my heart, my breathing, and my hopes. When I rescue my voice from underneath a hard swallow, it has the meek tones of a child who expects a scolding.

"Yes?"

"I'm sorry, Julie. She has denied contact with you."

Denied contact? My brain can't compute this. Technically, I know that this means the search is over—my birth mom's refusal to connect ends the process. But it can't be! I have so many unanswered questions.

I'm up and pacing the length of the sunroom, the phone at my ear. From the other side of the sunroom door, my dog Emmett watches me.

"But . . . did she at least fill out the medical questionnaire?" Anger leaks out.

My request for health history is more than just answers on a form. It's a way to connect with my birth mom and the only way to learn my birth father's name. It's the means to solve the entire puzzle of my existence. My birth mother's "denial of contact" means that everything I've been dreaming about, wanting and needing, is impossible. She has shut the door on me and squashed all my hopes and dreams.

"No. We didn't include the health forms in the first outreach. The agency's policy is to include them in the second round of correspondence. The goal of the first letter is simply to establish contact."

I huff. "Linda, I don't understand why it wasn't sent with the first outreach. A family health history was my goal from the beginning. Exactly what I didn't want to happen has happened. I've ended up with no contact and no health history. Will the judge allow us to go back to her?"

I look at Emmett. He paws at the sunroom door and his nose smudges the glass. I let him inside. As if he knows the tough spot where my heart has landed, he nuzzles my knee. I sniffle hard, damming up the tears his tenderness unleashes.

"No. The program dictates that once the birth relative rejects contact, we can't go back to them. They must initiate a future connection. I'm sorry. I was hoping that I could get your birth mom on the phone. From experience, once I'm able to talk to a birth parent, I'm successful in establishing an exchange of letters and photos. This did not play out as I expected."

"Linda, this is so unfair." Emmett licks my hand.

"Yes. Yes, it's unfair. Again, I'm so sorry. I can read the letter to you if you'd like. Perhaps it would help to hear her words?"

"I guess so." I shut my eyes and Linda begins with the date: February 5, 2011.

My birth mother's response flew through the postal service in record time. Three days. She penned it three days before today's snowstorm strangled the Midwest. Three days before JT went into surgery in Africa. It landed in Linda's inbox on my daughter's birthday. Three days before my own birthday. My world has tilted in three measly days.

Linda tells me:

Dear Confidential Intermediary:

I received your letter dated January 14, 2011. Yes, I am the person you refer to regarding the situation of February 11, 1959 in Chicago. I will be very specific. I do not want to have any connection with these two birth relatives in any way. I am taking you at your word that my confidentiality will be respected. There is no point in contacting my siblings or other relatives because they know nothing of this matter. A girlfriend and her mother helped me through all of this, and they are both deceased. My present family knows nothing of this. Do not try to call me because I have caller ID, and I will not answer your call. My confidentiality must be respected.

As I listen to Linda read my birth mom's message, I'm nearly doubled over in despair. Why wouldn't my birth mother want to know my sister and me? We're educated, well-mannered women who are not asking for money, just answers to questions. Hasn't my birth mom been waiting fifty years to know us? Deny contact, why would she do that? I'm her daughter, her long-lost child, and as far as we know, she has no other children. I don't understand.

Pricked by my birth mom's words, I say, "She sounds so angry.

Her note sounds so final. How can she refer to my birth as a 'situation'?"

Linda's voice is quiet and gentle. "The letter does have an angry tone to it. Keep in mind that we've caught her off guard. The outreach came to her out of the blue. She may settle down and change her mind. If she calls me at any point, I believe I can turn this around."

I pounce on the hope Linda offers. "What is the likelihood that she will change her mind?" Emmett's ears twitch, as if he intuits a shift in my mood.

Linda continues. "With birth mothers, anything can happen. I've seen some have a change of heart in days or weeks, and others never do. It's hard to know the extent of their trauma or how disruptive reintroducing a child they relinquished can be to their lives now."

Now it's Linda who sounds sad. It occurs to me how hard this might be on her—counseling the clients she's been cheering on.

"So all we do is wait? Wait for her to change her mind, and wait for her to contact you so we can ask her to fill out the health form?" This sounds like the "watchful waiting" doctors prescribe patients, like me, whose health scenario is too early to treat.

"Yes, at this point, that is all we're legally able to do."

While Linda's sympathy is soothing, my birth mom's stunning message brings on a fierce anger. I'm a child/woman spurned, and I refuse to accept the rejection. I want more, and I want what I want. I want all of it: the medical forms, to meet my birth mom, my birth father's name, and both branches of my genealogical tree filled in. My birth mom has a right to her privacy, but what about my right to know? Why do her rights trump mine? This feels like a cruel joke, a mistake, an error that Linda should rectify. In the two months that Linda has been working on my case, we have yet to meet in person. Now, I doubt that I'll get that chance.

I'm back on my feet, pacing. The dog has the good sense not to follow. "Linda, can you go back to the judge and ask permission to mail out the medical questionnaire? There's a hole in your agency's 'first outreach' policy. You see that, don't you?"

There's a pause on the line, then Linda says, "Let me talk to my supervisor. I understand your point. It may be up to the judge to rule on this."

I think about the judge, my judge, the one I met in the courthouse three months ago. While Judge Aurelia Pucinski is not personally overseeing my case, I want to believe that she might be keeping tabs on me. I recall how she wrote my name on her tablet along with my case number. This idea of a guardian angel judge emboldens me.

"I would like to pursue this as far as we can. If I need to get my doctors to provide medical reasons for the health forms to be sent to my birth mother, I will gladly do it." I glare out the snow-spattered windows.

"Okay, I will have to get back to you on this. Would you like a copy of the letter from your mother? Of course, I'll have to black out her identifying information, but I can send it to you." A bone. Linda has offered me the only bone in her pocket.

"Yes. I would like to have it." Even though I'm an emotional mess, I remember my manners. "Thanks for all you're doing. I'm not frustrated with you, Linda, just with this situation. You understand that, right?"

"Of course. I know this was not the result you wanted, but it still may turn around."

I let out a big sigh. "I hope you're right."

As I say this, the phone beeps. I check the caller ID. It's Molly.

"Linda, I'm sorry to rush off, but I have an important call coming in. Thanks again for your help." As I click over to take it, I see Steve stomping the snow off his boots on the side porch.

"Mom?" Molly is sobbing.

My heart is beating so fast, I stumble over my words. "Tell me
. . . what?"

"JT made it, Mom. She had a five percent chance and she came
through surgery. Her sister says the surgeons are hopeful. That it's
a miracle. She's on a heart–lung machine, but her progress is good.
She may come off it tonight."

"Oh, thank the Lord." Tears slide down my cheeks. "Dad's just
coming in. Let me tell him. Call you right back!"

I think of JT's mother, a woman I know well, whose motherly
heart must be full of thankfulness to the skilled surgical team. A
mother who did not lose her daughter today, who has been given
a second chance, and who will love her daughter back into good
health. And then because I cannot keep it from happening, my
thoughts go to my birth mom; the crushing disappointment and
sudden rejection lies heavily on my own heart. My birth mom will
not be loving me, one of her only children, back into any kind of
good health.

I rush across the sunroom toward the side door. Snow drips off
Steve's overcoat onto the tile. "Molly just called. JT made it. She's
alive." His arms are around me and his cold cheeks are warmed by
my tears.

Within the folds of his damp coat, I say, "I have more news.
Not so good."

He steps back and studies me.

"The CI called. My birth mother . . . she doesn't want to know
me. She denied all contact with both Jenny and me!"

My chin falls to my chest and I can't meet my husband's
searching brown eyes. The rage and resentment I experienced when
talking with Linda have vanished. Different feelings have replaced
them. My birth mom's rejection embarrasses me. Shames me. I feel
childlike. Unworthy. Less than. I think about Jenny and worry how
my sister will react when I call her later.

The bulky sleeves of Steve's damp overcoat suck me in. It's in his hug, one that's full of love and compassion, that I realize how conflicted I am. While I'm relieved and joyous about JT's prognosis, I'm devastated and demoralized by Linda's news. Why couldn't both precarious situations have had happy endings?

I know that in time I'll get over this wretched disappointment and shocking denial. I know I'll press Linda to petition the judge, and I'll swamp him with medical reasons for the right to send a second letter to my birth mom—one that includes a health questionnaire. My chest expands, and I let out a series of soft sighs. Perhaps before the judge rules, my birth mom will have a change of heart. Maybe.

When I pull away from my husband, his eyes never leave mine. "I told Molly I'd call her back. Let's call Colleen first and wish her 'happy birthday' before she heads out to celebrate with her Austin buddies. After that, we can sit with a glass of wine and talk about the rest of this." He nods in agreement.

In the kitchen, I notice that the snow has stopped falling. The trees and shrubs in the yard are painted an ethereal silver and white, but they droop under the load they carry. Just like me. Wild beams of light and clanking fill the street. The snowplows have come to clear us out. By Friday, a cold front is expected, one that will plunge the Midwest into a deep freeze. Just in time for my fifty-first birthday.

13

Table of Eight

The aroma of grilled food surrounds me as I follow the hostess and my parents toward our table at Gibson's, one of our favorite local steakhouses. The white-clothed tables are set too close together for Dad and his walker, so Mom stops to ask diners to scoot in their chairs. Behind me, the *tip-tap* of Jenny's fancy boots echo on the black-and-white tile. Turning, I catch her pocketing the stub for my parents' winter coats, and I match her smile, which says, *Maybe now we can relax.* Today, we are fifty-one.

My family, the Ryan clan, has an obsession with birthdays. As kids, our special day kicked off with homemade cupcakes that we passed around during school lunch. Mom would've made these the night before, frosted them after we went to bed, and placed them in a cardboard shirt box lined with wax paper. Birthday dinners were held in the formal dining room at the front of our house—a room normally off limits to my five siblings and me. Mom would spread a linen cloth over the long table and set it with her good china, crystal, and candlesticks, just as she did for the important holidays. At the end of the mirrored buffet, a stack of artfully wrapped gifts would compete with the Kirschbaum's Bakery cake—it wasn't a proper birthday without one of those. When no one was looking, I'd swipe a finger at the buttercream swirls.

In our household, the birthday person also had the honor of selecting whatever main course fancied them. One year, Jenny selected lasagna, while I chose beef stroganoff. Without hesitation, my mother prepared both dishes. Besides our immediate family, two other relatives were frequent guests at our parties: Aunt Addie, my godmother, and Grandma Mimi, my father's mother, who was our only living grandparent. Sharing my birthday with my sister elevated being the birthday girl to a different level. The anticipation of celebrating "our day" was like an electric current that ricocheted between us. The excitement refused to die out even when we dropped into our matching canopy beds at day's end.

With all that special effort and attention, my birthday has always been a day that got me out of bed with a bounce and a confident grin. Yet, when I awoke this morning and remembered what today was, my head stayed on the pillow. Steve had gone down to make the coffee, and I stretched under the warm covers and contemplated the frozen landscape beyond the bedroom window. I remembered. I knew exactly why my muscles wouldn't move and why I longed for tomorrow to hurry up. My birth mother's denial. Instead of relishing the day that has always honored me, I threw an arm over my face and let tears soak the pillowcase.

Tonight, I still don't feel much like celebrating, but Jenny made this dinner reservation weeks ago. Canceling on my twin, my parents, and my family is not an option. As we approach our table in the rear of the noisy restaurant, Jenny whispers in my ear, "Let's put Dad next to me. I can help him with his food."

"Okay. I'll sit next to Mom then. That'll give her a break from doting on Dad." I grin as I notice Jen's top. "Hey, nice sweater!" I say.

She looks down at her red cardigan and then over at my crimson cowl-necked sweater. She points at my dark gray slacks and we giggle. Our propensity to wear similar clothes by accident tickles my parents. When my mother notices our outfits, she'll undoubtedly rehash the old tale about how she dressed us alike until we could talk, and then because we demanded to be unique, she bought us the same outfits in different colors. Right now, it feels so good to laugh and to sideline the underlying strain that my birth mother's rejection inserted into our special day.

Jenny's face is a few inches from mine. "How are you holding up? Still angry?"

My voice is low. "Less angry today. Still stunned and very hurt. Oh, by the way, I got a message from Linda this afternoon. Her supervisor agreed. They'll petition the judge for a second outreach that will include the health form." Jenny's arm goes around my shoulders and I welcome her squeeze. "Let's sit before we have to explain what we're talking about."

"It's my plan to forget about all this adoption stuff tonight and enjoy the party." She nods at me.

Jenny settles my father across the round table from my mother and me. Over a shoulder, I glimpse our husbands coming in from the parking lot, their cheeks reddened from the frigid February wind. My mother sighs as she wrestles her large purse and two identical gift bags under her chair.

"Do you need some help?" I ask.

Straightening in her seat, Mom gives me a weak smile. "I'm fine, dear. My goodness, I don't know why I'm so out of breath." Her comment doesn't require an answer. Getting Dad spiffed up and to the nurse's station for his evening meds, and then down to the main entrance for our carpool probably consumed most of her afternoon. "It's good to get out," she adds.

"Yes, it really is." I pat her hand and remind myself that tonight is about celebrating with the people who want me in their life. Despite the underlying tensions, we're family.

Across the table, Jenny and I share a congratulatory grin. We've done it—we got them out to dinner and we're finally seated. The two empty chairs between Mom and Jenny are for my kids, Danny and Kassie. Having opted out of the chaotic episode of "load your grandparents and the walker into the back of your mother's Buick," they will arrive in a separate car.

A white-coated waiter appears. "Can I get you folks started on beverages?" In black embroidery on the waiter's chest is his name: Andrew. I watch my sister's face zero in on that.

The waiter nods at Jenny. "Ma'am, I'll start with you. What can I get you?"

Jenny flashes a grin. "Andrew, I'll have a martini with blue cheese olives, if you have them." Always the professional, my twin. In corporate sales training, they must teach to repeat someone's name, and look them in the eye to create connection.

Three days ago, I'd called Jenny after talking with the intermediary about the "denial of contact." My sister's reaction did not mirror mine. "I thought that might happen," she'd said.

Perhaps a corporate sales career is also an education in handling rejection well. As for me, I can't stop the ticker tape that runs through my brain: *She doesn't want us in her life.* Nothing I do alleviates the knots in my stomach or stems the tears that occasionally slip out. It's as if someone I cared about has just died, yet my sister appears to have assimilated the rejection just as she does when a large sales proposal falls through.

When it's my turn to order, I'm inclined to mess with my twin. "Andrew. One of my all-time favorite names. I'll have the house cab." Jenny smirks at her bread plate.

"What're you two giggling at?" Dad asks. Jenny leans over and catches Dad up on my well-meaning tease. Within seconds, the white napkin draping his enormous belly jiggles.

"You two." Dad beams.

Soon Danny and Kassie join the table, and Dad launches into a long-winded joke about a sinner who meets St. Peter at the pearly gates. From helping my father with his bills, I know that his middle desk drawer bursts with jokes and riddles. As he delivers the punch line, my father's dimples reach into his cheekbones.

"Good one, Gramps," Danny says.

I'm three sips into my cabernet when my mother scoots her chair in close to mine. Her deep brown eyes zero in on me. Not in the mood to hear any more tales about the latest struggles my younger siblings face with their jobs or kids, I look over at my dad in hopes that he'll launch into another corny joke.

"Julie?"

"Yeah, Mom?"

"I'm wondering what's happening with your birth mother search?" The question is offered as simply as if she's interested in tomorrow's weather.

Since I filed the paperwork to be assigned an intermediary in November, my mother has not asked a single question about that process. At first, I thought my father had neglected to mention I'd called on the way to the courthouse that day. Regardless, Mom has no clue that when I filed my petition on Election Day, I met Judge Aurelia Pucinski and our private conversation took the place of a hearing. Mom isn't aware that my intermediary's name is Linda, or that in early January a letter was sent to my birth mom. And she doesn't know that during these last three weeks, my gut tightened every time the phone rang.

Because my mother has disregarded the most crucial task I've ever set out to achieve, I've stopped sharing other aspects of my life with her. I've not mentioned the problems with my uterine fibroid or that my doctor suggested a hysterectomy or that I've deferred a decision until I receive a second opinion. I'm not just irritated and disappointed, I'm stung by my mother's lack of maternal support.

Part of me believes that her apathy is a punishment for seeking out my "other mother." I'm convinced that all those times she vowed to "help in any way she could," she was only mumbling words she thought she should say. What also hurts is that I would treasure another ally in this battle with my closed adoption. Thank God for Steve and Jenny and Steve's mom, Mary Lou—she's become one of my most trusted confidantes.

Turning away from my mother, I set my wine down and take a long sip of water. It's not just that my mother has chosen a public place to pose a question that is three months overdue. She's picked my birthday, a day on which I'm reeling from my birth mother's rejection, and a night I'm determined to set my adoption aside and have fun. When Jenny and I chose our seats, I pulled the short straw—I should have sat next to Dad. I peek at mom's cocktail glass. The Manhattan-on-the-rocks-with-a-cherry is now mostly a cherry perched on ice.

Andrew the waiter appears. "Has everyone had a chance to study the menu, or do you need more time?" *Oh yes, I need more time. On so many levels.*

When the waiter has taken our orders and retreated to the kitchen, I take a deep breath and turn back to my mother. "How interesting that you should ask that now. We got word through the intermediary earlier this week. At this time, my birth mother does not wish to connect with us. The CI is convinced this decision will change over time." As I say this, I shift my gaze to the single red rose at the center of the table. I refuse to let my mother see any of my inner turmoil, pain that she might detect in my hazel eyes.

Within seconds, my mother's hand caresses my back, as if to say, *I know this must be a wicked disappointment. I'm here for you.* I stiffen, wondering why she's silent and doesn't put this into words. When I don't say anything, my mom looks across the table at my father. Her hand still rests on my back, and I resist the urge to squirm out of it. Unable to catch my father's eye, Mom reaches for her cocktail. She rests back in her chair as if studying the reflection of the cherry in the ice. Stretching for my wineglass, I sit back too, grateful that a difficult moment has passed. My mother has finally expressed an interest in my adoption search, and I succeeded in not chewing her out for taking her time in doing so.

Mom whispers in my ear, "What a shame. I was looking forward to meeting her someday."

My breath leaves my chest.

Not for one second do I believe these words. I know my mom. I know that she will leave that cherry in the bottom of her Manhattan glass until it's ripe and full of vermouth, then she'll lift it on a spoon and close her eyes to savor every ounce of its fruity deliciousness. Just as convinced as I am of this effort, I know that my mother, the woman who raised me, does not want my birth mother anywhere near the family she put together. Her statement is perhaps a gift for my birthday, or maybe a peace offering for her months of silence. Because she has taught me to be a lady at all times, I keep my mouth shut and let my eyes wander over to Jenny, who is at this moment chuckling with my dad and Danny. I wish I were sitting over there, where the fun is.

My tongue loosens. "Mother, you're missing the point. Finding my biological relatives is about getting my health background. My four kids deserve a complete family medical history, too." I shake my head. Dinner at Gibson's on my birthday is about decadent pleasure, not the twisted drama of an adoption triangle. *Damn.*

Dad shouts across the table. "What're you two talking about?"

"Nothing to worry about, Jack." Mom waves off his words. "I'll tell you later."

Mom studies the filet that appears in front of her, and the worry lines between her eyebrows become a gorge. "What will you do?" she says softly to me. *Now I've worried her. Damn that, too.*

I ignore my entrée. "The judge needs to agree that my CI can send her a follow-up letter with the medical questionnaire. Legally, she doesn't have to return it, but if she does, it's only half my history. Since my birth father's name isn't on my original birth record, we can't contact him unless she provides his name. Which I'm guessing, she won't. A lot of ifs." Studying my baked potato, I add, "This could be it. All I ever get."

Painting the worst-case scenario is not about gaining my mother's sympathy. It's about making her feel bad that I've been going through all this without her knowing or caring.

Mom throws her arm around my shoulders, and it's as close to a hug as the chair will allow. This time her touch conveys how much she'd like to protect me from all things bad. I'm reminded of the many times she dried my tears and offered advice on how to handle the mean, "in-group" of girls. Her advice then: make your own clique of girls, friends you like and have something in common with. Sound advice that served me well.

As my mom looks into my face, I can almost see her mind working. She's trying to grab onto some meaningful piece of advice that is eluding her. "It's hard to know how this will turn out, but it sounds like you have the right people working on it. Honey, it's in their hands, now."

The smile I give my mom is not a grin, but it's a signal that I appreciate her words and that there is nothing more to be said. She's correct. I do have the right people advocating for me and they are doing their best. All I can do is to stay hopeful and keep pressing.

"Thanks, Mom. I think we should eat!"

She looks at her food and back at me. "Right. And then, we have two very special birthdays to celebrate."

14

Genes Don't Lie

Sleet collects on the windowsill while I proofread Kassie's English composition. The landline interrupts my mental cursing of her punctuation and grammar. "Hi, Jen. What's up?"

"Hey! For our birthday, my kids gave me a genetic testing kit from 23andMe. I think you should do it, too."

A few months back, I sent Ancestry my spit and ninety-nine dollars. Since signing up, I regularly scrutinize the list of third or fourth cousins who match with me, but the online messages I've sent aren't always answered. If I do receive a response, there's no consistent family names linking me to these distant relatives. Without my birth parents' true identities, I would need a sibling, a first cousin, or an aunt or uncle to register in order for the connections to be useful.

Sharing all of this with Jenny, I ask, "So you think that 23andMe is going to yield better results?"

Jenny launches into her pitch. "Number one: it's supposed to be more scientifically sound. Number two: 23andMe has picked up a different client base than Ancestry. Plus, you can contribute to research by participating in their surveys."

"What's the cost?" I don't know why I ask this. What's one more vial of spit and one more big bill if it produces the break we desperately need?

My sister presses. "We've nothing to lose by trying another DNA site. It could be weeks before the judge rules on your request for the second letter to our birth mother and waiting for her to change her mind feels like watching paint dry."

Jenny's sarcasm makes me giggle. My birth mother's denial of contact still has me in a funk, but my sister has admitted she's "over it." I've confided in Steve how weary I am of researching and spearheading each new assault on our closed adoption. While I'm considered "the searcher" in the eyes of the court, my twin sister benefits from my efforts. Her call today is a positive step toward squashing the seeds of discontent that have been sprouting inside my head.

Last week, Linda, our confidential intermediary, scheduled a hearing before the judge overseeing my case. Since then, I've asked her to add another item to my petition. I'm requesting that the judge allow two items to be asked of our birth mom: a complete medical questionnaire and the release of our birth father's name, so the same can be asked of him. To sway the judge, I've begun gathering documentation from my team of doctors that highlights my health issues: ovarian cysts, a uterine fibroid, and ductile calcifications that have now occurred in both breasts. If the judge rules against another outreach, genetic genealogy such as 23andMe may be our only hope in connecting with birth relatives someday.

"I'm signing up online right now," I say. "Did you know there's an option for twins? Let's sign up for that analysis, too."

After I hang up with Jenny, I envision all the relatives that this new test might provide. I look at the diploma above my desk. Indiana University was another one of those forks in the road where I'd planned on going left, but my relationship with my twin pulled me to the right. The combination of the gene test kit and the framed degree reminds me of the Twin Studies Program, which Jenny and I had participated in at IU over thirty years ago.

In March of our senior year in high school, I was set on attending Miami University and studying psychology. Eastern Illinois University was recruiting Jenny for volleyball. The only college where we'd both applied and been accepted was Indiana University. Toward the end of March, my parents planned a visit to IU. Leaving my three other siblings at home, the four of us packed up in the family station wagon and headed to Bloomington. Four rigorous years at Benet, our college prep high school, were closing out. Senior prom and graduation were about a month away, and the looming independence of college life tantalized us. Yet, there was an apprehension lurking below the excitement. Could my twin sister and I disentangle from one another and enjoy college apart?

Sometime during high school, I decided that I wanted to study psychology in college. My mother says that even as a toddler I was serious, an observer—I watched before joining in any group activity. People's personality traits, reactions, and behaviors fascinate me, as do the choices they make. Certainly, my adoption made me conscious of the "nature vs. nurture" debate, but my course of study was influenced more by the faulty family dynamics that erupted following my youngest sister's sudden death. I puzzled over my mother's grief and her bouts with depression. Subliminally, I may even have been on a quest to understand how a mother could give up not just one but two healthy newborns to a stranger to raise as her own.

On the trip down to Bloomington, my dad mentioned something that piqued my interest. "I read that Dr. Rose in the Psych. Department at Indiana is famous for his Twin Studies Program. You should ask about it during your tour. It might be something you and your sister should get involved in if you go there."

Dad was spot on about Dr. Rose and the Twin Studies Program. He was also right about IU being a strong college choice for both of us. Over that weekend, something else became obvious. Two young women who'd been inseparable since before they were born needed more time together before charting futures that would push them in different directions.

Four years later, Jenny received her degree from IU's College of Business, and I graduated from the Department of Psychology. While I never had the privilege of studying under the renowned IU Personality Psychologist, Professor Rose, Jenny and I did enroll in the Twin Studies Program. We underwent a battery of tests—personality inventories, physicals, questionnaires, interviews, and observation. For our cooperation, we received a compilation of the data.

The results astounded everyone. Our profiles were so similar that the researcher suggested we "could be considered identical twins." We wondered how this could be. Catholic Charities had told our adoptive parents that Jenny and I were fraternal twins, which in biological terms meant two eggs, two sperm, and two placentas. To be identical would mean that one egg was fertilized by one sperm and then divided, leaving two fetuses to develop in one placenta. The phrase, "could be considered identical twins," was nebulous. What were we really? Since there was no one who could answer this question with any certainty, Jenny and I have referred to ourselves as fraternal twins for fifty-one years.

Since my birthday and ordering the 23andMe test kit, life has been chaotic. Jenny has been caught up with her kitchen remodel, and I'm preoccupied with Kassie's spring track schedule. Since mailing in the 23andMe test kit three weeks ago, neither of us had given it a second thought until a few days ago when the results showed up in my email. The findings were a bombshell. Jenny and I are not fraternal twins—we're identical.

Today, Jenny is showing off her new kitchen and hosting our extended family for my mother's birthday celebration. The new cherry cabinets glisten in the afternoon sun, and the house still has that fresh paint smell.

"The place looks amazing," I tell her. My sister's face glows with pride.

In the front room, I greet my parents and siblings, and then I return to the kitchen to help my sister. I open the cake box and set the Kirschbaum's birthday cake on a fancy glass pedestal. Digging into my purse, I pull out candles and the envelope I promised to bring to Jenny.

I wave it at her. "Here's a copy of the 23andMe test results."

Jenny points across the kitchen. "Slip it into the top desk drawer." The envelope contains a computer printout showing how the genes of Twin1 are identical to Twin2.

"Shall I start the coffee?" Neither of us wants to discuss the test results anymore or the argument I had with my mother a couple of days ago concerning it.

My sister is pulling out dessert plates when Mom joins us in the kitchen. "Do you need help in here?"

I shake my head. "You're not supposed to be in here, birthday girl."

My tone is not quite as friendly as a birthday person deserves, so I offer my mother a weak smile as an apology. I also mean it to be a peace offering for the sharp comments I made to her forty-eight hours ago.

Once the 23andMe results landed in my inbox, I got my mother on the phone.

"I was told you were fraternal," Mom said. "Why would the sisters at St. Vincent's misrepresent that?"

In reply, I hadn't said, *Because no one cared enough to get the details right. Because the nuns weren't there and neither were you, so all of you perpetuated a lie.* No, I didn't say those things, but I wanted to. Since my birth mother's rejection earlier in the month, I'm quick to be cross with anyone connected to my closed adoption.

What I did say to my mother was this: "You're certain the nuns told you we were fraternal?" The words were in the air before I considered their effect. These days my mother is sensitive about her memory. In the background, Dad yelled for her.

"Haven't we always suspected you were identical because of the Twin Studies you did at Indiana?" Mom sounded impatient, which was no doubt a combination of my accusation and my father's hollering.

Coiled in my desk chair, I reminded her. "The researcher's conclusion was not definitive. The point is Jenny and I are identical twins that grew up believing we were fraternal. This is just like the baptismal certificate—you told us we were baptized at Holy Name, but we weren't. This is more of the same." I knew I was being difficult, that I was wearing her down with these countless assaults, but I was looking for someone to blame.

My mother sighed. "Your father needs me. We can continue this discussion another time. If the powers that be say you're identical, then that's what you are."

The manner in which my mother shifted the blame of this grievous error onto others was reasonable, and it was also predictable. I was blaming her, and she threw it off onto, as she called them, "the powers that be." I remember well that phrase from my childhood. As a kid, I thought "the powers that be" were a corps of unnamed saints responsible for handling questionable circumstances. As an adult, I realize that my mother used this phrase to explain away uncertainty and to end difficult conversations.

In my heart, I knew I should lay off my mom. She was sensitive and prone to gloomy spells. These mistakes in my adoption story were not her fault, but all the absent truths, the search dead ends, the denial of contact, and our case extension languishing before a judge had turned me into a fuming, finger-pointing victim.

From the sparkling new kitchen sink, Jenny gives me a look that means "tone it down." Then she looks at my mother. "Go get situated with Dad in the dining room. Julie, you take these forks and plates. It's time to sing 'Happy Birthday.'"

Before she leaves the room, Mom kisses each of us on the cheek. "I love you both. Thank you for going to the effort to make my birthday so special. I don't know what I'd do without either of you." She flutters a hand in front of her face, as if that gesture alone can wave off all the emotion swirling in the room.

"We love you too. Get in there, birthday girl!" I say.

Jenny carries the cake into the dining room where eighteen family members have gathered to sing. As I follow my sister, I think about what went wrong with the information surrounding our birth. Did some clerk in the Department of Vital Records guess at whether Jenny and I were fraternal because she couldn't locate the doctor who delivered us? Had one of the delivery nurses checked the wrong box on a form at the hospital? Or had the nuns at the orphanage invented their own truths? The mistake about our twindom ushers in a fresh batch of questions. Was I really the firstborn, or was Jenny?

As my mom blows out her birthday candles, I think about my "other mother." She is perhaps the only person who can provide answers to all these issues. If only she will change her mind about connecting with us.

I help my sister pass out the slices of chocolate cake, and as I move about my sister's house, I paste a benign smile on my face. I make an effort to sit with each of my siblings and catch up with their busy lives, but I'm preoccupied with my birth mother's rejection and the stunning news of being an identical twin.

After Mom is done unwrapping her gifts, I signal Steve that it's time to go home. All I want to do is get in my pajamas and watch TV. It doesn't matter what show we watch. I want to turn off my brain and forget about being adopted.

15

St. Vincent's

The parking lot behind St. Vincent's is full. I ease the Buick into a parallel spot next to the massive complex. Ahead of us, Chicago's LaSalle Street is a parade of buses, cars, and taxis. A stream of exhaust mixes with the chilly April air and drifts toward a homeless person propped against the St. Vincent's Center. Fifty years ago, the same red brick building serviced a different clientele—women, infants, and children. Back then it was known as the St. Vincent's Infant Home.

Today, Jenny and I have an appointment with Lisa Holmes-Francis, a Catholic Charities Post Adoption Services social worker. Besides a tour of the building where we spent the first three weeks of our lives, Lisa has promised to show us the third-floor chapel and its baptismal font. Last summer, we learned we'd been baptized in St. Vincent's chapel, not at Holy Name Cathedral as our parents had been led to believe.

"Are you ready to do this?" I ask my sister.

During the forty-minute drive into the city, Jenny transformed the passenger seat of my car into her own personal command center. While I navigated the Eisenhower Expressway, she plugged a headset into her phone and fielded calls from clients and colleagues. Between my sister's work schedule and the social worker's commitments, setting aside this timeslot has been two months in the making. I began working on it shortly after our birth mother denied contact with us in mid-February. Reconnecting with a time in my life that I can't recall has become increasingly important to me.

Jenny stows her things. "Yep, I'm ready!"

"Look, that's where the orphanage's playground must've been." I gesture toward the parking lot behind St. Vincent's, a seven-story building that takes up an entire city block.

On the back seat of my car is the paperback, *St. Vincent's: An Orphanage That Shined.* Grabbing it, I open to the page where sisters in winged headdresses pushed baby buggies while nurse's aides played games with toddlers and school-aged orphans.

I point up at the building. "Those stained glass windows must be the chapel." Looking down at the book in my hand, I shake my head. "No more babies. No more cribs. Not since 1972 when the place officially closed. That's when DCFS took over." Craning my neck at the north-facing wing, I say, "According to the book, the fifth floor was where the babies were cared for, and Sr. Mary Alice's office would've been there."

Jenny grins at me. She's read the stories about Sr. Mary Alice Rowan, St. Vincent's infamous prioress. One myth professed that Sr. Mary Alice need only open her office window and project her "vigorous voice" to gain the attention of the monsignor one block away at Holy Name Cathedral. Since reading all the tales in the paperback and recalling my mom's personal account of dealing with Sr. Mary Alice, the nun has become a vivid character for me.

Jenny opens the car door. "I'm really looking forward to meeting Lisa and seeing the chapel."

"I'm so glad you took the afternoon off." I dig for quarters in my purse.

I've been waiting eight months to see the insides of the St. Vincent Center. This is my second visit as an adult adoptee to the orphanage. Six months ago, I stopped in without an appointment and was turned away by security. Today, when Jenny and I walk through the front entrance together, it'll be the first time we've been back since our adoptive parents picked us up in March of 1959.

After I feed the parking meter, Jenny and I walk past the dozing street person. As we round the cornerstones of St. Vincent's, the butterflies in my gut speed up their little dance. I link my arm through my sister's and point at the grand entrance. The way the noon sun gleams off the wrought iron fencing makes it look like it just received a fresh coat of black enamel. The notion that my first home is still being well cared for pleases me. Where the front walk breaks from the cement sidewalk, the gates fold back like the welcoming arms of the sisters must've done when our orphanage was in its prime.

Jenny and I pause near the front door. "There's the plaque I was telling you about." She studies the sign. The St. Vincent's Infant and Child Asylum was established in 1887—a ninety-year history of caring for poor women and children.

I'm tempted to run my fingers over the brass rectangle, but instead I reach for a tissue. Facing the door stirs up mixed emotions. Here is where it all began. Our adoption. Our three-week stay here was because our birth mother chose not to include us in her life. We've returned weeks after learning that she has made the same choice again. Twice rejected. I dab the tissue at the corners of my eyes and smile thinly at Jenny. She squeezes my arm.

Stuffing the tissue back in my pocket, I remind myself about last year when I was turned away at this door. Coming here then without an appointment was a naïve blunder, one of many I've made getting this adoption probe on track. Today, Jenny and I will be allowed to enter because we found the right gatekeeper—Lisa, the Catholic Charities social worker. There's a lesson in that: never give up trying to find the right key to a locked door.

As Jenny holds the bulky door open for me, I think of Linda, my confidential intermediary. Next week, she has a hearing in front of the judge overseeing our case. Soon we'll learn whether he will allow Linda to send a second outreach to our birth mother, one that will include a health questionnaire. The judge will also rule on my second request: that our birth mom provide the name of our birth father. The thought of everything resting on Linda next week—convincing the judge that these requests are vital to my health and well-being—makes me more jittery than a third cup of coffee. My future rides on her skills as an advocate and negotiator, and yet I've never met her.

In the vestibule, Jenny and I sign in with security. I half expect to be turned away again, but when I mention the social worker's name, the guard nods. Cracking open my best smile, I give Jenny a thumbs-up.

We're in!

"While we wait for Lisa, let's have a look at the old photographs in the hallway over there." The guard nods his permission.

Everything is easier the second time around.

From my abbreviated visit months before, I know I won't see the two of us being cuddled by a nun or a nurse in any of the photographs. This time, as we stroll through the gallery, I scour the black-and-white photos for my brother. Two years younger than Jenny and me, Howie is also a veteran of St. Vincent's. When we reach the end of the photographs, I spot Lisa in the lobby by security.

The social worker and I met last month when I attended my first adoption support group meeting at the Lake Street offices. Jenny was out of town, so I convinced Howie to attend the meeting with me. My needs are different than his. He's considering whether to launch a search for his birth relatives, and I'm trying to deal with the anger and rejection broiling up my insides. My birth mom's refusal to connect and my inability to access information about my background have put me in a hard place. Acceptance and forgiveness are like foreign countries to me right now.

Lisa gives me a warm hug, and I introduce her to Jenny. "This is my twin sister."

Her eyes flick from Jenny to me several times. "Wow. You two really do look alike."

Jenny laughs and glances over at me. "About a month ago, we learned through DNA testing that we're identical." This isn't a setup. Jenny and I hadn't planned on bringing this up today.

Tagging on to my sister's comment, I'm conscious of keeping my voice free of accusation. "When we were adopted, Catholic Charities told my parents that we were fraternal twins. Perhaps you can shed light on how this mistake might have happened?"

A slight frown erases Lisa's smile. "Before coming over here to meet you, I studied your file. Your birth mother did not deliver you here at St. Vincent's but at a maternity hospital. Whatever information was sent over from the hospital is what would have been captured in the records. I'm sorry for the error, but I'm happy you found out the truth." So there it is, an apology, leaving me with no one to blame.

Lisa's perfectly arched eyebrows frame her blue-green eyes. Her smile reappears. "Since you've already viewed the old photographs down the hall, I'll show you a few other areas, and then we can finish in the chapel."

We follow Lisa to the old elevator. As she walks, the social worker gathers her long brown hair into one fist and then drops it behind her shoulders. I remember this habit of hers from the post-adoption support group meeting last month.

The format of the meeting was simple. After signing in, we went around the U-shaped conference table and stated our name, disclosed whether we were an adoptee, birth parent, or adoptive parent, and then we shared where we were in the search and reunion process. If we brought someone with us, we introduced them.

For the icebreaker piece, Lisa asked that we offer a response to this question: "If you could say one thing to the family member you seek, what would that be?"

Ethnically and racially diverse, the group members ran the spectrum in age from thirtysomethings to seventy-year-olds. With the exception of two birth mothers, the rest were adult adoptees, and all but three were women. The common thread: Catholic Charities had facilitated everyone's adoption. I was grateful that Howie and I had chosen seats at one end of the horseshoe. Since this was my first meeting, it settled my nerves to hear the group's answers before taking my turn.

More than half of us were waiting to hear back from a birth parent or birth daughter/son. From my recent experience of waiting weeks for my birth mom to answer Linda's outreach, I knew how excruciating passing the time can be. A woman, I guessed her to be in her late thirties, had been anticipating a response from her birth mother for over a year. When she broke down in sobs during her introduction, the Kleenex box at the center of the table shot over to her like a hockey puck.

Two older adoptees, both males, had yet to decide to send their first outreach letter. Howie fell in this category. For them, taking in the experiences of the group and deliberating over the pros and cons of search and reunion kept bringing them to the meetings. I understood their reluctance. Only twice in my fifty-one years had I seriously considered looking into my own adoption. If it hadn't been for the breast biopsy pushing me down this path, I might not have learned of the confidential intermediary program or Catholic Charities Post Adoption Services.

One of the birth mothers and a female adoptee shared their reunion stories. Both glowed like someone who'd recently fallen in love. They passed around photos of themselves beaming, wrapped in tight embraces with their newfound relatives. To the group's credit, each of us ogled at how much the searchers resembled their child or parent, and each attendee professed such joy and support for the searcher that I wondered why I'd delayed in joining such a compassionate crowd. Given the recent dismissal by my birth mom, I doubted I'd be sharing photos of my twin and me flanking our birth mother anytime soon. Nor could I envision Jenny and me sandwiched between both of our mothers—that thought almost made me laugh out loud.

When it was my turn to talk, I clasped my sweaty hands tightly in my lap. "I'm Julie. This is my first meeting. I'm an adoptee." I tried to make eye contact with the people across the table. "I also happen to be a twin. Thanks to Catholic Charities' policy of keeping twins together, my sister and I were adopted into the same family." I smiled at Lisa, our moderator, and then I looked down at the tabletop. "Due to health concerns, I began the search for my birth mother last year." I felt my brother's reassuring hand on my shoulder. "Last month, I learned that she didn't want to connect with us. I'm hoping she'll change her mind someday." When I glanced up, I caught the Kleenex box just in time.

Plucking a tissue, I introduced Howie. "He was adopted through Catholic Charities too and is considering a search for his birth relatives."

Lisa jumped in. "And Julie, how would you answer the ice-breaker question?"

The tissue balled up in my palm. I'd thought hard about this when the others spoke. The angry-rejected-adoptee-me, the one I'd been working hard at controlling these days, wanted to ask my birth mom: how could she look herself in the mirror every day—she who gave up not one, but two daughters, and rejected both of them. Twice. The person-that-was-me-before-this-adoption-search, the one I was desperately trying to reclaim 24/7, chose a different response to offer the group. "I would ask her if she has thought of my sister and me throughout her life, and if she ever wondered what had happened to us."

As we get on the elevator, Jenny touches Lisa's sleeve. "Thanks for taking the time to give us a tour of St. Vincent's today." My sister tips her head in my direction. "Seeing the place might provide some healing and closure."

Lisa's smile dimples her cheeks. "My pleasure. Showing off the building to St. Vincent alums is one of the best parts of my job. Most adoptees are thrilled to connect to this short period of their life, even if they have no desire to reunite with birth relatives."

In the short ride up in the elevator, Lisa gives us a brief history of the building and an overview of how the space is used now. "What were once areas for convalescing mothers or housing and dining for the staff have become Catholic Charities' offices and conference rooms." Some of Lisa's descriptions of what went on at St. Vincent's in the '50s, '60s, and '70s are a repeat of what I read in the paperback history, but there's no substitute for seeing the space in person.

Lisa holds the elevator door open and Jenny winks at me as we step out. She mouths the words, "This is fun."

My smile is thin. I suppose this little field trip to St. Vincent's is fun, but I'd describe it as meaningful, filling a hole I didn't know needed filling.

Down the long hallway, the linoleum tiles gleam, much like they would have glistened under Sr. Mary Alice's reign. I feel a pride I hadn't expected. If you were to be an orphan in 1959, this was probably the Cadillac of orphanages. I can almost hear the elaborately robed sisters swishing down the halls as they checked on their charges, evaluated the storeroom inventories, and assisted the army of nurses and their aides. The Daughters of Charity had truly run an impressive operation.

Jenny asks, "I read that besides being an orphanage, this was a maternity hospital, too."

Lisa answers. "You're correct. At one time there was a women's ward at St. Vincent's. Sometime in the mid-1950s, the mission changed. While some women did spend time here before they went into labor, the sisters no longer handled births. Let's go right, here."

We stop outside a conference room. Before Lisa can say another word, I ask a question that's been jabbing at me. "You said you peeked at our adoption file. Do you happen to know if our birth mother spent time with us here?"

Lisa's feet shift and she cocks her head at me. "She was not here with you. The records don't indicate what happened to her after your birth or when she signed the relinquishment papers. I'm sorry." I swallow hard. Not quite foundlings, we were, nonetheless, abandoned children. We had become wards of the state hours after taking our first breaths.

Turning slowly, Lisa directs our attention to a door at the end of the hall. "That conference room used to be the sisters' dining room. Would you like to peek inside?"

As we move inside the narrow room with its wall of windows, it's not hard to imagine the nuns pushed up to the huge conference table with their plates and silverware.

"They sure had a fabulous view of the Gold Coast. That's Holy Name Cathedral over there." I point toward the towering steeple poking through the landscape of buildings surrounding us.

The seat of the Archdiocese of Chicago. Twenty-seven years ago, Steve and I had been married at Holy Name. Even though I hadn't been baptized there, two of my daughters had. Such an honor.

"I have one more thing to show you on this floor. Come." We

stop in front of an office a few doors down. "This office belonged to Sr. Mary Alice. Do you know anything about her?"

Jenny and I giggle. "We both have copies of the book about St. Vincent's. We've read the stories."

Lisa laughs with us. "Sr. Mary Alice was quite a character. Stern, but an excellent administrator. She retired before the orphanage closed."

As we head back to the elevators and our final stop, the chapel, I ask another burning question. "Lisa, I shared with you at group about my birth mother's recent denial of contact. In your years of experience, how likely is it that she will change her mind?"

Lisa clears her throat. "Sometimes birth mothers need to work through the shock of their child contacting them, and then they reach out. Others never can turn that page for it brings back such traumatic memories for them." Lisa moves closer to me, and when she speaks, her voice is full of compassion. "It's not about her not wanting or loving you. It's about what's going on in her life. I wish I could look into a crystal ball and tell you six months from now she'll call, but these things are hard to predict."

Jenny nods several times. "That's very helpful." My sister's hazel eyes lock on mine. "Julie, let's hold on to that advice: there are factors in her life that are preventing her from making contact with us."

My sister's satisfied smile almost convinces me that the social worker is right about our birth mother's motives. Shoving my hands in my pocket, I look at Lisa. "Next week, the intermediary I'm working with has a hearing with the judge overseeing my case. We're trying to get our health history and also our birth father's name from her."

The social worker's blue eyes flash with interest. "That may be the straw that breaks the camel's back. Often the fear that their child is not okay will spur the parent into reacting." The icky feeling in my belly subsides. Perhaps there is reason to be optimistic.

"Keep in mind, this isn't a guarantee," Lisa says. Lisa, the social worker, and Linda, the intermediary, must have received the same training. Neither one of them offers false promises, and their information is always sobering.

My look is tentative. "It's been two months, and there's been no change of heart. The tone of her note suggested anger at having been contacted. I can only imagine the distress a second outreach might cause."

Again, Lisa doesn't hold back. "You can never predict how a birth mother will react. As I said at group, there's no rule book for them. Often there's such fear in being found out as having been an unwed mother, and the shame of that, as well as the pain of relinquishing a child. It will be enough to shut them down for quite some time."

Her words, while not consoling, are helping me to understand the possible mental state of my "other mother."

Jenny answers for both of us. "Thank you, Lisa, your perspective is invaluable."

"Ready to see the chapel?" Lisa asks with a grin. We nod.

Inside the elevator, Lisa tells us, "Other than some necessary updates, the chapel hasn't changed much since it was built. The marble baptismal font is the same one that was here when you were baptized, but it's in a new location at the back of the chapel. The marble bowl is in remarkable condition."

"I would love a picture of Jenny and me beside it, if you don't mind?"

"Of course." Lisa opens the door to the chapel.

Before us is a two-story room built large enough to hold around seventy-five people. Painted beige and with limited decorations, the focus of the room is the centered altar at the far end. From both sides of the towering space, religious-themed stained glass windows look down onto rows and rows of pine pews.

Lisa motions for us to walk through the worship space. "I'll meet you over there in the baptismal area."

My sister and I genuflect at the center aisle and then sit at the end of one of the pews. When I pull down the kneeler and lower my head, I'm overwhelmed with emotion again. *This is where I began my life. Jenny and me. A place where we were well cared for when we were between mothers, between homes, but still together. We've had such good lives ever since.* Staring at the crucifix over the altar, I offer thanks and consider what I might pray for. The judge. My birth mother. Linda. I pray for all of them, and I pray for myself, that the anger and hurt burning a hole in my core lessens sometime soon.

Jenny and I leave the pew and walk side by side down the center aisle toward the back of the chapel. Below a niche of windows, the marble baptismal font awaits. Sunlight streams in, and the cascading rainbow reminds me of that same refraction of light on my staircase at home that caused me to contact Worldwide Tracers. As I did then, should I interpret this rainbow as a sign too? Are my mom's "powers that be" offering guidance? Am I to hold out hope for my birth mother's change of heart, or am I being encouraged to move on with my life?

Lisa takes my side as we gather around the baptismal bowl. Now that we are up close, the sun from the windows makes the bowl look like it glows from within.

"So here's the font. As you can see, it's in excellent condition. Should I get a photo of the two of you now?"

As Lisa takes our cell phones and readies herself to take several pictures, I look into the bowl. The marble is a swirl of creamy whites with the faintest garnet veining. Right away, I think of the body and blood, two of Catholicism's most important symbols, and water, that which gives us life. I move closer to my sister so that the bowl is centered between us for the picture.

The two of us are silent as we gaze at the font and up at Lisa for more snapshots. I'm not sure if my sister and I are thinking the same things—about all the orphan babies who were blessed by the holy chrism at this bowl; about this sacrament, our first, when the water poured over our foreheads and expunged our original sin; about being held, not by our parents or the godparents they selected for us, but by strangers whose names we'll never know.

As I follow the deep red veining that snakes down one side toward the bowl's center, time slows for me. I imagine my infant self, sixteen days old, held by a nurse's aide, and my sister in the arms of another young nursing student. Cradled in these women's arms, I envision a look of wonder in their eyes, and yes, I see something else. Pity. My stand-in godparent felt sorry for me: *Such a beautiful baby with such pale skin, such big eyes, so innocent. Abandoned*, she's thinking. *Who could abandon this precious child?*

Yes, who could? Could I do it, abandon one of mine? The nurse studies my wrinkled brow, which means I'm about to wail. She smooths away my cry with the tip of a finger, brings me in close, and shoos away the heaving in my chest. She kisses me near my temple and whispers in my ear. I shush and study her lips, trying to discern her words. *There now*, she says, *you're next, here's your turn to be free of that original sin that mars your soul. Soon, you'll be clean, pure in God's eyes, and then you'll become the child of a mother who'll love you more than you ever imagined you could be loved.* While I cannot know that any of this transpired, it settles me to think that it might have, and I'm thankful. Grateful to that woman, my stand-in godparent, whoever she was.

"One more, look here," Lisa commands.

Again, Jenny and I smile at Lisa. *Click.* I gaze back at the bowl. The light cast through the window has moved on, and the bowl no longer glows. Yet, I feel different somehow. Perhaps it's me who's captured that light. It's as if the pity that I've often felt for that abandoned child-me and for the rejected adult-me has faded. Like my original sin, it has been washed away. I straighten my shoulders and stand tall. I'm proud to have had my baptism here in this lovely, secluded worship space, a chapel that belonged solely to the sisters and the orphans who once lived here. My sister and I may have passed through here quickly, but we are, without a doubt, alumnae of St. Vincent's. We were welcomed in 1959, and today we've been welcomed back. Our belonging is secure, and I will never forget where I came from.

The wadded tissue comes out of my pocket, and I turn to my sister. I hug her harder than I mean to, and she doesn't pull away. Lisa's footsteps echo as she hurries toward us. Jenny pats my shoulder, and then we smile shyly at one another. Our hazel eyes twinkle, and no words are needed. We know what's in our minds: the visit today to St. Vincent's is more meaningful than either of us expected, and we're glad we made the trip together.

16

The Second Outreach

Since my visit with Jenny to St. Vincent's last week, the Chicago area has been deluged by spring thunderstorms. In the sunroom, the dogs and I survey the yard. If the rain doesn't let up soon, my spring garden will be ruined. As troubled as I am about the condition of the yard, I'm even more uneasy about another outcome I cannot affect—Linda's hearing before the judge, which is scheduled for two days from now. We've made two requests: permission to contact my birth mom to request her health history and an appeal for my birth father's name.

The last time I spoke to Linda was nearly two weeks ago. While I don't believe anything has changed, I'm antsy. After five months of working with Linda, I know her schedule. Monday mornings she's in a staff meeting, midweek she's in court, and Friday afternoons, she's unavailable. I dial the Midwest Adoption Center.

"Julie, you've been on my mind today." If Linda's voice were a food, it would be warm syrup, the sweet, soft tone instilling confidence that everything she's tackling will turn out right. "The judge still hasn't acted on the two requests I've made on your behalf. I'm scheduled to meet with him in his chambers on Wednesday."

The date's been etched in my mind for weeks. "Any feeling on how he'll rule?"

"Honestly, I have no way of knowing. This judge is new to the confidential intermediary program. I've only dealt with him a few times. He took over for Judge Pucinski."

Six months ago, I met Judge Pucinski in her office on Election Day. The passion she expressed for adoptees' rights stuck with me and emboldened me to press on through my birth mother's denial and demand that an exception be made in my case. If Pucinski were the judge overseeing my case, I feel certain she'd rule in my favor on both counts.

Still soft, Linda's voice is serious. "Our request to mail out a second outreach to a birth mother who has already denied contact is unprecedented." I rub the knot forming in my neck.

As a result of my case, the Midwest Adoption Center had adjusted their policy. All first outreach letters are now accompanied by a health history form. The birth relative is requested to complete and return it regardless of whether they intend to make contact. While this new policy doesn't help my situation, I take solace in knowing that future MAC clients will benefit from my predicament.

"But, Linda—"

Linda speaks over me. "I plan to emphasize to the judge that MAC has changed their policy to rectify this mistake for future clients. The case can be made that we were in error on your behalf by not supplying the health history forms in the first outreach."

Slowly, I release my breath. There's so much at stake here. If the judge doesn't allow us to go back to our birth mom, our only recourse is to wait for her to change her mind—an event that Lisa from Catholic Charities pointed out may or may not happen.

The dogs follow me as I move to a different window in the sunroom. "Hopefully, the change in policy will sway the judge that my situation should be remedied too. Do you have everything you need from me?"

Linda is quick to answer. "I have all the records from your doctor, as well as his note advocating that a complete family medical background is necessary to ensure your ongoing good health."

One of the dogs nudges me. As I pat him on the head, I mull over my medical history. A painful ovarian cyst recently took over the top spot from my other female issues—the irritable uterine fibroid and biannual mammograms due to dense breast tissue. Next month, I have an appointment with a new gynecologist who will offer a second opinion regarding a hysterectomy. Even though we're identical twins, Jenny has not experienced any of these concerns, and we're both grateful for that.

Linda's voice grows serious again. "All that being said, with the change in Illinois adoption law making its way through the state legislature, the judge may feel that you will have a second chance in November to get at the information from your OBR."

This statement prickles me. "Please point out to him that the information on my OBR isn't going to help me. While you didn't come right out and say it in the Search Assessment, my birth mother's alias is on the OBR, and we know my birth father's name isn't listed there. Waiting for November isn't an option for me. The judge gives us this chance or we . . ." I hadn't expected to tear up. "Or all we can do is pray. Pray that my birth mom changes her mind someday."

The war I've waged these last few years with my adoption has worn me out. As I sink into a sunroom chair, my voice takes on a childish whine. "Judges are supposed to be fair. He has to consider all sides of this. I need him to allow the second outreach. And I need him to require that she provide my birth father's name."

Linda is silent, and I try to pull myself together. I've been forceful, but there's a lot riding on the judge's ruling. Without this chance, I'm a person whose background is a blank page. If the judge agrees with me, at least I'll have a chance of filling in half, maybe both sides, of my family history.

"Julie, as soon as I get out of the judge's chambers on Wednesday, I'll call you with the news." Linda's voice is comforting, but my head throbs with worry.

On Wednesday morning, instead of a nerve-racking stare-down with the landline, I decide to be productive. I head up the narrow pine staircase to the storage closet under an eave on the third floor. The mothball-scented, goofy-shaped closet is where out-of-season coats, luggage, Halloween costumes, and my sewing supplies coexist. The last time I hunted for something in there, it looked as if someone had waged a full-scale tantrum. Placing the cordless phone on the floor by the staircase, I begin sorting what to keep and what to give away.

My arms are draped with a sixties black-and-white jumpsuit and a toddler's glow-in-the-dark skeleton costume when the phone lets out a peal. I stumble past the piled luggage and grab the phone after the second ring.

"Oh, hi, Jen." Winded from my short sprint, I mutter, "I haven't heard from Linda yet." There's a trickle on my forehead and I brush it off, hoping it's sweat and not a spider.

"Okay, call me when you hear. I'm working from home today."

It's when I'm hauling the items that I plan to donate down the stairs that the landline echoes throughout the house. Dropping everything into a heap, I charge into the kitchen.

Linda!

She whispers, "Julie, I'm just out of the meeting with the judge."

Barely able to breathe, much less speak, my mind completes the scene for me. Linda is standing in the narrow hallway outside the cluster of judges' offices—the same corridor where I waited for

Judge Norton, the day I filed the CI paperwork. *Please, please have good news.*

"How did it go?" My chest feels like something heavy is sitting on it.

"The judge authorized the second outreach. We can send the medical questionnaire to your birth mother. However, he will not require her to supply your birth father's name."

When I speak, my voice is flat. "Well, that's something, I guess." I know I should be happy—I just won half of something.

Linda's voice warms. "If your mother voluntarily returns the health forms, perhaps she'll include his information. Of course, you do realize there's no guarantee that she will return any of this."

My eyes slam shut on Linda's disclaimer. Besides being disappointed with the partial ruling, I'm tired of no guarantees. I whisper, "Of course."

"I'll get the paperwork together and mail out the letter to your birth mom beginning of next week. I'll mail you a copy at the same time so you know when it will reach her."

"Thanks, Linda. This isn't all of what I'd hoped for. I know you did your best."

The initial disappointment of not getting everything I wanted is ebbing away, and resentment swoops in. I hate having to jump through so many hoops to get what other people take for granted— basic family health history and genealogy.

"If she calls me with any questions about this latest outreach, I know that I can convince her to connect with you. If I can just get her on the phone."

My laugh is weak. "I believe you, and I'm cheering for you to get that chance."

When I hang up, I look at the pile of donations near the kitchen. What a mess I created. Everything I tackle these days seems to be two steps forward and one back. I sit down at the kitchen desk and study the calendar. If Linda sends out the letter next week, and I allow for the mail delivery, my birth mom should have it by the end of April. That leaves roughly ten days for her to respond before . . . I circle Mother's Day on the calendar.

17

The Most Unusual Mother's Day Gift

The dogs see me through the back door as I tighten the laces on the old sneakers I use for gardening. The pair prance around on the back steps and bark crazily for me to join them in the yard. Instead, I slip into the chair at the kitchen desk and slide out of their view. A mug of fresh coffee in my hand, I study the oversized desk calendar that I've kept since the kids were little.

It's never been my habit to cross off the squares on the family calendar—I fell into doing this recently. After my tour of St. Vincent's in mid-April, I dug out a black Sharpie and began slashing through each day as it passed. When I started this routine, I had my eye on the upcoming hearing, the date when Linda was to meet with the Circuit Court judge overseeing my case. When he ruled in our favor—allowing a second letter to be sent to our birth mother in spite of her demand for no contact—I continued marking up the calendar because it made me feel in control of something. My new focus became Mother's Day, May 8.

As I think about this now, picking Mother's Day was arbitrary.

When Linda called with the judge's ruling, I was standing over this desk, and I'd flipped the page to May. I calculated the turnaround time between the second outreach letter leaving Linda's office and my birth mom receiving it. I figured if she returned it promptly, then Mother's Day was a reasonable target.

On that April day, I came to another conclusion. Jenny and I belong to that cohort of people who believe that if rules are in place, we should follow them. The thought of being tardy for an appointment or a dinner reservation makes our pulses soar. Since our mom runs late for just about everything, I presumed that we inherited our need for punctuality and rule-following from one of our biological relatives. If my birth mom were the parent who passed on the "rule-follower gene," then not only would she comply with the judge's order to return the health forms, she'd be quick about it.

As confident as I felt about those deductions several weeks ago, now as I pick up the black pen to cross off yesterday's date, there are knots in my stomach. My heart informs my head: your birth mom denied contact with you and Jenny a few days before your birthday. She's likely to do the same thing around Mother's Day. While there are still a few days left for Linda to inform me that my birth mom refused to fill out the forms, I remind myself what Lisa from Catholic Charities said during our tour of St. Vincent's: *Often the fear that their child is not okay will spur the parent into reacting.* Trying to be realistic and hopeful at the same time isn't easy.

The black pen drags through the square that was yesterday, and I study what else remains for the week. It's Friday—I know Linda isn't in the office this afternoon. Anything that might arrive in the mail from my birth mom today will sit in Linda's inbox until Monday. Snickering at myself, I realize that we're about to miss the silly Mother's Day deadline I conjured up.

I smooth out a crease on the calendar. The rest of May is crazy busy. Steve and I head to Austin after Mother's Day for Colleen's graduation from the University of Texas. After that, Kassie will be knee-deep in her freshman year final exams, and then Molly travels home from New York. She plans to visit our friend JT, who is rehabbing at home from her cardiac surgery in South Africa. We won't see Danny until August—the summer collegiate football program starts as soon as his sophomore classes end at West Point. He'll finish out the summer at Camp Buckner in a cadet leadership development course.

As I think about the small brunch planned for Mother's Day this year, I can't help but sigh several times. Of all my four kids, only Kassie will be home to celebrate with me on Sunday. During the years they were growing up, I'd been served coffee and breakfast in bed, their handmade cards stacked neatly on the tray, and then we'd meet my siblings and my parents for brunch in a restaurant. Maybe next year we can all be together.

A scaled-back Mother's Day is a letdown I refuse to dwell on. In its place, I pick up the thoughts that kept me awake last night. I could have this return-the-health-forms scenario all wrong. Maybe my birth mom didn't open the letter from Linda's office. What if she collected the mail, spotted the envelope, tore it to pieces, and walked it out to the trash? *Please don't let her do that.* Tossing the Sharpie across the desk, I vow to get as far from the ugly, marked-up calendar as possible. Mother's Day has quickly become less of a guiding light and more of a ridiculous reminder: I am twice a daughter, but like all the other fifty-one Mother's Days in my life, I will honor only one of my mothers with a card and flowers.

At the sink, I fill a water bottle to take out to the garden. It's here I remind myself of another possibility involving my birth mom and the health forms, one I'm afraid to hope for, though my heart desperately prays for it even when I sleep. My heart wants my "other mother" to read Linda's letter, for her to pick up the phone, and to ask, "What is this all about? Are my daughters all right?"

If this were to happen—if my birth mother were to call Linda—then Linda might persuade her to return the medical history forms and consider exchanging letters and pictures with Jenny and me. I believe in Linda and trust her. If my birth mom were to call Linda, then Linda might ask for my birth father's name, and then, snap, the glorious details of my personal story—one that has been hidden for over fifty years—would fall into place.

As I open the back door, the collies scramble, and they're all wiggles and whines and sloppy licks. Wagging their bushy tails, they race past me into the garden where flats of pink petunias and white begonias are waiting for me to plant. When I pick up the trowel, a batch of tears surprises me.

There's something else that a call to Linda from my birth mother would signify. It would mean that my "other mother" actually cared about what was happening in her daughters' lives. I would know that she was thinking about us, worried about us, and cared enough to shed her anger or fear or whatever shame was holding her back in order to take this step. This effort would go a long way in pushing aside the waves of my own anger and thoughts of being "less than," which her rejection spiked. If my birth mom phoned Linda, it would demonstrate that I was important to her after all.

Wiping the tears on the sleeve of my denim shirt, I leave the painful place where my heart landed over the health forms and set to work. The morning sun warms the back of my neck and a nice breeze sends the sweet fragrance of the iris and peonies in my direction. As I dig in the first flat of the petunias, I'm grateful that the abundant spring rains have loosened the soil. Such a simple thing—loose soil. It makes gardening so effortless, so pleasurable. The repetitive task of making holes in the dirt settles me, and my mind wanders.

To give a small plant enough of what it needs to thrive—it's just like children. Once they're rooted, all they require is love and attention. This gets me ruminating about mothers and Mother's Day. There's the irony of mothering four almost-grown children while still seeking my own mothering. My relationship with my mom has improved since our conversation at my birthday dinner. Her reaction to the judge's recent ruling about the health forms was dear: "I will pray that you receive those back."

Then there's the conversation with my mother-in-law, Mary Lou, who called last night. "Thanks for the flowers. I just love hyacinths and narcissus." When I laugh out loud, the dogs stare at me with sudden interest. It's typical of my mother-in-law to call daffodils by their botanical name. She's the most well-read person I know. Thinking of her now makes me so deeply grateful that I'm close to tears. Without Mary Lou's maternal advice, clear wisdom, and daily checking-in, I don't know where I'd have landed this past year. She's not just my husband's mother, she's my friend. Without Steve and Jenny and Mary Lou, I'd be so low on the ladder of life, I'd have fallen off by now.

And as I must do, as our whole family will do, I remind myself of what else this Sunday represents. May 8 is not only Mother's Day, it's my youngest sister's birthday. If, thirty-five years ago, the doctors could have saved her from the virus that complicated an undiagnosed heart condition, thirty-nine candles would land on her birthday cake this year. For all of us, Sunday will be a day when delight mixes with a bit of sorrow. For Mom, there is one less child to mother, and I know she will reflect on that as she opens our cards and gifts.

When the last flat of begonias is planted, I get up and stretch. I resolve to not let my adoption search saga tarnish the joy and appreciation I have for both being a mother and for the women who mother me. Perhaps it's the sunshine and the beautiful morning, or the satisfaction of the well-tended garden, but my mind tingles with more reasons to be grateful. I'm not just thankful for my mom and my mother-in-law. I appreciate all my mothers. One has offered me solace and friendship. One gave me the gift of life, and the other offered me a life that helped me thrive.

These thoughts, as well as the tidy, full garden, bring a smile to my face. Before I bundle up my tools and garden debris to haul to the garage, I place my cell phone in the breast pocket of my work shirt. The dogs traipse after me into the driveway, fascinated with all the smells emerging from a garage usually off-limits. Their frantic silliness to beat out the other for the best sniff brings out another smile. A light heart is a welcome change.

It is when I'm hanging the garden tools on the pegs in the back corner of the garage-that-used-to-be-a-barn that my cell phone goes off. First, I feel it buzz in my breast pocket and then the jazzy ringtone Kassie set up for me plays its tune. By the time I shed my dirty gardening gloves, the call has gone to voice mail.

Linda!

Oh, my! Closing my eyes, I cradle the cell phone and slide it up to my chest. All the possible scenarios I envisioned this morning flood back to me. She'll return the health forms. She won't comply. She'll call Linda. Which one is it? As I retrieve Linda's message, my heart locks into an erratic hip-hop.

Linda's voice cheers. "Your birth mother returned the medical questionnaire. It was in the morning mail. I'll redact the personal information and send it out to you Monday. I'm so happy that you'll finally receive some of the family medical history that you've worked so hard to get. If you pick this up and have questions, I'll be in the office for at least another hour. Happy Mother's Day, Julie!"

My fingers freeze around the cell phone, and I stare out from the gloomy garage into a spring morning dazzling with sunshine.

Nearly blinded by the light, I whisper to the empty garage, "I can't believe it. The waiting is over."

Just as I imagined, my birth mom returned the forms in record time, and I don't have to agonize anymore about how she'll react. I'm pleased by having intuited something about her that wasn't on any form or document. We share a few personality traits, my birth mom, Jenny, and I. Whatever else I can know about her will be on those health forms. I got what I've worked for all these months, but . . . she didn't call Linda. My birth mom didn't take the time to call. Tears cloud out the sunshine. I let them trickle over the ridges of my freckled cheeks and settle in the crumpled neck of my shirt.

Just over three years ago, my doctor ordered the breast biopsy that launched me on the path I've been on, more or less, ever since. And now, two days before Mother's Day, my stranger mother has given me a gift. Next to my desire to meet and get to know her, this medical form is all I've been thinking about for the last year. As I lean against the wall of the garage, I think about Linda the intermediary, Lisa the social worker, my husband who sparked this battle for information, and my twin who walked beside me through the hills and valleys of the search. So many wonderful people have helped me get to this moment. Bless them all! Including the woman who gave me life and sent this most unusual Mother's Day gift— my family medical history. Maybe, as Lisa had suggested, this was all she could offer given what is going on in her life.

Stepping away from the corner of the musty garage, I pick up an old tennis ball and step into the bright yard. The dogs cock their heads at me and take off after my first throw. As I toss, and they retrieve, the dirty yellow ball again and again, I laugh and giggle and ruffle their fluffy coats. "Good dogs. Go get it." Each time, I throw harder and faster, and before you know it, I'm doubled over, panting and sweating and tearing up.

"It's all over," I mumble again.

The collies saunter over, drop the ball, and watch it roll to my feet. They move closer and when I crouch, they lick away my salty tears. Lifting a corner of my shirt, I wipe off the sloppy mess on my face and check my cell phone for the time of day.

With the dogs on my heels, I take off toward the house. I want a pad of paper nearby when I ask Linda what's on the forms.

18

※

Poked and Prodded

Zigzagging around the travelers at Chicago's Union Station, I avoid the crowded escalator and bound up the nearly empty staircase. Winded at the top, I press toward the Canal Street doors where the taxis wait. In thirty minutes, I have an appointment with my new gynecologist in the medical district near Northwestern Hospital. In decent traffic, it should be a twenty-minute cab ride, which leaves me with only ten minutes to spare.

When I rattle off Dr. Stanley's address to the driver, I don't have to tell him to hurry because he lurches into city traffic and runs a yellow light at the corner. Unwilling to complain, I search for a seat belt. When the cabbie banks a hard left on another yellow, I brace for the jolt and reach for my purse as it slides across the seat. Whether it's the anticipation of discussing my health with a new doctor or due to this frantic taxi ride, my mouth tastes sour. I scour my bag for a breath mint and check the folder I prepared for Dr. Stanley—a copy of the medical information from my birth mom that I received from Linda's office about two weeks ago.

As my driver barrels over the Columbus Street bridge, I gather my purse in a bear hug, putting pressure against my belly, the abdomen that has a history of ovarian cysts and a problematic uterine fibroid, the one Dr. Stanley will palpate and examine and then determine if he agrees with my previous physician's diagnosis—a full hysterectomy. As the medical district comes into sight, I loosen my clenched jaw. In minutes, I hope to learn what one biological aunt's uterine cancer and another's breast cancer means for my own health outlook.

"Right here will be fine," I say to the driver, handing him five dollars extra for getting me to my appointment both in record time and in one piece.

Once I complete the stack of new patient forms, I carry them up to the receptionist's window. Seconds later, a nurse bedecked in pastel patterned scrubs opens the door to the exam rooms. Before she calls my name, I look up. The benign smile she offers across the crowded waiting room does nothing to quell the jitters in my gut.

"Welcome, Mrs. McGue. Dr. Stanley would like to see you in his office first. Right this way."

As we step into the hallway, I hand her the file from my purse. "I brought some medical history. This is new information. I didn't have access to it when my records were sent over."

This instant is like turning in a final exam, one that you've studied for and labored over, but one with only enough time to answer half the questions. As pleased as I am to have my birth mother's health details, it saddens me that I may never have my birth father's name or his background.

When we reach the doctor's office, the nurse places my records on his desk. "Please have a seat. Dr. Stanley should be here in a minute."

After she leaves, I stare at the stack of files the nurse laid down. One folder is about an inch thick and the other is the one I presented a minute ago. The hefty one I assume contains the medical records my previous doctor forwarded. As I consider the pile, it occurs to me that the history of my life could be condensed into a short stack of folders. There is the adoption file that my parents presented me in their apartment and the one at Catholic Charities. There's a thin one that the search agency, Worldwide Tracers, created during their feeble effort to solve my case. No doubt, Linda has a thick case file on me, which the judge will ask her to close out soon due to my birth mother's refusal to connect.

When I'm contemplating this, how all lives could probably be distilled down to a few labeled folders, the office door cracks hard against the backstop. Dr. Stanley is an abundance of energy and smiles and apologies for running late. He shakes my hand, and his boyish grin disarms me. I half expect him to share a humorous anecdote, but he doesn't.

He plops into his swivel desk chair and settles his dark blue eyes on me. "Tell me what concerns have brought you in today."

As I explain my recent health issues and being adopted, Dr. Stanley peppers me with questions. I launch into my reservations about a hysterectomy, my efforts to attain my birth mom's health history, my inability to get the same from my birth father, and my concerns about the cancers that two biological aunts have faced.

Dr. Stanley doesn't hesitate. "This is what I'd like to do. I'll do an exam, and then I'd like to meet back here so we can talk some more. Sound good?"

I nod and try to keep up with Dr. Stanley, as he leads me down the hallway to an open patient room. "The nurse will be right in to get you set up and draw some blood." He pauses and smiles at me, his dark hair looking almost blue in the fluorescent light. "We're going to take good care of you."

When the nurse returns me to Dr. Stanley's office, he's behind the desk, engrossed in paperwork. He smiles and motions me to sit. Whether it's the blood work or the worry about what his next words will be, I'm light-headed.

Dr. Stanley closes my folders. "Okay. So you have a maternal aunt who had uterine cancer decades ago, and another aunt diagnosed with breast cancer a few years back." He pats the folders and continues. "While these facts are interesting to note, your biological mother is healthy from what I see here. I find that most relevant. As for you, you're in perimenopause and I expect that your fibroid will go down as you enter menopause. I plan to continue to monitor it every six months with a pelvic exam and an ultrasound. We'll stay on top of your mammograms, but I didn't detect any abnormalities today."

He pauses and I lean in toward his desk. "I'm not recommending a hysterectomy at this time. Let's just see how you do."

"More watchful waiting, then?" I ask, afraid to breathe, to smile, to hope.

When he nods, I can feel the color return to my cheeks. No surgery, just a reasonably normal checkup.

Dr. Stanley clears his throat. "One other thing." My eyes widen as I look over at him. "If you haven't had one already, schedule a colonoscopy. Your maternal grandmother's bouts with colon cancer should be taken seriously." He lays his hand on the folder I brought. "Looks like you have longevity in your family. With your grandparents into their late eighties when they died, you can look forward to a long life."

"Thanks," is all I can muster, but Dr. Stanley's prognosis makes me want to jump up and hug him.

When I reach his office door, Dr. Stanley stops me. "Congratulations on getting a portion of your medical history. I'm sorry your birth mom isn't present in your life, but as you said, 'you just never know.'" He shakes my hand. "Nice to meet you, Mrs. McGue. It's my pleasure to be taking care of you."

Outside the medical office, I press the elevator button and hoist my purse to my shoulder. The gesture is effortless, and I wonder how my purse could feel lighter than when I arrived. Inside the elevator, I look the other two passengers in the eye and offer a cheerful, "Good morning." Against the elevator wall, my blouse drapes loosely across my back—it feels lighter too. When I step into the warm June day, I notice that the tightness in my lower back is gone. I hadn't realized how much tension my body was holding as a result of my concern surrounding this appointment.

Even though it's quite warm for a two-mile walk to Union Station, I decide to forego another harrowing cab ride. The sun peeks around one of the tall office buildings, and I welcome its warmth on my face. Pleased with my new doctor, I'm overjoyed with his outlook. For the first time in months, I feel calm about the changes in my body.

Setting out on foot, I consider the next few months. Other than keeping up with the demands of my family, I have nothing to struggle for. Or against. No more adoption battles to wage except one—working on accepting my birth mother's decision and forgiving her for choosing not to include me in her life.

19

Target

As I pull into the sweltering Target parking lot, I'm chagrined that the few shady spots by the road are taken. Sliding my car into an open slot butting against the cart corral, I hope that no rushed, overheated shoppers will ding my doors. The August heat wave has all of us on edge. I'd rather be at the pool or at home in the air-conditioning than battling with families in the school supply aisle.

"Do you have a good idea what you need?" I ask Kassie. A rising high school sophomore, she holds up her school supply list, and we dart into the chilly superstore.

On our return to the parking lot, my car is hotter than a pizza oven. Windows fly down and I push the AC to the max. As Kassie and I wait for the suffocating car to cool, my cell phone belts out the melody I've assigned to Linda, my intermediary.

Two weeks ago, I received a copy of an order of dismissal from Linda's office. Because six months has lapsed since my birth mother denied contact, the judge overseeing my case is mandated to dismiss it. I assume that Linda is calling today to confirm that the judge signed that order, to say her goodbyes to me as a client, and to wish me good luck in life.

"Hi, Linda. I've been expecting your call." My voice has that controlled calm of someone seasoned at fielding disappointing news.

To my surprise, her silky voice gurgles with pleasure. "You won't believe how I've spent the last hour and a half."

My already elevated pulse spikes. "How?"

"Your birth mother called." Linda's voice squeaks with excitement. "She's changed her mind."

"What?" I'm certain that I misheard her over the blasting AC.

Linda slows down as she repeats herself. "Your birth mom called, and I got her to change her mind about contact."

Just before Mother's Day, I'd prayed for my birth mother to do just this—call Linda, express concern about Jenny and me, and be persuaded to connect with us. Instead, my "stranger mother" returned the health forms without an accompanying note. Since then, I've been leaning on Lisa at Catholic Charities and my post-adoption support group. I've made significant progress in accepting my situation: I'm an adult adoptee from the closed adoption era who is fortunate to have half of her health background.

Perhaps it's the ungodly heat and humidity, or the mayhem of the school supply aisle, but when I find my voice, threaded through it are sarcasm and surprise and joy and mistrust and indignation. "She's changed her mind? After all this time?"

Why am I suddenly so important to her?

Linda rattles on, and I listen. She's so pleased to share this groundbreaking news that she doesn't notice how quiet I've become. The mother who has rejected me twice now in fifty-one years called to inquire about the State of Illinois "preference" forms. She'd been going over the paperwork that Linda had sent along with the outreaches, and she'd read that in November, the Illinois Department of Vital Records could release original birth records to adoptees who request them. If a birth parent chose to block that release, they needed to sign a "preference" form. My birth mother was calling

Linda to ask how she could block my request for the OBR. Until today, they had never spoken on the phone. Linda had stated multiple times that if she could speak to my birth mother by phone, the probability of some sort of reunion would go up dramatically.

And so, it is. In the midst of a record-setting Chicago heat wave, on a Thursday afternoon in early August, as I sit in a barely cooled car in a Target parking lot with my teenage daughter and all her school supplies, my birth mother has called Linda. After nearly nine months of waiting—the irony of which isn't lost on me—I am on the other side of "this," the thing that is my search for identity, family, and belonging. The timing is absurd.

I want to laugh, and I want to cry. "Now, after all this time? You've got to be kidding."

Kassie's blonde head snaps up. I mouth the bewildering words in her direction: *Birth mother called!* She kicks a sandaled foot toward the door. Her gesture is a sentiment shared by family and friends: *We're over her—give her the boot!* Their attitude: no one enjoys watching a cowering dog receive repeated abuse.

Linda must sense that her newest challenge is to convince me to be receptive to my birth mom's abrupt overture. "She's been worried about you. The judge's order to comply with the medical questionnaire has been weighing on her." *Aha! Lisa the social worker was right. This was what got her attention and forced the breakthrough.*

"*Sooo* concerned that she waited nearly four months to check in?" A multitude of emotions grapple with one another, and testy emerges as the winner. My daughter flicks me a thumbs-up.

Linda is unfazed by my attitude, a trait that makes her good at what she does—uniting estranged and reluctant birth relatives. "She belongs to a prayer ministry. Due to the medical issues detailed in the judge's order, she placed you and your sister on the ministry's active prayer list. When your birth mother talked about the prayer circle and your health, her voice cracked."

She does care about me! Us!

There are other obstacles my seventy-eight-year-old birth mother faced before making today's call. I learn that her dear friend is battling a terminal cancer, that my stepfather is the parent of two adult adoptees, and that he's unaware of her pregnancy that occurred twenty-two years before their marriage. My request to reunite landed in the middle of all that.

Linda ticks off more items. "She's well-educated. Her father was French and very laid-back. Her mother was German, and strict— she kept a KPER list for the entire family. I don't know what that is," Linda admits.

I snort. "I do. We used one every time we went on a Girl Scout outing with my daughters' troops. It's a chore list." Rules, preparation, and organization are inherited family traits. Now I know which parent handed off all that to me.

"She said your grandmother would have disowned her if she'd discovered the pregnancy. Your birth father and she argued extensively about a forced marriage. She came with a girlfriend to Chicago where she connected with Catholic Charities." This information corroborates the intake interview notes from Catholic Charities, facts I received nearly a year ago.

"After exchanging letters and pictures through my office, your birth mom is open to meeting you and your sister." Linda waits for this to settle in before launching the celebratory balloon. "This fall."

"This fall?" I'm incredulous. Fall sounds so far away; it's still summer.

After three years of assorted doctor's visits, a myriad of adoption search starts and stops, dead ends, and legal obstacles, the woman who gave birth to my identical twin and me and left us with an orphanage wants to get to know us. When she returned the medical history months ago, I'd lost all hope of ever meeting her. I'm struggling to shift gears.

"This is amazing, Linda." I choke up. "Great . . . great job. I can . . . hardly believe it."

Kassie's face twists in concern. "Mom, are you okay? What's going on?"

I turn to her. "My birth mom she changed her mind and . . . she wants a reunion."

"Linda, can I call you back? I need a minute."

Reaching across the console, I hug my innocent, precious child. My daughter. A daughter I brought into the world. A daughter I treasure having in my life. After all these years of wondering, I'm going to have the chance to know the mother who brought me into the world. Kassie's arms hold me tight, and she's crying, too. I love that she's here with me, the only witness to this spectacular moment.

On the drive home, my brain hopscotches. How should I begin the first letter to my birth mother? What should I call her—Mother or Birth Mother? Not Mom! What events of the last fifty years should I highlight? Should I type the note or write it out in my best cursive? Linda advised that Jenny and I compose separate letters, and that our first exchange include a small collection of pictures, a mixture of baby photos and recent ones.

Rushing to my desk in the kitchen, I get Jenny on the first try.

"Wow. Wow. Wow! I can't believe she had a change of heart right before the judge was to dismiss our case." Jenny hasn't gotten her own call from Linda, because technically I'm the "searcher."

"Linda said our birth mom's been worried about our health since she received that second outreach with the medical questionnaire." I get my giggle ready. I know what's coming.

Jenny fumes. "Well . . . with all that worry she sure took her sweet time. It's been months, for Christ's sake."

I whip off details that Linda broke to me minutes ago. Linda confirmed that our "other mother," having married later in life, never had any other children.

"Ah, that makes me sad. Very sad," Jenny says. Both of us are quiet.

It's me who cuts into the pause. "I was really hoping that we'd have some siblings, even as complicated as that would be."

"Me too. A brother would have been nice." Jenny sighs. "So her husband doesn't know about us yet?"

"Nope. She told Linda that she expects him to react well to the news, but she's waiting for the right time." Neither of us puts a voice to the doubt in the back of our minds: What if she decides not to tell him after getting us all revved up?

"Okay, Jules. What's the next step?"

"We each draft a letter, send it to Linda, along with photos. There can be no identifying information in the letters. Just generalities. It's got to do with privacy. Then we wait for our birth mom to write back. When Linda receives something from her, she'll let us know. We can either pick it up from her office or she'll send them to me. That's the drill. It all changes once our birth mom decides she's ready for direct contact."

My mind is churning with what-ifs and what-thens. Like, what if my birth mom doesn't write back? What if we have to wait months for her to reply? What if she doesn't want to meet us after exchanging letters? And the biggest game changer for me is: What if she won't give us the name of our birth father?

"Does Linda have a feel for how long this writing back-and-forth could go?" Jenny asks.

"The policy is that after the exchange of three letters each, she either wants to meet us or we're done."

Jenny is the first to speak. "I think that after the call with Linda today, she's committed."

My sister's optimism buoys me, but there is another concern pinching me. "What should we do about Mom and Dad?"

Envisioning how to introduce this latest search twist with our adoptive parents tightens my core. I might start with, *Hey, Mom. How's your day?* Then she'd say, *Good, honey. What's new?* Then I might add, *Oh, by the way I just learned that my birth mother wants a reunion with us after all.*

"I think . . . I think we wait for a while," Jenny says.

I pounce. "Isn't it better to get this all out in the open, sooner rather than later? And don't forget what happened at our birthday dinner at Gibson's. Mom said that she was looking forward to meeting our birth mother. Don't you think she wants to be in on this?" As I make my point, my voice is a steady whine.

The silence between us is uncomfortable. "You can tell her if you want. I think we should wait. There's still so much more that could unfold."

Jenny's reticence means that if I don't want to wait, I'll be spearheading the disclosure to our parents. Suddenly, disturbing my parents as they enjoy another one of their long weekends at the cottage doesn't appeal to me either. What feels right is to relish this amazing turn of events and avoid conflict.

"All right. We can wait to see how the letter writing goes. Perhaps we tell Mom and Dad once we talk to our birth mom. Definitely after we meet her."

"That works for me. Anything else?"

"Just one quick thing. Have you thought about how you're going to sign your letter? Linda says we can't use our real names."

Jenny is quick. "How about Twin1 and Twin2?" Both of us crack up. It's reminiscent of Thing One and Thing Two, characters from a favorite Dr. Seuss book.

"Let's use our birth names," I say. "I'll be Ann Marie and you be Mary Ann."

"I can't wait to ask her about that silly name reversal thing. Wonder if she did that or the sisters at St. Vincent's?" Jenny's question is just one of many I've been scribbling down.

When we're done, I continue to sit at the kitchen desk and reflect upon the questions Jenny and I discussed. I'm reminded of the chatter at our July adoption support meeting. The birth mothers in the group claimed that answering the questions of the child they gave up is inordinately painful. They avoid the hard ones if they can. I wonder if the mother I'm about to get to know is worried about the questions we will ask of her, and if she will have difficulty providing honest answers.

20

The First Call

I yell up the stairs, "Kassie your ride is here!" At the cubbies, I hand her a sack lunch and kiss her forehead.

"Thanks! Bye, Mom." She stops at the side door, her white blouse untucked from the plaid uniform skirt. "Hey, good luck. I hope today's the day."

Grinning, I say, "Me, too, honey. Me too."

Just thinking about the "release" form—the one that Linda is waiting for that will grant her permission to give my birth mom's real name and address to me—is enough to get my heartburn flaring.

Since Monday, I've been trading emails with Linda and the exchange has worn me out. I'd write, "Any word yet?" and her quick reply would be, "Nothing in today's mail."

I head upstairs to dress. As I tidy up the bedroom, I pick up my journal and scan some of the last entries:

6 weeks ago: *Call from Linda. I was sitting in the Target parking lot of all places. B-mom changed her mind!!! Rocked my world. Glad Kassie was there. Gathering photos of me as baby and now. Writing my first letter. Hard to take out names and identifying details. Signed it: Your Daughter, Ann Marie. Can't believe this is finally happening. Pinch me.*

4 1/2 weeks ago: *Linda forwarded the first letter from B-mom. She signed it: Love, Your Birth Mother. I lovvvve that she said "love." She included lotsa pix. I look like her when she was younger. Sent her another letter. Signed it, Love, Ann Marie. Wonder how many more letters we will have to write, before . . . So many things to hope for.*

3 weeks ago: *Another letter from B-mom. More pics. I framed the most current one and put it on my desk. Keep staring at it. Trying to memorize everything about her. Wish she were smiling in it tho. Want to see if I have her smile. Linda calls. B-mom doesn't want to write any more letters. Wants to exchange info and talk on phone!!! Yeah. At last. Big step. I wonder what her voice will sound like.*

2 weeks ago*: Linda sends us our release forms. Jen and I send ours right back. Can't wait to learn B-mom's real name, where she lives. Any time now. So excited I can hardly fall asleep at night. Jenny started a family bet. We all put in our guesses as to which Midwest state B-mom lives in. I picked Minnesota. Steve picked Iowa. Jenny picked Wisconsin. The kids picked Michigan, Ohio, and Indiana.*

10 days ago*: Linda calls. B-mom's friend with cancer died. Because of funeral and family, she can't get to PO box to pick up release form. B-mom has PO box just to communicate with Linda. B-mom hasn't told her husband about us yet. Ugh! So nervous. Praying like crazy that she doesn't chicken out. Lisa from CC is right—B-moms are unpredictable.*

7 days ago*: Linda calls. Still no release from B-mom. She's playing phone tag with B-mom. I'm really nervous. What if she changes her mind—AGAIN? We're so close . . . don't drop us now. . . .*

6 days ago*: Linda calls. She heard from B-mom today. She mailed the release. Whew. Prayers answered. Told her husband—it went well. Thank the Lord! He sounds like a dream. Linda is waiting for the form and will call me when it comes.*

Yesterday*: Still nothing . . . hope the release isn't lost in the mail. Should be any day now. I hope before the weekend . . . I can't wait to get to know her better.*

After I stow the journal in the nightstand, I decide that I need something else to do today besides sitting by the computer or waiting by the phone. Yanking out exercise clothes, I take off for the gym. When I come out of my workout, I've a missed call and a voice mail from Linda. Why had I parked the Buick at the far end of the lot, and why do my car keys always settle at the bottom of my purse?

Linda picks up on the second ring. "I received your birth mother's signed release. Do you want to come in, or should I mail the information?"

"I'll be there in a half hour."

The twenty-three-minute drive to the adoption center should be effortless at nine thirty on a Thursday morning, but I fumble with the navigation system and the Bluetooth. Jenny's phone is off—she's in the air, heading to a work conference.

At his office, Steve picks up right away. "Good for you. Remember that I've got five dollars on Iowa."

His quip relaxes me, but only for an instant. As I speed north to the unfamiliar Chicago suburb, I regret that after all these months of working with Linda, I've never taken the time to visit the Midwest Adoption Center and meet her. Finding MAC's office building, meeting my intermediary, and receiving my birth mom's name are all going to happen on the same day.

Still wearing my Lycra exercise tights and jazzy purple tee, I slam the Buick's door and rush into the office complex. Oblivious to looks from the white-shirt-and-blazer crowd, I scan the building directory and take the stairs down two at a time. Countless office suites blur past me as I race toward the door at the end of the corridor.

At reception, Shanika, the administrator I'd spoken to the day after meeting Ray, "the History Cop," welcomes me with a glistening smile. "Linda is waiting for you in her office. Right this way."

We stroll past several offices populated with smartly dressed workers. I tug at the hem of my purple tee and reach up to straighten my ponytail.

Shanika sticks her head inside an open door. "Linda? Julie is here." She gestures for me to step through the doorway.

Inside, a thirtysomething woman, several inches shorter than me, hurries around a big desk. As Linda approaches me, her soft brown curls flutter around her neck.

"Welcome, Julie. What a wonderful occasion to finally get to meet you." We shake hands and I notice that her eyes are much bluer than her online photo.

"Even though we've never met, I'd have recognized your voice anywhere." I look down at my clothes. "Sorry, I was at the gym when I got your message."

Linda giggles. "That's understandable. I'm glad this worked out for you to come in. Please, sit. I have everything ready for you."

As she swivels around to the credenza, I dig for my reading glasses and concentrate on getting my breathing under control. When Linda turns back, a single sheet of paper is in her hand. "Are you ready?"

I nod.

Linda places the document on the desk. The moment progresses as if in slow motion. I'm not conscious of the center's phones chirping around us, nor that my heart is beating as if I'm still on the treadmill. All I'm focused on is Linda's slender hands inching the piece of paper across the faux wood desktop toward me. She releases the paper, and my right hand with the chewed-up cuticles picks it up. I read and reread the "classic old lady" name. My mind struggles with the name, rolling it around like a tongue does with too much peanut butter. When my birth mother's address finally computes, I realize that Jenny has won the family contest. Wisconsin!

Glancing up from the paper, I quiz Linda. "Shirley Faye Wilkinson. Is that her married name?"

I'm puzzled. I don't really know what I expected her name to be. I guess I thought that her alias, Ann Jensen, would be part of her real name, but it isn't. It's way off. I'll have to practice saying Shirley Faye Wilkinson out loud. In my head, I've been calling her: my "other mother" or "first mother," or Ann Jensen.

Linda explains. "Wilkinson is her married name. Her maiden name was Desjardins, which, your mother informed me, means "from the gardens" in French." This makes me wonder if Shirley loves to putter in the yard like me.

I grin at Linda. "Now I understand why all those months ago, you said, 'It's an uncommon name. She shouldn't be too hard to find.'" I whisper her name again in perfect high school French, "Shirley Faye Desjardins Wilkinson."

Linda leans across her desk, and our eyes meet. "Your mother would like to call you tomorrow. Will three o'clock work for you?"

Back in the Buick, I place the paper with Shirley's name and address in the passenger seat beside me. Folding it and stuffing it into my purse had felt irreverent. During the drive home, I glance over at it, making certain that what just happened in Linda's office is real. I have found my birth mom, and I know her real name. Tomorrow, I'm going to talk to Shirley Wilkinson for the first time. I'm not just an adopted orphan anymore—I'm a bona fide acknowledged offspring.

It's a few minutes before three o'clock, and I'm locked in a stare-down with the caller ID in the kitchen. Rocking on the toes of my sneakers, I'm more tense than a bride before she walks down the aisle and nearly as excited as a child waiting to see what Santa left under the Christmas tree. Next to the phone, I've lined up Kleenex, a pad of paper, and the typed sheet I picked up from Linda's office yesterday. Like the scorching afternoon when I sat in the Target parking lot, this moment has an otherworldly feel. It's as if I've stepped out of my skin, and I'm watching someone else squirm and fidget and stare at the phone on the desk.

Since Jenny is at her work conference, she'll have her own call with Shirley tomorrow. There's a part of me that feels guilt over hearing my birth mom's voice before Jenny, but that's how things have worked out. Another part of me believes that because *our* adoption search has been *my* task since the day that I retrieved our adoption papers, I've earned the honor of being the first daughter to speak to Shirley.

As I stand here waiting for the phone to ring, I'm curious about how Shirley broke the news to Howard, my stepdad. Just how do you tell a man whom you've been married to for thirty years, "Oh, by the way, you know how you thought I'd never been a mother? Something happened to me when I was in my twenties, long before I met you. . . ."

To set the right atmosphere for divulging such a deep dark secret, do you sit on the damask sofa in the living room or book the back booth at a quiet restaurant? Does he hug and console you for all you dealt with in those difficult days? Does he forgive your secret-keeping and encourage you to get on with meeting your long-lost daughters, or have there been daily arguments ever since?

Two minutes to go. I look at the list of questions I've prepared.

My stomach tightens as I read the first one: Get your birth father's name! As I underline this for the third time, the phone erupts, sending shrill notes into the empty kitchen.

Deep breath. You're ready. Sit, and pick up after the second ring. "Hello."

"Julie? I'm still getting used to calling you that. For all these years I've thought of you as Ann Marie." My birth mother's voice is loud and commanding like the schoolteacher that she was for decades.

"Hello, Shirley." Closing my eyes, I finger a tissue. "Is it okay if I call you that?" I'm hoping she doesn't ask me to call her "Mom"— that name is reserved for someone else.

There's a pause, and then, "Yes. Shirley is fine."

Shirley launches into an explanation of why she picked this time to call. As she talks, my inner voice repeats the mantra: *I'm talking to her. I'm really talking to her.* I glance at the tissue box. I'm not going to need it. I'm too happy to cry.

"Linda said telling your husband was difficult, but it went well."

"Yes." Shirley explains how she asked Howard to join her in their front room once the funeral activities were over. She told him about everything: the unwed pregnancy, the move to Chicago with her girlfriend, the ensuing years of sadness and loss.

"Howard was tearful because he knew all too well how badly a woman in my condition, in that era, would've been treated by family and friends and society." From there, Shirley informs me how she met Howard—they'd been introduced by a mutual friend. A widower, he had two adopted children from his first marriage.

"He sounds like a wonderful man. I look forward to meeting him sometime."

Shirley jumps on this. "He's very accepting about meeting both you and Jenny." I hadn't meant to presume, but it's a huge relief to hear Shirley affirm that one of our next steps is getting together in person.

For the third time, Steve appears in the doorway of the kitchen. His thumbs-up is more a question than a statement. In return, mine is a grand gesture. I'm so full of joy—happiness I can only liken to that moment when I saw each of my newborn children for the first time.

Shirley continues to glide from one topic to another like she's clicking off items from a list. Her energy amazes me. She barely catches a breath as she brings up the PO box, the shuttle there every few days to check for letters from Linda, and the buckets of tears she shed in the parking lot when she saw our baby photos. I learn about her big family, being one of twelve, and life on a Wisconsin dairy farm. As she talks, I scratch out a timeline of her life on my notepad. Many miles away, I imagine she is at her desk doing the same with the highlights from mine.

We are halfway into the two-hour call, when I sling out the question burning my insides. "What's his name? My birth father. Who was he?"

Both Linda and Lisa have coached me on this topic. I should expect that Shirley might not recall my birth father's name, or she might choose not to reveal it. She hesitates, then struggles with the spelling of his last name, but then there it is: Dick Thomson. I roll it around in my head. Dick Thomson. What is that? British or Irish? I hope that he will not be as difficult to locate as Shirley. Circling his name on the notepad, I can't wait to hand it off to Linda.

This is when I allow myself to gloat. My lopsided family tree is sprouting leaves on its naked branches. Pride fills me up—I finally have a pedigree like almost everyone I know! Emboldened, I ask more questions about my birth father, but Shirley provides only a few more facts. They were co-teachers at an elementary school, and he was one of only a few male teachers.

"Where was he from?" My pen poises over the next blank sheet on my notepad. I'm ready to begin a new timeline.

"From up north. North Dakota, I think. I'm not certain." Shirley whispers when she speaks of *him*. She does not call *him* by his name. He is just *him*.

Determined to write something under his name besides North Dakota and teacher, I say, "Catholic Charities said that he was younger than you."

"Yes, he was. By how much, I'm not sure." Her hesitancy has put the skids on our dialogue, and I wonder what she's holding back or why she's reluctant to share more.

"Was it two years or three, do you think?" After I ask this, there's so much silence that I think the call has dropped. "Shirley?"

"I just don't know," she says firmly.

Her voice stops me cold, so I shift to a new topic and vow to come back to *him* later if I can. We touch on a variety of things such as her stepkids and her relationship with them. We talk about sports, and how it was a big thing in her family. This drifts us into a subject I can dwell on for hours: my four kids. She oohs and aahs over my tales, things I'd glossed over in my letters.

Throughout our call, I discuss my parents sparingly, sharing only that I was raised Catholic, that my folks were good parents, and that my mom had also been an elementary teacher. I can't say why I shelter them from Shirley. Perhaps it is for fear of making her feel bad about not parenting me and Jenny, or to protect their privacy, or an unconscious need to keep my two "family worlds" separate for the time being.

Before the I-love-yous and talk-soons, we settle on a range of dates for Jenny and me to visit. When the call ends, I sit still, protecting my abundant joy as if it has a glass veneer, and then I finger the pages of my notes, studying them as if someone else has scribbled in my hand. I stare at the Kleenex, at the phone, at my files, and all the while a victorious smile remains fixed.

I've done it. Three long years of missteps and roadblocks, and thanks to Linda, I'm finally on the other side of *this*. Slumping back into the desk chair, I close my eyes and give thanks to a god who I'd sworn had forgotten my name. Then I shove away from the desk, gather my notes, and yell for Steve.

21

The First Meeting

Yesterday, the turkey leftovers vanished from the fridge, and my kids returned to where they needed to be. Colleen and Molly are back at their jobs in Florida and New York, and Danny is in class at West Point. When Kassie left for high school this morning, Jenny and Dan's car was in our driveway. As I zipped up my suitcase, I could hardly believe that the day I've been thinking of and dreaming about for most of my life had finally arrived. I'm finally going to meet my birth mom, Shirley Faye Desjardins Wilkinson, in person.

Steve and I loaded our small suitcases into the trunk of Jenny's car, and then the four of us headed to the interstate for our reunion. As we drove north toward Wisconsin, the western skies bulged with dark blue clouds, and a winter storm covered the Midwest with frigid air. Throughout the four-hour car ride, Jenny and I stole looks at one another and babbled like teenagers. We didn't voice it aloud, but our apprehension over this first meeting with Shirley factored into our disjointed dialogue.

It's been on our minds for weeks. Phone conversations and writing letters is one thing; getting along in person is something else entirely. So far, our reunion has been chugging along without a hitch, but what will it be like when we're sitting across from one another trying to make conversation? Is the transition from pen pals to a deep mother-and-daughter bond possible? The internal pressures are enormous, and the early start to the day weighs on us.

By midafternoon when we reach the hotel, the four of us droop like flowers in desperate need of water. It's been a day of too much coffee and not-quite-long-enough catnaps. Shirley and Howard are due to meet us in the hotel lobby in twenty minutes. Jenny and I commandeer a set of matching gray lobby chairs, which give us a clear view of the parking lot and main entrance. Our identical profiles are mirrored in the expanse of windows overlooking the Hyatt's grounds. Looking around, I reflect upon the obstacles that preceded this trip: too many airport shuttles with the big kids, Dad's ER visit, the annual chaotic Thanksgiving dinner in my dining room, wrangling a house sitter for Kassie and the dogs, and keeping our parents from knowing about this trip to meet Shirley. For a week now, those factors have layered over the mounting excitement of meeting Shirley for the first time. If someone tapped my shoulder right now, I might crumble into a thousand pieces. I peek at my watch. Where are they?

Jenny scrutinizes the parking lot. "There's a van. Shirley said they'd be driving a van, right?"

I look over to where Jenny points. "She said a gray van."

Steve hands Jenny and me a cup of lukewarm lobby coffee and rejoins Dan on the sofa behind us where they discuss football and the weather.

Jenny is on the edge of her chair. "I can't tell if it's gray or silver."

Squinting out the window, my belly tightens.

"Never mind, it's leaving." Jenny points to her watch.

Shirley and Howard are now ten minutes late. My sister's look seems to ask, *Do you think she's decided not to come after all?* I shrug.

All the planning to get to this day, the roadblocks, the buildup. I'm almost undone. I don't know whether to pace the lobby or sit here with my sister and stare at the snow-sprinkled lot. Draining the weak hotel coffee, I send the cup sailing toward a trash can. A narrow miss. I wonder if this is a habit of my birth mother's—being late, or "tardy" as a schoolteacher would say. Shirley has just earned her first black mark in the report card of our reunion.

"There it is." Jenny catapults off her chair.

A dark gray van edges into the far end of the parking lot, but we can't see who's in it. The vehicle weaves through the rows of cars and pulls into a parking spot near the front entrance. By the time the driver's door finally opens, my chest is on fire.

A stooped, white-haired man with wire-rimmed glasses shuffles around the rear bumper and offers his hand to someone we can't see in the front seat. Our first view is black sensible boots peeking below dark slacks. A gray-haired woman steadies herself and tugs a black puffy winter coat down around her hips. She fluffs her short gray curls and smiles at the man. They nod at one another and she releases his arm. As her face comes into view, I recognize the woman I've come to know from a handful of photographs.

Shirley!

Jenny grins at me, and we glide toward the hotel entrance. Our feet move, but our eyes are glued to our "first mother." I'm determined not to blink for fear that this scene will vanish like a mirage. Shirley reaches for Howard's arm again as they navigate the icy patches freckling the sidewalk. Like my mom and dad, they are careful where they step. Under one elbow, my new stepdad grips two small white boxes. They're so cute together—it doesn't matter that they're twenty minutes late.

As Shirley plods toward the entrance, she appears smaller than I'd gleaned from the pictures included with her letters. Jenny and I are at least three inches taller than her. I detect a stoop to Shirley's shoulders, and because I can't avoid it, I compare her to my mom. My two mothers are about the same height and build. Even their short gray hair is permed and styled with the same heavy shield of hairspray. When Shirley's dark eyes flash over to Howard, I can't tell if they're a chocolate brown like my mom's, or if they contain flecks of gold and green like Jenny's and mine.

Shoulder to shoulder, Jenny and I stand a few feet from the revolving door. Riveted here, I eye my twin. Her face glows with the anticipation of a child unwrapping a marvelous surprise. A gentle smile plays on her lips, and I assume that this is what my face looks like, too. In seconds, we'll be gazing into the face of the woman we've been trying to find for three years. The thrill of it is numbing.

When I glance back to the entrance, Shirley and Howard are just outside the revolving doors, stomping snow free of their boots. Jenny and I wave like fanatics, but the pair are oblivious, which sends us into a fit of girlish giggles. When at last she spies Jenny and me, Shirley's lips soften into a shy smile. Her quick glance at Howard seems to say, *They're here, we're here, this is happening, and I need you by my side.*

As soon as Shirley enters the hotel lobby, Jenny and I encircle her, the length of our long arms pressing her in close to our hearts. Within our embrace, Shirley peers up into our faces. Instead of the emotional sobs that I'd expected, the three of us beam. Our smiles are sparkly and broad, full of joy and wonder and expectation and promise. Around us, our husbands' cameras bombard us like paparazzi.

Shirley's voice pierces the silence of our triangle. "You both are so tall."

We laugh nervously, and Shirley breaks free.

"Julie and Jenny, this is Howard."

My birth mom's deep-set eyes glisten as she introduces her

husband. I marvel at how tightly her cheekbones wear her skin and at the hint of crow's feet near the eyes that Jenny and I and Danny and Kassie inherited. Besides the stylish gray hair, only the thickness at her jawline gives away my birth mom's seventy-eight years.

Howard hugs me and then Jen. "I'm happy to meet you. Three weeks ago, I didn't know I was about to be a father again." Delighted with his little joke, Howard grins at Shirley.

When my birth mom leads Howard over to the guys, I whisper to Jenny, "Now we know where we got this bumpy nose and these high cheekbones." My sister winks.

Steve offers to help Shirley out of her coat, and as she fumbles with the clasps, I study her hands. Her fingers are long and flutter from the wrist like a pianist's. Her nails sparkle with pink polish. Staring at my own fingers and hands, I recognize how Shirley's right hand dominates, and how her right pointer finger gets more exercise than the other nine. I also notice that while Jenny and I have inherited our mother's gestures, our full lips and straight teeth have come from another end of our gene pool.

Once all the introductions have been made, Jenny slips her arm through Shirley's. "We've got a nice corner over here to sit before dinner."

I take Shirley's other arm. "Do we have time for a drink first?"

"We do. The French Bistro is just down the road in another hotel. I picked it because I thought it would be fun to celebrate your French ancestry tonight. Next time around, let's try a German restaurant and celebrate that half."

"Sounds wonderful."

Sinking into a lobby chair, I mentally correct Shirley—being German is half of her background but only one-fourth of mine. Not until Linda locates Dick Thomson, will our full heritage be revealed.

Shirley twists around in her chair. "Howard?"

He glances over from where he stands in conversation with the guys, and she gestures at the white boxes. Shuffling over, he presents them to Jenny and me.

Shirley points at the boxes. "This is why we were late. Howard was delayed at the florist. He surprised me with one too."

She pats her lapel where a yellow rose wrapped in white ribbon is pinned. Shirley informs us that the yellow rose is "her" flower—she'd carried a bouquet of yellow roses on their wedding day.

Jenny and I ooh and aah over our stepdad's thoughtfulness. Between more camera flashes, I catch Steve's eye and read his lips, *You did it.* I give him a thumbs-up.

Our drinks arrive, and Shirley gathers everyone close. "I was going to save this speech for dinner, but now seems like a good time. I think we need a toast. To Julie. Here's to your persistence, dear girl. Without that we would not be sitting here today."

Her words open a dam of tears all around. Through sniffles and "Here, heres," we clink coffee cups and beer mugs and diet cokes. The concierge charges over and offers to snap more pictures. Just as we finish posing for another family photo, my cell phone goes off, and then Jenny's. Six grandchildren are briefly introduced to their biological grandmother. The loop linking three generations of biological strangers has officially closed. A warm peacefulness settles over me.

After an hour of drinks and pictures in the Hyatt lobby, the six of us pile into the Wilkinsons' gray van and head a mile down the road. With Howard at the wheel, our car pool has the feel of a bona fide family outing—as if we've been piling into the family van for a dinner out all our lives. When we arrive at the French Bistro, Shirley leaves us at the hostess station to speak with the manager who's handing out menus in the dining room. The restaurant radiates splendor with white tablecloths, candles, and glitzy holiday decorations. Classic Christmas music drifts around skirted tables, waiters hustle, glasses clink, and silver domes reveal steaming entrées. At a table in the corner, six diners lift their glasses and laugh. As I watch them, I can't help but hope that over time our cluster of strangers, who at this moment are fearful of saying the wrong thing, might become like that table of merry diners.

Howard's face shines with pride as he divulges the countless trips Shirley made to the Bistro these past weeks. "Instead of the main dining room, she reserved a private room with a set menu. She wanted everything perfect for your visit."

When Shirley returns with the manager, our party of six is led back to a small room off the entry. Once the French doors close behind us, the lively music from the restaurant's main areas fades. The room is as quiet as a church, and the focal point is a long table draped in a white cloth with votive candles flickering at its center.

Shirley waves her hand around. "I thought this private room would be a perfect spot to get to know one another without any interruptions." She grips the back of a chair, and her eyes flick over to Howard. Shirley's speech must be prearranged because he acknowledges her look with a slight nod, and then clears his throat several times.

"There are people in Shirley's life that don't know about you girls yet. This arrangement protects her from having to explain who all of you are."

His words send shock waves down my spine.

Instead of joyously proclaiming from the nearest mountain-top that Shirley's girls have come back into her life, Jenny and I are to remain hidden. The realization that Shirley isn't ready to acknowledge our existence to anyone besides Howard sickens me. The announcement makes me feel as if I've been naughty, or that I'm not cool enough to be introduced to my biological family.

My ego puts a stop to this vein of thinking. It isn't me who should be feeling any of this. I consider Shirley. Why is she asking Jenny and me to be complicit in a scheme of prolonged secret-keeping?

Not for one second have I felt unworthy or ashamed of my existence. Such notions are foreign to me. My adoptive parents have always treated me with great pride. Every one of my accomplishments and achievements have been touted and bragged about, often to an embarrassing degree. I twitch an eyebrow at Jenny, but she avoids my gaze.

With the elephant released into the room, Shirley signals that everyone should be seated. Jenny pulls out the chair next to Shirley, and I walk around the table to sit across from them. Steve scoots between Howard and me, and Dan takes the spot at the head of the table. No one is on my right, which is probably a good thing for I twitch and fidget. I want to move, to fling open the doors, take a walk around the block, or invite the waitress to return and chat with us. I had no idea that the first outing with my birth mom would be awkward and elicit such complicated feelings. The glass veneer of my joy over having my birth mom in my life has developed a small crack.

When the waitress brings a tray of champagne flutes into the room, Howard rises from his seat. "I was very surprised when Shirley sat me down a few weeks ago to tell me about Jenny and Julie, but it explained a lot of things. Certain times of the year she'd be quiet, go to church, and retreat into prayer. I didn't know why she'd suddenly become so sad. Now I do. We're glad you're here. Welcome."

After his toast, Shirley takes over. "To you, Howard, for making this secret so easy to share." Her hand trembles, but Shirley's steady gaze speaks volumes about the bond between them.

Shirley tilts her glass in my direction. "To you, dear Julie. As I said earlier, without your perseverance, we would not be sitting here tonight. To your health. Now that it has put us together, may it never be a concern again. To you dear Jenny, for supporting your sister, and encouraging her to press on with this difficult task. And to you men, for your love and devotion to your wives. We're glad you're here, too." Her gentle and warm words assuage some of my earlier discomfort.

Before the first course appears, Shirley reaches into the many tote bags near her chair, and removes two large packets that she hands to Jenny and me.

"Inside this envelope is your ancestry. I included the research from a relative who traced my father's lineage back through Canada and into Europe. Stacked behind that are copies of various family photos."

Emptying the envelope, I flip through the contents. Each and every page is labeled in Shirley's neat script with names and dates and places. I'm speechless. For fifty-one years, I could only guess at my background, but now here it is in one tight little bundle. It's more precious to me than fine jewelry. As I peruse the documents, I forget about the earlier disgrace—my role as the family secret.

After we finish our French onion soup, Shirley gives Jenny and me a family history lesson. She explains about the Native Americans in our lineage and expounds about our ancestors from eastern Germany. They boarded a transatlantic ship from Hamburg to make a new life for themselves in the upper Midwest. When I get to the photo of Poppa, my great-great-grandfather, it's evident who passed on Danny's ability to grow an impressive beard.

When the waitress serves an apple tart with fresh coffee, Jenny catches my eye.

"Now we have something for you, Shirley." I remove a small gift bag from my purse. "Your seventy-ninth birthday is nearly here. This is an early gift from Jenny and me. From all of us."

All eyes are on Shirley as she lifts the small jeweler's box from the gift bag.

"Oh my," she says as the little white box springs open.

Nestled in the center of the pendant's filigreed design, two amethysts flank a blue topaz—Shirley's birthstone in the middle of Jenny's and mine.

"Thank you, girls. I love it." Dabbing her eyes, Shirley bows her head for Jenny's help with the clasp.

Barely three months ago, we were still the lost girls, but now we are the daughters found. This is infinitely better.

When we exit the Bistro, I hold Shirley's elbow, and she whispers to me, "I'm so thrilled that you're here. I'm glad your dad's health is improved and that the weather didn't interfere with your trip. Such a blessing to have you in our lives now."

Kissing her cheek, I tell her, "I'm glad that everything worked out for us to come. The weeks will fly by, and then it will be time for you to visit us in Chicago. For our birthday!"

She squeezes my arm.

Perhaps it's due to the strong dessert coffee, or to the emotional surge from the day's activities, but when Shirley and Howard drop the four of us off at the hotel, none of us head to the elevators.

Steve shrugs out of his camel overcoat. "Shall we have a nightcap in the bar?"

"Definitely." My eyes go to my twin. I've been dying to get her reaction to meeting Shirley. To the dinner. To the packet. To the gift. To everything.

"Good plan." Jenny flashes a wicked smile.

Watching her saunter toward the bar, Dan's laugh echoes around us. "I know what she'll be ordering. A very dirty martini with blue cheese olives."

Our hearty laughs fill the lobby. My sister commandeers a cushy corner booth in the nearly empty lobby bar. She signals for the bartender, and we toss our warm coats and gloves over extra chairs, making our corner look like a mob has settled in for the night.

"I'll have a cabernet," I say to the bartender.

The young man looks less than thrilled that four more fans have joined him in watching Monday Night Football. When he returns with our drinks, Jenny launches into a rehash of our reunion dinner.

"I'm in love with Howard. He couldn't be cuter. He's so nice to Shirley and such a dear about all these surprises that have landed in his lap."

Steve raises his wineglass. "Here's to Howard."

I clink my glass with the others. "Shirley sure has dealt with a lot. In order to meet us she has to reveal a fifty-year-old secret to her husband, her dear friend is dying of cancer, and the whole time she was fending us off through Linda."

It sounds like I've excused my birth mother for turning away from us ten months ago, but in truth that scar is still healing. It's only been six weeks since our first phone call and three short months since I wrote the first letter to Shirley. I wonder if our relationship will bloom into one of those deep bonds between a mother and daughter, one in which multiple phone calls are necessary before the day can close.

A bad taste creeps into my mouth. I'm worried about disclosing this weekend to my folks. Despite Mom's endearing words at our birthday dinner last year, "What a shame. I was looking forward to meeting her someday," I doubt that she's ready to accept Shirley in our lives.

Steve's gaze skims over Jenny and me. "The similarities between Shirley and you two are astounding. It's not just the eye color and cheekbones, it's your hands and gestures."

Jenny peers into her martini. "I thought the restaurant was charming and the food delicious, but I would've preferred eating in the main dining room." She locks eyes with me. "There wasn't any music piped in that room to fill the awkward pauses."

Shaking my head in agreement, I open my mouth but hesitate

to speak. Perhaps now is not the time to bring up Howard's statement about us still being a closely held secret. I could use a good night's sleep before hashing it out with my sister. A call to Linda or Lisa might offer strategies on how to best handle it going forward.

Jenny leans over and pats the folder of genealogy sticking out from her purse.

"Good job, Julie. You did it. You found her. Today was incredible."

Jenny's praise means a lot. "We did it together." I raise my nearly empty glass.

"Not to be a spoiler—" I begin.

"Don't say it." Jenny laughs. "Enjoy this moment."

"Well, we do have to think about it—"

Jenny cuts me off. "Telling Mom and Dad is for another day. Drink up! I'm ready for bed."

Steve calls for the check, and I smile as I watch him. Had my husband not insisted, for the sake of my health and for the benefit of our four kids, I'm not certain that I'd have gone down the adoption search path at all. Now that I'm in good health, the breast biopsy looks like a blessing of sorts. Life is funny that way.

Laughing, Jenny tries to wrangle the check away from Steve. "All right, we'll get breakfast then."

My sister's infectious giggle brings on my own. My twin. If I hadn't had her to ride each wave of this tumultuous search with me, I'm not sure I would have waded in so deep. The intricate layers of our twindom positively affected how we dealt with each decision point in a very complicated project. Because of our deep bond, the stress or disappointment or anger that popped up have been easier to manage. While the emotional load has been heavy, it was spread over two sets of shoulders.

As our weary but happy group heads to the hotel elevators, another thought pops into my head. Not once did the snafus in our adoption search come between my sister and me. That's something to be grateful for, too. With the search for Dick Thomson already up and running, I'm confident that we'll survive another one. This time Linda leads the charge from the onset, and she's armed with a real name instead of an alias. With one reunion off to a glorious start, I hope that our birth dad will want to get to know us, too.

22

❧

That Woman

D oubt and regret sneak out of the house, shadow me across the driveway, and climb into the Buick with me. I wish I didn't have to venture out on such a wintry night. Even more than that, I wish that tonight's conversation with my parents was in the record books, and that I was already in bed watching the ten o'clock news with Steve.

Like me, my car needs time to warm up to tonight's task. After I crank up the defroster, I grab the ice scraper and chisel at the frosty windshield until my wrist throbs. Jenny and I have waited nearly four months to tell our parents about our birth mom reentering our lives, something I very much regret.

Back in August, when we learned that Shirley had changed her mind about connecting with us, I'd wanted to share the development right away. Jenny convinced me that our reunion was still too new, too tentative, so it would be smarter to let things "unfold." She wasn't wrong really, but now Christmas looms, a hectic time to reveal such an important turn of events.

When we progressed from exchanging cards and letters with Shirley to planning a visit to Wisconsin, Jenny and I decided the time was right to tell our parents. Circumstances forced us to post-pone it. Dad was hospitalized with an intestinal issue, and Mom visited him every day. Making our disclosure in the middle of that crisis would have stressed my mom to the breaking point. We didn't want that, so we put off revealing our big news once again.

When last week's face-to-face reunion with Shirley turned out well, Jenny and I got out our calendars. I was adamant that we shouldn't wait for the New Year to roll in, but the problem was find-ing a date that would work for both of us. Jenny was scheduled to return from an overseas business trip just as my family was leaving for our annual vacation to Montana. I was the one who persuaded Jenny that I could handle dropping the bomb all by myself.

I send the last bit of ice careening off the Buick's windshield and climb into the warm car. There was never going to be the "right" time to talk about our reunion with Shirley. Tonight's the night. Telling my parents is on me, and I must present it in the kindest, gentlest way possible.

Signing in at the main desk, I hustle past the chaotic commu-nity room and make a beeline for my folks' apartment.

At the door, I gather myself up with a couple of big breaths and let the door knocker fall.

From the other side, Dad shouts, "It's open, Jules."

I swallow hard. Of course, it's open. They're expecting me. My purse drops to the floor and I slide sloppy boots from my feet. When I straighten up, Mom is in the foyer.

She gives me a friendly squeeze. "What can I get you?"

Avoiding her dark brown eyes, I say, "Nothing, thanks. I just had dinner."

"Your dad's in here."

As I follow Mom toward the den, the entire scene feels like déjà vu. It's as if the same things are being said in the same order as the last time that I was in this apartment to discuss my adoption. And just like three years ago, when my parents handed over my adoption papers, my heart races as if I've run up a flight of stairs.

To get into the den, I must pass the large photo of the cottage on Lake Michigan, my folks' happy place. The fate of the cottage is another tough conversation, but one I plan to defer until the new year.

Dad smiles and waves from his comfy recliner, and Mom plops down on the loveseat. Nothing in their cozy sitting room has changed. On the coffee table are my mom's devotionals, a tangle of rosary beads, and a glass of chardonnay. Maggie, the ancient terrier, lifts her head and blinks wildly at me as if she knows I'm about to challenge her people to their limit.

As always, I kiss my father's cheek and squeeze his stooped shoulders. This time I drop into one of the armchairs opposite the loveseat instead of dragging out Dad's desk chair. The TV blares, and my dad struggles to locate the remote.

"What're you watching?" I'm not quite ready to launch into my spiel.

"Just news. Shootings and Middle East crises. More of the same." Normally, Dad would relate a humorous anecdote from the day, but not tonight.

"How are you feeling?"

His complexion is pale, almost gray, and his cheekbones protrude now more than ever from the apples of his cheeks. His sudden weight loss is from the stint in the hospital, but it's more obvious to me tonight than when I saw him at Thanksgiving. On the end table, there's a white box. The lid is off and there are more empty brown wrappers than there are candies inside.

I smile at my dad. "I see you're well enough for a Pixie or two."

Dad's eyes gleam with the tease, but not as bright as they used to. For a second, I reconsider the errand that has brought me out on this nasty December night. Out of the corner of my eye, I see Mom pick up her wineglass and swirl the golden liquid.

Twisting my hands in my lap, I blurt, "I have some shocking news to share."

Mom's head snaps up, and Dad drops the remote to his lap.

"It's not bad news." I assure them with a wimpy smile. "My birth mother contacted my confidential intermediary. She's changed her mind about meeting Jenny and me."

My mother blinks and her knuckles whiten around the stem of her wineglass.

Dad clears his throat. "Why that's wonderful, Jules. Now, besides the health history she gave you, you can learn more about your ancestry."

At that instant, I want to leap up, give my dad a suffocating hug, and thank him for being such a dear human being, but I don't. I'm waiting for my mom to say something. Anything. The dog groans and rolls over, wiggling against the carpet. The three of us watch her as she does this over and over. Finally, Mom reaches down and massages Maggie's belly. My mother's silence is like a slap. My cheeks burn.

Words pile out before I can gather them back into my mouth. "I've met her. This past weekend. She's married to a nice man named Howard. He was a widower with two adopted children when she married him. How about that for a twist?"

Smiling wanly at my mother, I'm hoping that she'll respond to the irony of my birth mother having stepkids who are adoptees like me, but her eyes follow the dog's antics. Anxious to get all the answers to their questions out in the open, I rattle off details and explanations. I want to be done with this and go home and sleep like a baby.

Mom's face is hard to read, but Dad leans forward. "What's her name? Where does she live?"

As I answer him, I try not to flaunt the joy in my heart. "She's from a large family—one of twelve. Isn't that a coincidence, Mom? You, being the youngest of twelve."

My mother nods, but her eyes never leave the dog's pink belly.

I carry on like a teenager trying to talk my way out of trouble. "Shirley is German and French and there's some American Indian thrown in there, too. She gave Jenny and me all sorts of pictures of our ancestors." Pasting on my best fake smile, I spread my hands wide. "Now I can finally start my family tree on that ancestry site."

Exhausted, I peek at my mom who gapes at my father. Dad pales as he comprehends the meaning of her look—Mom is appalled at his excitement over my shocking news. The tremors in Dad's left hand resume. I suck in my breath. My reunion update has put Dad in a hard place with my mother.

When my mom clears her throat to speak, Dad and I are like magnets. "And your birth father, have you met him too?" Her voice is as icy as the Buick's windshield.

I gulp hard. "Nope. We're looking for him. The intermediary, I mean, is looking for him. We have his name, now. Thanks to Shirley. If you recall, we didn't have that before."

Encouraged that Mom has entered the conversation, I try something I think might appeal to her sensitivities.

"Shirley wanted me to say how thankful she is to both of you for taking such good care of us." She had teared up when expressing this sentiment to me.

Mom is on this before my last word is in the air. "My goodness, there's no need to thank us. We did what all parents should do: love and nurture the child that was given to them."

With that, my mom drains the chardonnay and clanks the goblet down on the glass top of the coffee table. The nuances of my mother's statement settle into the room like the aftershocks of an earthquake. My mom is giving herself credit for acting like a responsible parent, leaving no doubt about her judgment of the woman who gave up twin daughters.

Looking from my dad's pale face to my mother's flushed one, I play the last card in my losing hand. "She looks forward to meeting you both sometime."

My mother jumps to her feet as if I've insulted her. The dog startles and yelps.

"I ... do not want ... that woman ... in MY life."

There it is.

Whether it's the wine or her anger that has loosened my mother's tongue, there's no lingering doubt as to where she stands regarding our reunion with Shirley. Dad sinks into his recliner like a rag doll. His face is ashen, and I suspect my own face has lost its healthy color, too. My mother has hijacked tonight's dialogue, and it's become all about her—what she wants and doesn't want. Something clicks in my head, a door closing. I'm done being so forthcoming with her about my adoption search.

"Now, honey," Dad starts to say, but he stops when she glares at him over tightly crossed arms.

"It's okay, Dad. Really. Mom, you don't have to meet her if you don't want to. The point in my coming here tonight was to be open and honest with you. You've nothing to worry about. Even though Shirley is in my life, you'll always be my parents."

My mother melts into the sofa and reaches for my father's hand. Her shoulders have the look of the weary, or of a person who may regret tomorrow what she said tonight.

We're passing out of the difficult moment, but I can't help pressing her. "You've confused me though. I thought you wanted to meet her. That's what you'd said on my birthday, that night at Gibson's. You'd asked how my search was progressing. You said that you always wanted to meet her. Remember?"

Mom's voice is so weak that I have to lean in to hear her. She studies the veins in her hand that is clasped firmly in my father's. "I don't remember saying that."

189

Dad's blue eyes meet mine. "If you want us to meet Shirley, we'd be delighted. Wouldn't we, honey?"

My heart melts. "Thanks, Dad."

When I'm in the doorway to leave, Dad says, "We love you. Keep us posted about your birth father." He squeezes my mother's hand as if this will encourage her to speak up and agree, but Mom's eyes close.

"I will." Saying my goodbyes, I try not to hurry out the door.

The cold air in the parking lot makes me gasp, but the fresh air feels good on my face. It clears my head, makes me feel alive, relieved.

The deed is done.

In the short walk to the car, I consider what I hadn't mentioned to my parents. Linda's team has been unable to locate my birth dad, Dick Thomson, and she's asked me several times about the spelling of his last name. Was I sure that Shirley spelled Thomson without a "p"? All I can offer is that Shirley struggled with it. Given how buttoned up she is about *him*, I'm reluctant to quiz her again. As a result, Linda's office is searching for every permutation of "Richard or Dick Thomson." There's a stream of males with my birth father's name, all from North Dakota, born between 1934 and 1936. Knowing his exact birthdate and birthplace would help narrow the search.

Climbing into the car, I think about my mother's reaction—she acted worse than I'd expected. The wine is partly to blame, but so is my timing. Delivering the news in the afternoon instead of after dinner might have shown her in a better light, might have produced a warmer response. Maybe.

A bit of conversation that I had with Lisa at the back of St. Vincent's chapel comes back to me. The social worker had quizzed me. "How is your relationship with your adoptive mom?"

Snickering, I'd told her, "Throughout our lives, Mom and Dad reiterated that they'd help us if we ever wanted to search. When the day came, it was obvious that my father supported it, but my mother did not."

Lisa had said, "We see this a lot. The world your mom created for her family is threatened. She's afraid she'll lose you."

I was incredulous. "At my age?"

"Yes, at any age. It's the day they never wanted to come."

When I explained to Lisa about my mother's words at my birthday dinner, she shook her head. "You cannot fear what will not happen."

Tonight, Lisa's words had played out. My mom defended her right to be my mother and threw a net around our family unit, one that did not include birth relatives. Her love was angry, fiercely protective, and selfish, but it was honest. Over the course of my life, I have known my mother's love to be other things: kind and gentle, effusive and expansive. More often than not, Mom offered the perfect remedy to the hurts and struggles I experienced as a growing girl. What disappoints me now is that her love cannot extend beyond her own needs and fears. She can't transcend those limitations and recognize what I need as her daughter, as an adoptee. She isn't there yet, and I'm not certain she'll ever make that leap. While Jenny may be shocked at my mother's exact words tonight, I doubt that she'll be surprised.

My head in my hands, I remind myself: I did not choose to be adopted, and my heart is big enough to love two mothers and two sets of parents. If only my mother wouldn't make me feel so bad about it.

23

The Birthday Box

2012

When the car honks, I grab the bouquet of flowers for Shirley and scoot out the side door.

"Happy birthday, Jen!" I proclaim as I slide into her sedan.

Jenny's grin lights up her eyes. "To you, too! Those are pretty! Shirley will love them."

Today is our fifty-second birthday. It's the first birthday that we'll celebrate with Shirley and Howard. Planning the activities for her three-day visit has consumed Jenny and me for weeks. It's been a good kind of busy, one that makes us joyful with anticipation, a huge contrast to how miserable we felt on this day last year when she'd denied contact with us.

After I assure Jenny that Shirley's flight is on time, she pulls out of my driveway, and we head south on the interstate toward Chicago's Midway airport. On the same interstate, Steve is with Kassie and Colleen traveling in the opposite direction to meet Molly's flight at O'Hare. Everyone but Danny has finagled a trip home to celebrate my birthday and to meet Shirley and Howard. After the airport run, the girls will have lunch with my parents. We will meet up with them at our house after Jenny and I drop Shirley and

Howard's luggage off at their hotel. Watching Shirley's face as she meets her granddaughters for the first time is something I can't wait to witness.

Jenny sneaks a peek at me. "Are you ready for another night of birthday cake and presents?"

I snicker.

Tonight will be the second evening in a row that Jenny and I will celebrate our birthday. Since the "I do not want that woman in my life" episode two months ago, neither my mom nor I have brought up Shirley, our blossoming reunion, or the search for my birth dad. If either of my parents wondered what this year's birthday might mean to Shirley, Jenny, and me, or how the three of us might be honoring it, they haven't asked, and we haven't offered.

My mom's attitude and Shirley's visit proposed a dilemma for Jenny and me. Figuring out when and how to schedule separate birthday parties with two sets of parents is delicate business. Now I understand the struggles divorced families face. I suggested to Shirley that they come on Saturday, our actual birthday, and Jenny asked my parents if Friday night would work for them. To our huge relief, plans were set in motion.

Jenny frowns at the road. "It's too bad last night's snow flurries forced us to eat in the senior center dining room versus that yummy Italian restaurant I booked."

"I know. I don't mind having lunch there once in a while, but the dinner menu is pretty limited."

"Especially for a birthday dinner!" Jenny snorts.

"The food was fine, but Mom and Dad seemed off to me."

Jenny's eyes remain fixed on the road. "Perhaps they suspected that we're celebrating our real birthday with Shirley and Howard tonight."

"Maybe, but keep in mind Mom is the one who doesn't want Shirley in her life. I would've loved nothing more than to have a photo taken on my birthday with my two mothers. She has made this such a painful thing."

Jenny pats my hand.

I stare out the car window and think about last night. Jenny and I and our husbands met my parents for supper at their usual five-thirty seating. The hostess sat us at a table for six in a corner, so Dad had room for his walker. Mom and Dad presented us with matching cards and gifts, and then a few of the high school servers popped out the kitchen doors with two candlelit cupcakes. Nearby tables clapped when the servers performed "Happy Birthday" a cappella. It was nice, but not as festive as last year when we had dinner out at Gibson's.

Last evening, my mom had not been her typical, sociable self. Her brown eyes had that far-off look of someone who might have slept poorly. Her contribution to the dinner chatter had been stiff and slow, not peppered with a cute story or a chuckle at Dad's silly jokes. As the dessert plates were cleared, I reminded her that Steve and I had to leave soon to pick up Colleen from the airport.

Mom had said, "How nice. Say hello to her for me."

Jenny nudged me under the table, and I picked up the beat.

"Molly flies in tomorrow morning. She and Colleen and Kassie are planning to have lunch with you tomorrow. Is that still okay?"

"Oh, right. Yes, that'd be fine."

Mom's eyes sped past mine as she signaled the waitress for more coffee. If my mother suspected that she'd been re-prioritized, she never let on. If the shuffling of birthday dinners had triggered a gloomy spell, Dad didn't hint at it.

The insistent tone of Jenny's voice brings me back to the moment. "Okay, Jules. We're nearing the exit for the airport. Can you tell if that sign says the parking garage is full?"

"You're good. Turn there."

Reaching down for the flowers, I banish the sour notes of last evening's dinner and welcome the excited stirrings in my stomach. Our first birthday with Shirley and Howard is about to begin.

From the kitchen island where I prep a shrimp dish, I have a clear view of the family room addition we put on the back of our old Victorian. Steve has the fireplace roaring, soft music plays in the background, and animated conversation filters back to me. I observe how easily Steve chats with Howard, and how Shirley's spirited laughter draws in Jenny and Colleen and Molly. The scene infuses me with a peaceful, content feeling. Family. Only my youngest children are missing from this scene. Kassie left an hour ago for her high school Valentine's dance, and Danny checked in with me from West Point earlier in the day. It's been a great birthday so far, with more memories yet to make.

As I place the shrimp dish down with the other appetizers, Jenny says, "I think Colleen looks so much like you, Shirley."

The pair sits close together on the sectional, and I pause to study them. Colleen, who turned twenty-six three days ago, has Shirley's build, but her brown eyes are a darker shade of brown like Steve's.

Molly is not to be overshadowed by her older sister. "What about me? Shirley, do I look like any of your sisters? Or nieces?"

She cocks her head and stares at Molly. "Well, I guess you look like my sister Betty. She's tall like you are, and when she was younger, she had dark, wavy hair. Lots of it."

All of us giggle. Managing Molly's thick hair has always been a challenge.

Pleased by Shirley's explanation, Molly poses another question. "How about Kassie? Who does she look like?" As Shirley considers this, her gaze drifts toward the flames in the fireplace.

If you didn't know my girls but were forced to gather them from a crowded room, the task would be a challenge. One is short, one is very tall, and one is of average height. Hair color runs the spectrum from thick and dark to thin and light brown to blond with reddish tones. Kassie does not closely resemble any of her siblings or Steve or me. I connect the dots: Kassie must take after my birth father, Dick Thomson.

I shoo the dogs outside, and the open door ushers in a nose-tightening crispness. "Oh, it's gotten chilly."

Steve reaches for another shrimp. "The cold front has moved in. Nothing but blue skies for the rest of the weekend."

Shirley tosses her gray curls. "We've been praying all week that the weather wouldn't interfere with our trip for the twins' birthday." She grins at Jenny and me. "Father God came through for us—no rescheduling necessary."

Howard's voice carries across the room. "Amen to that."

The room fills with laughter, an acknowledgment of how difficult this weekend was to put together.

Looking first at her watch and then at me, Shirley says, "I think we should open your gifts before dinner."

Jenny grins. "Let's do it!"

Shirley signals to Howard. "Would you help me pass out the packages to the girls?"

There it is again: the girls. I've been hearing that label all my life, but from my birth mom it seems fresh and new.

Towering on the window seat are the two large, bulky gift bags Shirley stuffed in my trunk an hour ago. As Shirley and Howard retrieve the presents, I think about our family rituals. The window seat is where I pile our wrapped packages on Christmas Eve. Steve and I are the ones who pass out those gifts to our family, just as Howard and Shirley do now. While the continuum of gift giving is a bit backward, the familiar routine lights up a corner of my heart.

"Okay, girls, now I want you to lift out what's in the bags. At the same time."

Shirley twists her hands. Her brown eyes hopscotch from Jenny and me to Howard, and then back to us again. We do as we are told. Jenny and I flip out tufts of frail tissue in a kaleidoscope of colors. The yellow, pink, and orange paper, which coordinates with the enormous gift bags, smothers our feet.

"This is heavy." I struggle to lift the item weighing down the bag. "It's a box? Wait it's a trunk, isn't it?" I peer at Shirley and she nods—a nervous smile plays on her lips. "The pattern on it is so pretty!"

Jenny studies the trunk on my lap. "They match!" We're used to receiving similar gifts from family on our birthday.

Sliding my hand across the patterned paper decorating the trunk, I discover a metal clasp. A closer look reveals the paper to be a patchwork of phrases all dealing with love. Of course, "love"—my birthday precedes Valentine's Day by seventy-two hours. My heart remembers. Last year, because of Shirley's rejection, loss not love was the theme of my fifty-first birthday. I pat the treasure box, wanting to savor the moment. For most of my life, receiving a birthday gift from my birth mom had seemed unlikely or impossible.

"I don't know how you fit this in your suitcases," Jenny says, laughing.

Shirley giggles quietly as Howard answers. "That was the easy part. The suitcase I mean. When Shirley was filling the little trunks last night, we noticed that one of them was damaged. We traipsed all over town to two other TJ Maxx stores until we found the right one."

My smile fills the room. I love that my birth mother shops at my favorite haunt, and I'm honored that she went to such lengths to assemble such a unique birthday present.

Shirley speaks over the light chatter. "Open the first package on top. Both of you, at the same time."

With one quick glance at me, Jenny nods and we flip open the lids. The box is crammed with items neatly wrapped in white tissue.

There are so many gifts that I wonder, *Are there fifty-two? One gift for every year that she's missed celebrating with us?*

Jenny holds up the same red object as the one in my arms. "A Valentine Bear. How sweet!" The plush toy fits in the palm of my hand, and I snuggle it up against my cheek.

Through quivering lips, Shirley whispers, "It's an early Valentine. I know it's a plaything, but I wasn't able to give you girls any toys while you were growing up. Forgive me as I catch up."

"Keep opening, Mom!" Molly begs.

We unwrap a myriad of other small presents. There's stationery with our initials, chocolate hearts, a small plaque that proclaims the meaning of our adoptive names, and a silver chain with a dangling charm—the letter "J" in cursive script.

"You've spoiled us, Shirley." I struggle to get up, so I can give her a proper thank-you hug.

Her face serious, Shirley stops us. "There's one more gift at the bottom."

"Oh, I see it now," Jenny says.

Nestled at the bottom of the trunk is a square of white tissue. I'd mistaken it for cushioning, a protective layer for the gifts piled on top. As I free the white bundle from the bottom of the trunk, I peek over at my twin. When she's ready, we tear away the thin paper and reveal a fold of soft fabric in a mellow shade of green. I pet it, raising the nap of the microfiber. Smaller than an afghan, the coverlet is the size of . . . Oh my! A baby blanket.

My eyes flick toward Shirley. She dabs a tissue under the wire frames of her eyeglasses. "I never got to . . . Sorry, I didn't think I'd cry. Give me a moment."

While Shirley collects herself, I think of that day in October when we first talked by phone. She hadn't cried then, nor had she teared up in November when we first met. Finally, on our birthday are the tears I've been longing to see. Shirley's emotion means that placing us for adoption had seared her. She had missed our presence in her life and regretted losing her chance at motherhood.

This emotional moment reminds me of a confession made by one of the birth mothers in my adoption support group: *I wanted to be strong for my child. I didn't want her to see me a mushy mess.* After she disclosed this, the adoptees, including myself, had shouted at her, *No, we want to see you vulnerable. We need to know that our adoption hurt you, that we meant something to you, and that you never stopped thinking about us.* The tears that Shirley allows now are more meaningful than any of the presents in the birthday box.

Before Jenny and I can free ourselves from the packages and tissues, Howard is at Shirley's chair, his palms settling into her shoulders. She pats his hands and smiles up at him.

"I'm fine," she whispers.

To us, Shirley admits, "I just never had the chance to hold you girls, much less to see you, which was what the nurses and nuns had advised. These are baby blankets. I know you don't need them, but I wanted you to have them."

We go to her and loop our arms around her shoulders.

I kiss her soft, damp cheek. "Thank you. Thank you for everything. All of it."

As I say this, I'm thinking more about her tears than the blanket, symbols of what adoption took from all of us.

Steve puts the fire out, and we gather our coats. We tumble into the cold cars lining the driveway and head out for dinner. During the short drive in the dark, I reflect on the many birthday gifts I've received over the years, what it means to be gifted, and that adoption is like regifting. I consider this new mother of mine. Shirley is a woman who gave up the most precious gift life can bestow: a child. That she could do this, that she did this, I still can't fathom, even though I know her story and her reasons.

In the rearview mirror, I study my daughters bundled into scarves and gloves, chattering and giggling like best friends in the back seat. Being deprived of mothering any of my four children would be for me an unrelenting sorrow. As a birth mother, Shirley's breakdown tonight proved that was true for her, too.

Gazing up at the streetlights guiding us to the restaurant, I'm grateful for this moment of solitude before a bustling restaurant shifts our group into party mode. I think about the candles on the cake that Shirley will see Jenny and me blow out for the first time, about the fuzzy green baby blanket I nestled back into the birthday box, and about what my fifty-second birthday has come to signify. For all of us tonight, the healing of adoption loss has begun.

24

The Wall of Smiles

Because today is the last day of Shirley and Howard's three-day visit, it feels more like a Saturday than a Monday. The past weekend has been a whirlwind of family camaraderie, stories and laughter, kisses and hugs, and lots and lots of cake and gifts. Before their flight home this afternoon, there's one more event planned. We have an appointment at the Midwest Adoption Center to meet Linda.

Jenny's silver car turns into my driveway right on time. Two heads bob in the front seat, one gray and the other light brown. I can only imagine what grand tale is being shared between my sister and birth mom right now. Throughout our birthday weekend, Jenny and I have done our best to catch Shirley and Howard up on our fifty-year history in the Chicago area.

Loaded down with my purse and fancy camera, I hustle out the side door. With each careful step down the icy driveway, my anticipation builds. Our reunion is in its sixth glorious month, and I can't wait to introduce Jenny and Shirley to Linda. A snapshot of the four of us in MAC's offices will be the weekend's capstone.

As I buckle up in the back seat, I ask, "Have we worn you out this weekend, Shirley?"

She chuckles. "Not really. I've enjoyed spending time with each of you girls. We've kept quite the schedule! It was a good idea for Howard to rest up at the hotel this morning though."

Jenny's eyes flick to mine in the rearview mirror. "Shirley was telling me that yesterday afternoon you gave them a driving tour of our old stomping grounds."

I shake my head in wonder. "Yep. We hit all the highlights. Our childhood homes and schools—including Benet where Kassie is in class right now—and then we went downtown and drove past the townhouse where Steve and I lived when Colleen and Molly were born—all that took up most of the afternoon. Last night, we were so pooped that only a Chicago-style pizza sounded good!"

"It was this thick." Shirley demonstrates, and we all laugh. "I'm still stuffed."

"When you were in the city, did you drive by St. Vincent's?" Jenny asks.

Shirley doesn't answer, so I do. "Yes, but the wind was so fierce that we parked on the street and didn't get out."

Reaching through the seats, I pat Shirley's shoulder. She giggles softly.

Jenny steals a glance at Shirley. "Were you ever inside St. Vincent's?"

My birth mom's eyes remain glued on the thick traffic ahead. When she answers, her voice is so low that my seat belt prevents me from hearing all that she says.

"No, I signed the paperwork at Catholic Charities. After that, I wasn't given any information about the two of you. The nuns said it was better that way."

Jenny and I trade a knowing look in the mirror. It's evident that Shirley is quite comfortable learning about our childhood and the events of our adult lives, but when it comes to placing us for adoption, that subject generates an impregnable fortress of pain.

For several miles, only the muted tones of the radio circulate in the car.

When we near O'Hare, I break the silence. "Jen, the exit you want is coming up."

The sedan turns into MAC's office complex, and we luck into a parking spot close to the shoveled walkway. I help Shirley out of the car. At her neck, a silver chain catches the brilliant morning sun. My fingers search for the matching chain and charm dangling around my neck. When Jenny appears at Shirley's elbow, she points at our jewelry.

"Looks like we all have on the matching heart necklaces you gave us for Valentine's Day."

Grinning, I raise the silver open-heart charm away from my breastbone. Shirley lifts hers, and Jenny follows suit. Our eyes twinkle as we lean forward and clink the charms like one does with a glass of champagne. The wonder of the three of us choosing to wear the Valentine necklaces for our visit to Linda banishes the uncomfortable moment in the car.

I thread my arm through Shirley's. "Let's go meet Linda!"

As Jenny holds open the lobby door for us, excitement bubbles in my belly. Each step toward MAC's lower level offices reminds me of the day I'd sprinted down the hallway to receive Shirley's real name. On that chilly fall day, I'd been dressed in workout clothes and sneakers, not trousers and a turtleneck adorned with a silver heart. Today, instead of racing toward Linda's office for clues about Shirley, I'm walking through the door with her.

"Here we are!"

Pushing open MAC's door, I smile at Shanika. Six months ago, I'd landed in front of this same receptionist. Alone, trembling with anticipation, I'd wished that my twin were standing next to me like she'd done at all the other critical moments in our lives. On that beautiful autumn day, I couldn't have envisioned that in time I'd be back at Shanika's desk, accompanied by both my twin sister and my birth mother. The closure fills me with pleasure and gratitude.

Shanika shakes my hand, and when she looks at Jenny, she covers her mouth. Her eyes dart from Jenny to me and settle on Shirley. I giggle as I introduce everyone.

"Oh, my. I knew you were a twin, but this is incredible. Ladies, welcome to the Midwest Adoption Center. We've been expecting you."

Shirley chuckles at all the attention our twindom brings. "These girls just had a birthday, one that I wasn't going to miss this year. We've had a full weekend. Squeezing in time to meet Linda, who put us together, is the icing on the cake."

Shanika looks down the hallway. "And here comes Linda."

"Hello, everyone. I'm so glad you made it to our offices today." Linda beams at me.

The glance that passes between us is an entire conversation. Her blue eyes convey the significance of our presence and acknowledge the challenges we overcame to stand here. In her gaze, I see the pain of that snowy day, one year ago, when she delivered the news of Shirley's "no contact." The satisfaction in having turned Shirley's phone call last August from a question about a form into an exchange of letters is evident, too. And I detect pleasure and pride—Linda's diligence and tenacity ensured that today's jubilant get-together became a reality.

Linda offers her hand to Jenny. "I know who this is!"

"And this must be—" The rest of Linda's words are muffled by Shirley's hug. I don't have to look at Jenny to know tears collect in the corners of her hazel eyes, too.

"Thank you, thank you, Linda. Without you, none of this would be possible." Shirley refuses to let Linda go. She has her by both shoulders, her brown eyes holding the gaze of the social worker, forty years her junior.

Through tears, I survey the office. Shanika's head lowers as if in prayer, and behind Linda and Shirley, three grinning faces peer out from cubicles. The curious support is touching. Witnessing a gathering such as ours—a birth mom connecting with not just one but both daughters lost to adoption—is probably not a frequent office event. Our visit is just as important to the staff as it is to us. It's an emotional reminder of how their efforts impact the strangers they try to help.

A shy smile warms Linda's face. "It's been my pleasure, Shirley. This has been an unusual case with a very happy ending."

Shirley grips Linda's arm. "There was a time when I thought I'd never step foot in this office. I was so angry, so shocked at receiving that first letter. I was afraid . . . afraid that my husband would intercept the mail. That's why all the letters had to be mailed to the post office box. Thank you for working with me on that." Shirley pauses as if waiting to be forgiven for the difficulties she caused.

Linda tosses her brown curls. "I understood your fear. It's not uncommon for a birth mother to keep an unwed pregnancy a secret from the man she marries. The culture at the time Julie and Jenny were born promoted this practice. Your reactions were perfectly understandable."

Shirley skims our faces as if wanting the rest of us to understand her behavior, too. "My reputation was at stake. I knew I couldn't raise two girls by myself. I would never have been hired as a teacher if anyone found out about my predicament. My own family would have disowned me. I had no choice but to consider adoption."

Linda breaks the tender moment. "As an intermediary, we've been coached to handle complex situations such as yours, Shirley." Linda nods at me and smiles. "I'm confident that if I can get a birth relative on the phone, I'll convince them to make the first step toward connecting with lost family members."

Jenny whispers in my ear, "She's good. It may have taken almost a year, but Linda made this happen as quickly as was humanly possible."

Linda's speech is familiar to me. She first made this promise on that snowy Tuesday when she read Shirley's rejection letter over the phone, and she restated this vow when the second outreach was mailed. I think about her counsel over the denial of contact, and her assistance in composing the first letter to Shirley. Having Linda on our case has been an incredible blessing.

Linda steps away from Shanika's desk. "Would you like to meet the rest of the staff? I can give you a brief tour, and afterward we can chat more in my office."

"We want a picture with you too, Linda." I pat my camera.

"I'd like that, too."

In every office we glimpse, there's one thing in common: files. Everywhere the eye lands, a tray overflows with labeled folders, someone huddles over documents, or the drawer of a file cabinet is open. We learn that each folder represents a new, pending, or closed case. The clients are either adult adoptees like us, or people from the foster care system.

Linda explains MAC's mission. "We connect children, families, and adults affected by adoption or foster care so that they can find out more information regarding their background. Success rates vary, and as Julie knows, we're limited to the timelines dictated by the court."

We saunter into Linda's office, and my eyes go immediately to her desk. It's free of files, uncluttered, just as it was the day when I arrived in my workout clothes. That day my chest had been tight with anxiety, and it had nearly exploded once Shirley's contact info was in my sweaty palms. Even now, my pulse pounds.

"How long have you been with MAC?" Jenny asks.

As Linda answers Jenny's question, my eyes wander the room. Linda's office is bigger than I remembered. Had there always been two chairs opposite her desk? Was the conference table in the far corner stacked with file boxes last fall, too? I slip past our little group to study the bulletin board on the wall.

"Linda, is this what I think it is?"

Linda joins me. "That's my 'Wall of Smiles.' Often my clients send me photos of themselves with the birth relatives I've helped them find. Whenever I'm having a rough day on a case, I peek over here from my desk. I can see the positive aspects of my job, and it reminds me why I do this."

"Wow. Wow!" Shirley exclaims, echoing our thoughts.

"So cool. Time to get your Nikon out, Jules," my twin says.

"Huddle up, Linda and Shirley. Then I'll get Jenny with Shirley and Linda." I snap away.

"Let me ask a colleague to take one of Julie and me. We need a group shot, too." Within seconds, the center's director has my camera in her hand.

Linda glows. "Jenny and Julie, you'll be my first set of twins on the board. Don't forget to send me copies."

My eyes dance from Linda to Shirley and then up to the bulletin board. We've done it. We've come full circle. As I look at the proud, happy faces of adoptees and their found families, I hope that a photo of my twin and me with my birth father will make it to Linda's "Wall of Smiles," too.

I'm tucking my camera away when Jenny asks, "Can you join us for lunch, Linda?"

"I'm afraid I can't. I have another appointment."

As Jenny and Shirley enter the hallway, I pull Linda back into her office. "Where are we with the search for Dick Thomson?"

Linda's voice is low. "I was going to call you about this. We're tracing three leads, but none of them appear to be quite the right age. The research department has used up a lot of time. You may need to quiz Shirley about the spelling of his name."

I stiffen. I'm reluctant to burst the bubble of our reunion by badgering Shirley with questions about my birth father. The topic of *him* is as uncomfortable to her as the subject of placing Jenny and me for adoption.

I sigh. "Let's follow the three leads for a bit. If nothing materializes, I'll figure out a way to quiz her about this."

Linda's gaze is direct. "Birth mothers often misremember the details surrounding their unwed pregnancy. Or they invent an entire new reality. She may not have given you the correct name. She does know you're searching for him, right?"

"Yes. She knows. When the time is right, I'll ask her about the spelling."

"I understand, Julie, but keep in mind the time limit on the case. We have six months left, and if there's no progress, the judge will dismiss. I'm sorry."

With nothing else to say, I follow Linda toward reception. I plea silently for a break in the case, one that doesn't involve pressuring Shirley or threaten the status of our reunion.

In the reception area, Shirley wraps Linda in another hug. "Thank you, thank you, Linda! Meeting you today tops off a beautiful weekend."

Linda walks us to the office door, and I wave goodbye to Shanika. I expect to speak to her more in the days ahead. As I walk behind Jenny and Shirley to the elevator, my mind jumps around like one of those tiny crazy balls you win at a fair. I weigh the visit with Linda and her "Wall of Smiles" against the birthday festivities with Shirley and my girls. I crowd into the elevator with my sister and birth mom and take a deep breath. The long, perfect weekend is coming to a close.

Jenny raises an eyebrow at me. "Ready to grab lunch?" I give her a thumbs-up.

As I guide Shirley to the car, she grins up at me. "I'm so glad to have met Linda today. I'm even more glad that you chose *her* to find *me*."

"Me too," I say. "Me too."

We exit the office complex, and I hope that my birth dad will issue the same praise when Linda locates him.

Part Three

FINDING HIM

When one door closes, another door opens;
But we often look so long and so regretfully
upon the closed door
that we do not see the one which has opened for us.
~ Alexander Graham Bell

25

The Resolution

2013

Steve and I arrived in Montana two days ago to prep our mountain home for the holidays. Our four kids and their guests will arrive in Big Sky tomorrow. I'm putting the finishing touches on the Christmas tree and fireplace mantels. I laugh to myself as I do this. It used to irritate me that the holiday decorating had become my job, and that my family acted like it killed them to throw a few ornaments on the tree. We've sailed past those times. After a long day of travel, I know they will comment on how festive the log home looks, and then they'll dig out their ski gear and goggles.

After testing the last string of lights, I park myself near the fire. The heavy snow on the deck and railings obliterates my view of the town center and valley below. The peace and solitude in the house combined with the magic of the holiday nudge me into reflection.

It occurs to me that when we've come to the mountains these last few winters, I've either been reeling from Mom's reaction to Shirley reentering my life, or beginning and ending a search for one of my birth parents through Linda's office. These last years have been consumed by adoption searches and the adjustment to their results. Adding another log to the fire, I settle near the hearth and consider the events of the past two years.

After Shirley and Howard's visit in February 2012 for our birthday, pressing family matters usurped the limelight. While I wanted to dwell in the ecstasy of our reunion, it became impossible to do so. As Dad and I prepped for tax season, a review of their financial situation made a difficult decision abundantly clear. It was time to sell "the cottage," their beloved weekend home in Palisades Park, Michigan.

Thirty years of beach bonfires, toasting marshmallows, and July 4th fireworks over Lake Michigan were about to come to a screeching halt. The string of summer friendships, with neighbors like the Williams family next door, would have to be fostered in other ways. Since lakefront property in Palisades Park, a private beach community, rarely goes on the market, Dad wanted to try to sell it by word-of-mouth. Listing it on the community portal got us a nibble right away, and within weeks we had a signed contract—cash, full price, all furnishings included, and a closing in thirty days.

Relieved, Dad said the deal was heaven-sent. Even though my parents avoided the hassle of listing and clearing out their lake house, the sudden sale devastated my mom. On a wintry night, Mom collapsed and was sent to the ER—poor diet and not enough proper liquids. Jenny called to share the shocking news just as I was leaving a different hospital with Steve where he'd undergone a planned medical procedure. Inwardly, I resented that daily life had hijacked my shiny-and-new reunion with Shirley. I'd just begun to get to know her better.

By mid-March, the situation with my parents had settled down, so Danny and I planned a road trip to Wisconsin. Shirley was tickled that Danny, the only one of my children who'd been absent over my birthday weekend, was willing to sacrifice part of his spring break to meet her. Over dinner at a Red Lobster, Danny invited

Shirley and Howard to join our family for an important annual event: "America's Game," the Army–Navy football match-up held every year in December.

On that special December weekend in 2012, my entire family descended upon Baltimore to cheer for Danny and his Army team. At the dinner that followed another disappointing and predictable Army loss, Shirley became the centerpiece. Jenny and I surprised her with an eightieth birthday cake. When our corner of a popular, local restaurant erupted in "Happy Birthday," Shirley made no effort to hide her tears. We were thrilled to show her off and touched by her show of emotion.

Over these past two years, Jenny and I have made several trips up to Wisconsin to visit Shirley and Howard. One of the first outings was for Mother's Day, and Howard surprised the three of us with a cake decorated with the words, "Happy First Mother's Day." That weekend, Shirley presented Jenny and me with a small photo album chronicling our "firsts": first meeting, first hug, first dinner, first birthdays, and snapshots of her first meeting with Linda. She arranged another surprise for us. One of her younger sisters, Vivian, joined us for cake and coffee in Shirley's kitchen. Even though Aunt Vivian's visit was brief, Jenny and I were ecstatic that Shirley had widened the circle of "who knows"—even if only by one person.

For as many crescendos that our Mother's Day weekend hit, there was a countering down beat. In setting up the trip, Jenny and I chose a hotel close to Shirley's home, one that had a decent lobby restaurant. When we met them for dinner, Shirley requested the hostess seat us in a back corner. As we strolled through the dining room, she was like a jittery bird looking for its next meal, her head pressed to her chest as her eyes darted here and there.

When Shirley excused herself from the table, Howard enlightened Jenny and me.

"She's afraid she'll run into someone she knows, and then she'll have explaining to do."

Jenny poked me under the table, and the embarrassed-angry mood that I'd experienced at the Bistro dinner made an unwelcome return.

The situation worsened when the waitress asked, "Are we celebrating anything special tonight?"

Shirley was quick to say, "No. These friends are just visiting for the weekend."

Across the table, Jenny raised her eyebrow at me. My cheeks warmed, and I found it difficult to engage in further table talk. Shirley's word choice, "these friends," had seared me. Even to a complete stranger, she couldn't bring herself to introduce us as her daughters. The incident upset Jenny and me so much that when we returned home, I contacted Lisa at Catholic Charities for advice.

She said, "You have to let her know how that makes you feel."

While I appreciated Lisa's wise words, Jenny and I believed that confronting Shirley with our feelings was risky—and it might threaten our reunion. Like the spelling of my birth dad's last name, insisting that Shirley introduce us as "family" was a discussion that had to wait for the right moment.

In September 2012, Linda notified me that MAC's research department had exhausted the list of Richard and "Dick" Thomsons that fit our search parameters. We had no choice—it was time to ask Shirley more questions about *him*. Jenny and I returned to Wisconsin in October with a mission. The stakes were high. If we couldn't derive any new information from Shirley about our birth dad, the judge would dismiss our case in November.

When Jenny and I arrived on that brilliant fall day, the three of us sat in Shirley's cozy kitchen, catching up over coffee while

Howard read the newspaper in the family room. My coffee grew cold as I deliberated over the right moment to introduce my questions. When our chatter reached a lull, I seized the chance.

"Shirley, I brought some documents that I'd like to go over with you."

Pulling out the notes from Shirley's intake interview with Catholic Charities, I pointed to the description of my birth dad.

"Does this sound right? Was he two or three years younger than you?"

She read it and blinked several times before answering. "I think three years is right."

Avoiding her eyes, I pressed on. "In our first conversation, you mentioned that he was from North Dakota and that his name is Dick Thomson. T-H-O-M-S-O-N, is that right?"

Shirley raised her eyes and squinted at Howard in the next room, as if to ask his help with this, but he'd dozed off.

"Yes, I think that's how you spell it."

I swallowed hard. Shirley's uncertainty meant that we had no idea whether Linda's team had been searching for the right man or not. I thought of all the hours they'd clocked, and all the time we'd wasted.

Leaning in toward my birth mom, I touched her arm. My eyes begged her to come up with more useful details.

"I'm sorry if this upsets you, but Linda is having a tough time finding *him*. I'd really like to have his health history. There might be something there that my doctors need to know."

Shirley didn't acknowledge my impassioned plea. To my bewilderment, she shouted across the room to her napping husband.

"Hear that, Howard? They can't find *him*—Linda can't locate their birth father."

When he stirred, Shirley stood and cleared away our coffee cups.

Deflated, Jenny and I went home from Wisconsin empty-handed.

We needed a break, a surprise clue, anything to keep the search moving forward. If one didn't appear in the next six weeks, our family tree and health history would be frozen as it was—half-done.

A week before Thanksgiving, Linda called. "The judge signed the order of dismissal today. I'm sorry. You know you can call me anytime you have a question, or if there's a new development in your case."

Even though I knew the dismissal was coming, the judgment had hit me hard. The dogs and I spent many hours traipsing through the neighborhood as I weighed our options. The only thing left in my search arsenal were the ancestry sites, but filtering out which names belonged to Shirley's side of the family and who might line up with my birth dad was an enormous task. For the better part of 2013, I dabbled with this assignment.

Stoking the fire one last time, I gather up the remnants of my holiday decorating. As I close the boxes, I think about the mountains and how I can't imagine being anywhere else for the holidays with my family. We've been coming here since the kids were little—over ten years. It's a place full of beautiful memories, a retreat that insists that worries from home are sidelined, and a spot where inspiration often lands in my lap.

The notion of making New Year's resolutions began last night over appetizers and cocktails. The six of us and four guests gathered in the great room by the huge fireplace. Ragtag tired from a day on the slopes, we scattered across the sofa and replayed the afternoon's adventures. We laughed about how the thick powder put the skids on our skis, resulting in near misses with other skiers and unyielding trees.

Instead of dressing for the New Year's Eve dinner and fireworks planned at the main lodge, we took turns voicing a favorite memory from the past year and proclaiming our brightest intentions for 2014. I restated the obvious. My favorite memory was incorporating

Shirley into all our lives. Connecting with my birth mother and filling in the details of my personal story was a wish I had not dared to hope for before 2011. I'm content and complete in a way I hadn't known I was lacking. As far as resolutions, I offered up a few measly ones: lose five pounds, learn to meditate, and take up yoga.

As the group went around stating their own New Year's goals, my mind drifted. Were yoga and meditation all I really wanted to tackle in the upcoming year? What about working on the memoir that I'd been on-and-off-again writing since I'd begun looking for Shirley, and what about the failed search for my birth father? How did those fit into the boring list I'd rattled off to the group? Cleaning up the cocktail party and rushing to change for the evening's festivities, I completely forgot about resolutions until this morning, New Year's Day.

The snowplow clanks and scrapes in the driveway outside our bedroom, making sleep impossible for me. Under the deliciously warm comforter, I consider getting up, starting the coffee, and assembling the makings of a tasty New Year's brunch for my family and guests. A glance at the clock reminds me I have plenty of time before any of that has to happen, but I get up anyway and pour fresh grounds into Mr. Coffee. The coffee maker coughs out its dark, rich aroma, wafting a wake-up call throughout the hushed mountain house, but I'm the only one waiting for the first cup.

I take my mug into the great room and turn the lights on the Christmas tree, and then I go to the wall of windows and study the clouds. They skim over distant mountain ranges as effortlessly as skaters on ice. On the other side of the glass, fresh snow mounds on the deck and railings. The ridge of pencil-thin lodgepole pines bordering our property sway in the morning winds like couples in a slow dance. In the yard below the deck, a trail of small, tight animal tracks snakes through the pine ridge toward the garage. Another creature besides me is up early meeting the new year.

The first morning of 2014 is stunning and bright and inspiring. I stand at the windows looking out at the frozen landscape, warmed by the log house, enveloped in a blanket of pure silence. Sipping my coffee, I pick up last night's thread of resolutions. Am I ready to tackle what I'd briefly considered last evening: renew my writing project and rethink how to find my birth dad? I just don't know.

Finishing the coffee, I head to shower and dress. As the shower steams up, I consider my writing again. Diving back into my story about the search for birth relatives isn't just a want; it's an unmet need. To make more time for it, I resolve to find a writing program in Chicago, and then I reflect again about the ornery goal of finding my birth dad. As fulfilled as I am having Shirley in my life, crafting a memoir without closure regarding *him* feels like a half-told tale. As the warm water softens my tense muscles, I feel like I'm missing something obvious, but the elusive thought won't crystallize. Other than an intermediary, what else can I do to locate my birth father?

The warmth of the shower room soothes me. Closing my eyes, I think of Shirley. I recall our first phone conversation when she'd offered *his* name, Dick Thomson. Just as she did on our visit to her home, Shirley had stumbled over the spelling of *his* last name. I etch the letters D-I-C-K on the shower door and repeat his full name aloud. Where are you, Dick Thomson, and why can't we find you?

I guess I'm not surprised that finding *him* has proven as difficult as finding Shirley had been. I turn off the hot water, but the glass refuge remains steamed up. On the inside of the door, I retrace the fading letters D-I-C-K. Unless I can come up with an idea, it appears that the search for my birth dad will remain an unsolved mystery.

Dressing, I glance through the bathroom windows and spot more animal tracks near the hot tub under the deck. As I follow the animal's meandering course, I wonder what had been prowling around, and what had it sought? An obscure notion flashes in.

If I wanted to identify the creature circling my mountain home, I would locate its prints in a nature guidebook. Failing at that, I would consult one of the local wildlife experts.

A local expert. That's it!

Linda is an expert in adoption search and reunion, but her office is in Illinois. I was adopted in Chicago, but my birth parents were co-teachers in an elementary school in rural Wisconsin. Shirley was living there when she became pregnant. Could there be an expert in Wisconsin who might serve as my local guide in tracking down Dick Thomson?

Dashing to my laptop, I query genealogical societies and land on a website where genealogists are arrayed by state. Under Wisconsin, there's only one person, and she's listed under Madison. What is the chance of that? Only one expert in the state of Wisconsin who traces family lineage, and she's right where I need her to be. Copying Jenny, I shoot off an email to Sandy Thalmann at Authentic Origins.

My list of 2014 resolutions just got its headliner.

26

The Genealogist

2014

Since New Year's Day, I've been trading emails with Sandy, the genealogist I discovered on the genealogical society's website. Today, we've scheduled a call to discuss the details of my case.

"Is this Sandy Thalmann? Am I pronouncing your name correctly?"

"Yes! It's nice to speak to you, Julie. One thing I didn't mention in my emails is that I'm adopted too. I got into this line of work so that I could research my birth family. A few years ago, I located my biological father."

My certified genealogist is also an adoptee. This has to be a good sign.

"That's wonderful. How is it getting to know him?"

Sandy pauses before answering. "I'm not in active contact with him. Per his wishes."

Her reply is smooth and practiced, but I've lived the heartache in her words. After all the months I've spent attending adoption support group meetings, I should know better than to assume anyone's search story has a happy ending. Sandy's outcome gives me a reality check—despite my efforts to find Dick Thomson, I could end up in the same predicament.

Because of my recent experience with Shirley, I say, "Perhaps he'll change his mind over time."

"I never give up hope, but it's been a few years now. Through my research, I learned that I have half siblings. My birth father asked me not to contact them." Sandy offers a shy giggle. "I do monitor the events in their lives, though."

I'm in awe at how steady Sandy's voice is as she delivers this sobering news. It appears that my new search angel—a woman not nearly as old as I am, but clearly further along in the adoption search and reunion curve—has accepted the outcome of her adoption journey.

Something Linda said comes back to me. "Birth parents don't always want to acknowledge the children they had out of wedlock. However unfair it feels, it's their right to do so." Recalling her words makes me sit straighter in the chair at my kitchen desk.

Pleasantries aside, Sandy is all business. "Let's get to the details of your case. Share with me the information you've collected, and we can discuss how to proceed."

In laying it all out for her, I start with the breast biopsy and finish with Shirley's change of heart, our reunion, and Linda's yearlong efforts to find my birth dad. As I do this, I flip through the file on my desk. The sheer number of documents that I've amassed over five years should bolster me, but the situation between Sandy and her biological family has flattened my optimism.

"Make copies. Send them to me and I'll sift through everything. I have to ask you the obvious question though. Why don't you come right out and ask your birth mother if she gave you the right name?"

I explain what happened. I'd asked Shirley if we had the right spelling and she seemed uncertain.

"She is very prickly about my birth father. Anytime a conversation circles back to *him*, she changes the subject. Our reunion has been amazing, and I'm afraid to jeopardize that."

Nurturing my relationship with Shirley is important to me, but I also want to find my biological father. I hate that these goals are in opposition with one another.

Sandy's voice is soft. "I get it."

"I'm hoping with your help, I won't need to ask Shirley any more questions about *him*."

My inner censor, the one that judges everything I tackle, pesters me: *How will you inform Shirley should Sandy locate Dick Thomson? One thing at a time*, I scold the annoying critic. *Find him first, tell her later!*

"When I receive your files and the deposit, we can discuss where I should concentrate my efforts. We'll chart the course together. Does this sound good to you?"

"Yes. All that sounds fine."

Sandy's leadership gives me confidence, and I ease back into the desk chair. After organizing the files for Sandy, I pick up the phone. Jenny is working from home today.

For the next ten days I pretend to be engaged in everyday life—bagging Kassie's sack lunches, appearing at her high school track events, and scratching out lesson plans for my religious ed class. Around the edges of these duties, I check my phone and computer for messages from Sandy. On New Year's Day, I'd resolved to resume writing about my adoption search journey, but I have yet to write a single word. Waiting for the outcome of Sandy's research has eroded my ability to focus on anything else.

It's midweek before I hear from Sandy. Because I've been lecturing a restless crop of eighth graders on the Beatitudes at church, my phone is off. Anxious to make it to my car without slipping on black ice, I trudge slowly through the chaotic parking lot. The day's dimming light, the rowdy class, and the mayhem in the church lot have me longing for a warm, quiet space. Inside the Buick, I crank up the heat and just sit. Powering up my cell is an afterthought. When I spot the email from Sandy, my pulse rockets:

Thank you, Julie. I received your packet and payment yesterday. I've browsed through your documents. My first piece of research will be to venture over to the office where central records are stored. Both of your birth parents were public school teachers. During the era when your parents taught, there was a special designation that followed their names in the city directories: P/S, for teacher in public schools. I hope to find your birth parents' addresses, and whether they lived alone or had roommates. If they lived in an apartment complex, I'll copy down the neighbors' information just in case we need that later on. Let me know if this direction is agreeable to you. All the best, Sandy

I fire off a reply. "Yes, this sounds like an excellent plan!"

For the next twenty-four hours, all I can think about is Sandy's research in the city directories. It is when I'm pulling the makings of dinner out of the fridge, that I glance at my phone. An email from Sandy! It's lengthy, so I clamber to my computer where I can read it on a larger screen.

I hold my breath as I read:

Julie, I located your birth mother in the city directories, but there's no man named Dick Thomson in the rolls. Perhaps your birth father lived outside the city limits, which means more digging. I discovered that your birth mom's neighbor, Elaine, was also a public school teacher. She may know something about your birth parents, so I'd suggest that you call or write her. I'm including her contact information at the bottom

*of this email. I've some personal business tomorrow, so I plan
to get back to your case on Monday. Have a good weekend. Let
me know if you reach Elaine! Take care, Sandy.*

For three days, I dial Elaine's phone number, but speak only
to an ancient answering machine. If Elaine has pushed past eighty
like Shirley, she might be one of those lucky snowbirds in Florida.
After checking in with Jenny, I send a note to Elaine in which I ask
her about Shirley and if she knew anything about my birth father.
When the post office opens on Monday, I drop off the letter to my
birth mother's neighbor from over fifty years ago. It's anyone's guess
as to whether she'll respond with a lead on Dick Thomson.

When Sandy and I enter our third week of exchanging status
emails, I'm reluctant to admit that we're in a rut. Each morning after
I send Kassie off to high school, I relax at the kitchen table with a
second cup of coffee. *Today's the day. I know it.* Yet, the repeated
exchange of "Nothing from Elaine" and "Haven't found anything
on Dick or Richard Thomson" eats at me. Spending another year
swirling in a failed search for my birth dad, as I did with Linda's
team at the Midwest Adoption Center, isn't how I want to spend my
time or energies anymore.

Last night, I called Jenny. "How much more do you want to
spend on this search for Dick?"

"We could give Sandy another few weeks. If she can't locate
him by our birthday, I say we stop."

Jenny's sigh means she's as frustrated as I am.

"I know. I hear you," I say. "We've been at this search stuff off
and on for five years. I'm exhausted too."

As discouraged as we are, our one-sided family tree and inade-
quate health history demand that we stick with it.

"Not to mention how much money we've spent. Where are we
at?" Jenny asks.

"All in? The total for both searches? Probably over a grand each is my guess." My words are soft, apologetic.

"It's okay, Jules. Let's give Sandy two more weeks and then reevaluate where we are. Okay?"

"Deal."

The traffic coming back from Kassie's indoor track meet is brutal. I turn down the radio and reflect on last evening's conversation with my twin. Quitting the probe for Dick due to search fatigue and rising costs doesn't feel right. The bottom line is that having only one birth parent in my life feels like failure. Just as we were closing in on Dick Thomson, he's slipped away. Blasting the radio as Pink chants the opening notes of "Try," I nearly miss my cell phone's ring.

Sandy's voice stutters like she's just sprinted down the block.

"I'm glad I caught you. Today I went back to the city directories and pulled all the folks whose last names begin with 'T.'"

"Oh?"

"This is where it gets interesting. There's a man listed as a public school teacher whose name is Dick Thomlinson. It's enough similar to Dick Thomson that I did some preliminary research on him. It turns out that like your birth father, Dick Thomlinson is from North Dakota. He's described as having a fair complexion and blue eyes. In 1958–59, Dick Thomlinson would have been around twenty-three. This matches with what you sent me from Catholic Charities."

Sandy takes a big breath, and so do I.

"So you think this guy is my birth dad? Not Dick Thomson?"

"I do. I do. Here's our next step."

When Sandy pauses, my pulse plummets. I think I know where this is going: call Shirley and ask. I start to interrupt, but Sandy cuts me off.

"I know you don't want to confront your birth mother. Dick

Thomlinson taught at Eisenhower School. Do you know if that's where your birth mother was a teacher?"

At home, there's a file in my desk that contains the timeline I constructed when I first spoke with Shirley on the phone.

"I don't remember. I need my notes. As soon as I get home, I'll call you back."

Pulling off the interstate, I can't get home fast enough. I refuse to acknowledge the inner critics: How could Shirley have mangled his last name, and did she do it on purpose? With my winter coat still on, I rush into the house and send the file drawer cascading. Perspiration beads on my forehead as I flip page after page. As I scan, read, and reread, my head sinks into my hands. Emmett, the male collie, meanders over and presses his head into my lap.

Massaging the cinnamon tufts behind the dog's ears, I sniffle. "It's not here, Emmett. It's not here. Nothing about Eisenhower School."

I glance back and forth between the papers strewn across the desk and my dog's loving eyes. Removing my smoldering jacket, I hit redial.

"Sandy, I don't have the name of the school on any of these pages. I don't think she ever told me."

"Do you think you can ask her? If she taught at Eisenhower in 1958, then Dick Thomlinson might be the man we're looking for, and then you can reach out to him for validation."

Sandy's words freeze me in place. If I ask this question, Shirley will be on the defensive. I've been the instigator of all the searches, the daughter prying for family history, and the twin with all the health issues. Emmett blinks at me.

I know what has to happen.

Sighing, I say, "It's probably best if Jenny is the one to ask Shirley about Eisenhower School. Perhaps she can pose this question without setting off any red flags." I stroke Emmett. "Sandy, this is great work. Amazing. I'm so grateful…."

I'm unable to finish my praises. Relief, in the form of heavy emotion, is washing over me. Years of dead ends and now this stunning breakthrough.

"We got lucky with this. I owe the staff person in the archives a big thank-you for her diligence." Sandy's voice sparkles, offering hope.

I find my voice. "Thank them for me too! I'll call you as soon as we confirm Eisenhower is where my birth parents taught together."

27

The Football Player

"Jenny, you're not going to believe what the genealogist found. She went back into the city archives. . . ." My words tumble out so fast I have to start over.

Too revved up to sit at the kitchen desk, I pace the kitchen. It's hard for me to believe what I'm saying to my sister. After all the false leads, Sandy has located a man she thinks is our birth dad. If her research is correct, then the man we should have been looking for all this time is Dick Thomlinson!

"This is incredible. What happens next?" Jenny asks.

"Well . . . Can you ask Shirley if she taught at Eisenhower School? If I ask, she'll know something's up."

Neither of us speaks.

The longer I'm silent, the clearer my message is to my twin—I not only want her to call Shirley and ask about Eisenhower School, I expect her to do it. Up to this point, I've done all the figuring, the contacting, and the following up on two full adoption searches. This is the first time I've asked Jenny to take the lead. For our search to proceed, she must do this.

"I guess I can do it," she says finally. "This is what I'm thinking. . . ."

Jenny usually chats with Shirley on Sunday afternoons. Drawing upon the fact that Jenny's stepdaughters attended school in Wisconsin, she plans to thread the Eisenhower School question into their dialogue somehow. My jaw tightens just thinking about what rides on Shirley's answer.

On Sunday afternoon at three thirty, I plop down in the middle of the family room sectional—the exact spot where Shirley sat a few years ago as she got to know her granddaughters: Colleen, Molly, and Kassie. This is the same room where I opened the birthday box, unfolded the green baby blanket, and was touched by Shirley's heartwarming tears. I never would have guessed that two years later I'd still be entrenched in the search for my birth dad.

As I wait for Jenny's call, I'm reminded of those days when I anticipated hearing from Linda. There's a light flutter in my chest, much like what you feel before houseguests ring the doorbell. For the umpteenth time, I check my cell phone.

Kassie has taken over the dining room table with her ACT prep materials. I'm glad for the company. With the two of us at home, the dogs are conflicted; they meander from room to room, pleading for attention. Picking up the remote, I channel surf.

When Jenny's text comes in, I jump. *Talking to her now.*

I type with both thumbs like Kassie does. *On pins and needles here.*

A smiley emoji flies back.

For the next thirty minutes, my eyes are on the TV, but my head is with Jenny and the conversation she's having with Shirley. I worry whether Jenny will have the courage, or the chance, to ask about Eisenhower School. Perhaps Shirley will deflect Jenny's questions like she did when I quizzed her about Dick's last name.

I snatch up my cell before the second ring. "Hey!"

"Eisenhower School, baby!" Jenny gloats. "Dick Thomlinson is our man."

On my feet, I cheer. "You did it. We did it! Yes, yes, yes!"

Kassie yells from the dining room. "Mom, what's going on?"

"It's Aunt Jenny. We got the news we wanted!"

"Jen, tell me all of it. How did you work the question in?"

I'm so proud of my sister. This moment is so big that I consider driving to her house, two towns over, with a bottle of champagne. We've finally caught a break. Jenny shares the play-by-play while I lie limp on the sofa. There's a sense of peace inside of me that I haven't felt for a very long time.

After Jenny hangs up, I leave Sandy a voice mail. "Your research paid off. Shirley taught at Eisenhower! Dick Thomlinson is probably our birth dad. Jenny and I will work on crafting a letter to send to him. I can't thank you enough. You've changed my life."

In the two weeks that follow, Sandy shoots me a dozen emails with research attachments about Richard "Dick" Thomlinson and his family. She's been working my case for eight weeks, and the file on my birth dad has bloomed from a meager report into a tome the size of a college textbook. Anything that Sandy forwards, I study eagerly. I also scour the internet and Ancestry.com to find answers to a growing list of questions. Jenny and I draft the outreach letter to send to Dr. Richard Allen Thomlinson, my birth father the retired college professor. Besides Sandy's input, I want Linda to weigh in.

In one of her emails, Sandy asks, "Did your Ancestry.com results show Native American roots?"

She attaches census records that show Dick's father was one-half Native American. His family grew up near a Chippewa Indian reservation. If we can confirm that he's our birth father, that would make Jenny and me one-eighth Chippewa. Wow, I didn't see that coming.

From the depths of my purse, I unearth a mirror. My fair, freckly complexion, hazel eyes, and light brown hair are more consistent with the Scotch–Irish on my ancestry report than anything else. Turning to the side, I study my profile. Having Native American on both sides of my lineage seems absurd. I'd always thought of myself as German and Irish, because that's what my adoptive parents had been told by the adoption agency. When I learned that Shirley was French and German with a smattering of Potawatomi, I had trouble assimilating it. If I have this much Native American in my background, my brain will be teased once again.

Sandy orders more documents from archives and national databases, and she requisitions birth certificates, marriage records, and death notices. She scours census data and newspaper articles for anything to do with Richard Allen Thomlinson. Even though we have no other likely suspects, we're trying to prove definitively that this man is our birth father. I ask Sandy to locate pictures of him.

Besides the relationship with Shirley, Dick Thomlinson has had two other women in his life. Late in the summer of 1959, six months following my birth, Dick became engaged to a fellow teacher from Eisenhower School. I skip over the details of Dick's second marriage to read the final pages. Dick and his first wife had two children, a girl and a boy, who are four and six years younger than Jenny and me.

A brother and a sister?

When I searched for Shirley, I'd fostered a fantasy of having other siblings. When Sandy sends me the names of Dick's children, I hustle to my computer. Richie and his wife live in a suburb only ten miles away—the same suburb where my adoptive mother was raised with her twelve brothers and sisters. There's little to discover about my younger sister, Cynthia, just that she's married and lives in downtown Chicago. The idea that my birth dad and siblings all live within driving distance launches crazy stalking schemes and notions of reaching out on Facebook or snagging an email address and connecting that way. Yet, Jenny and I want more proof that we're related to Dick Thomlinson before contacting him or his kids.

Sandy sends me a collection of grainy, photocopied newspaper clippings. When I print out these articles, I feel like I'm studying for a final exam. I read and reread, puzzling into place the pieces of a man's life, a man I think is my biological father. While Dick was in college, his parents died within a year of one another of hypertension and heart disease. As troubling as that information is, I'm more concerned about Dick's only sister, Frances, dying of breast cancer at thirty-nine.

If Frances is my biological aunt, then breast cancer is a more serious health concern for all the women in my family than any of us imagined. I feel queasy. If we can confirm all of this, what new tests will Dr. Stanley order for me? The exhilaration I felt several minutes ago about two potential siblings has been squashed by family health issues. A thought occurs to me. When I send Dick Thomlinson an outreach letter, I should request a DNA test.

When Sandy calls later in the day, I assume she wants to discuss the draft of the outreach letter I'd sent her that morning.

She's so excited that I have trouble discerning her words. "Julie, are you able to receive faxes at home?"

"Yes, but it would take me a few minutes to hook it up. Why? What did you find?"

I offer up a silent plea: *Let this be good news, not bad.*

"Two documents I requested last week just came in. One is a teacher photo from the university where Dick Thomlinson was a professor. The other is a yearbook photo from the state college where he played football."

"Wow. Fax them over. Thanks, Sandy."

This is the first mention of Dick Thomlinson being a college athlete. College football, just like my only son, Danny. It would be crazy if Dick Thomlinson were a muscled-up fullback like Danny.

After I set up the fax machine, I stare out the window. Colleen, the oldest of my four kids, was a walk-on on the women's rowing team at Notre Dame. My middle daughter, Molly, played forward on an Ivy League women's basketball team, and Danny plays fullback for the US Military Academy. My "mystery gene" produced three collegiate athletes. Did I inherit that gene from a college professor whose roots began on a Chippewa Indian reservation?

Glaring at the fax machine, I plead with it to beep and jolt into action. Within seconds, I get my wish. Yellow lights flash followed by the familiar screeching sound. As the fax emerges, I make out a young man's head, his fair hair closely cropped. Flipping it upright, I stand openmouthed for a moment, too startled to move.

"Holy Mother of God. You've got to be kidding me."

It's a yearbook photo of a young man about twenty wearing a college jersey. He's crouched in a football stance, his helmet in his hands, a cocky smile spread across his face. The camera reveals freckles and fair skin. Dick Thomlinson.

I laugh. While the black-and-white picture in my hand may have come from a 1956 yearbook, it could also have been taken this year. The picture I'm holding is supposed to be my birth father, but I'm looking at my son, Danny.

"We've done it!" My shout rouses the dogs.

Studying the photo, I murmur, "We found you, Dick Thomlinson. In spite of everything, we found you."

28

Unexpected Consequences

When I share the photo of Dick Thomlinson in his college football jersey with friends and family, it's impossible to contain my excitement. We ogle the young man's sure smile, the hairline cowlick in the same spot as Danny's, and the thick stocky build that they have in common. It's not enough that I believe "young Dick" shares a likeness to my son—I want others to see it and believe it, too. If the photo convinces the people I care about, then it must be true that Dr. Richard Allen Thomlinson is my birth father.

Sandy's original fax is pinned to the bulletin board above my desk. When I glance up, my birth dad is centered between Kassie's prom invite and her glossy senior portrait. Five years of searching for birth relatives have taken up most of Kassie's high school years, and all of Danny's tenure on the Army football team. If Dick agrees to talk with Jenny and me, I wonder if he'll be impressed that his grandson played college football just as he did.

The thought of Dick Thomlinson learning about the accomplishments of my family sends tickles whirling in my belly. Those tickles equal the number of doubts pounding my temples. Will Dick reject my contact just as Shirley did, and will he block me from meeting his children like Sandy's birth dad had done? The photo on the bulletin board is an important reminder: I'm not imagining things, and I didn't invent this man's likeness to my family. It also builds my confidence and urges me to get the outreach letter ready to mail to *him*.

As March slips into April, I compile Linda's and Sandy's comments into a first draft, and then Jenny and I burn up the evening hours implementing our small edits. Due to Dick's sister's early death from breast cancer and Shirley's mishandling of Dick's last name, Jenny and I agree—we will ask Dick Thomlinson to undergo DNA testing. In an attachment to our letter to him, I offer to cover the DNA testing fee, propose quality labs near his home, and include the medical questionnaire that Linda provided. By the time our family attorney signs off on the final document, April is over. Since receiving the fax of Dick as a college athlete, six excruciating weeks have elapsed.

Before I tuck the final version of the letter with all its attachments into an envelope, I review it.

Dear Dick:

I am writing you about a personal matter the history of which goes back to 1958. I'm adopted and was raised in Chicago. About five years ago, due to health issues, I began to research my biological background.

In the past several years, I was able to locate my birth mother, Shirley Desjardins, who gave me her medical history and genealogy, as well as a description of my birth father and the circumstances surrounding her unwed pregnancy. I learned that you were teachers together. The information she provided has led me to you now.

I assure you that I have no interest in disrupting your life. I'm seeking confirmation as to whether you are my birth father, and if so, some medical history about your family. I'm very open to talking to you personally about this situation, assuage any concerns you may have, and address the questions that this matter has brought to your attention.

I live in the Chicago suburbs. I have a twin sister who was adopted with me. I have been married for thirty years to the same man, and we have four children. I'm well educated, well respected in my community, and financially stable.

It's extremely important for my personal health that my doctors have a complete family medical background on file. I have enclosed a medical history questionnaire for your convenience. I'm seeking closure regarding my "personal story."

I can only imagine the shock you must feel in receiving this letter. I understand that you will need time to absorb this information. I hope that you will contact me in the next few weeks; otherwise, I will contact you.

I look forward to hearing from you, and I would be happy to provide pictures and more detailed information should you wish.

Sincerely,

Julie Ryan McGue

My favorite postmaster, a middle-aged man with neatly trimmed sideburns, and Lennon-style spectacles, encourages me to send the letter by certified mail. "You can track it that way," he says.

"That's a brilliant idea."

Tracing the packet's progress as it travels two hundred miles west where Illinois meets up with Iowa offers me some control in this nerve-racking situation.

"This way you can check when the package is delivered and signed for." As the mailman tosses the packet into a mail bin, I send with it my deepest wish: Acknowledge me! Don't dismiss me like a dirty little secret!

In between showing up at Kassie's end-of-the-year events, I monitor the progress of the certified delivery. Within two days, my letter is received and signed for, but it doesn't say by whom. I imagine the scene, the face at the townhouse door signing for a letter that opens up another door, one from the past that had felt forever closed. If it's the second wife doing the signing and opening and reading, then Dick may be doing a lot of explaining right now. Musing about this as the dogs and I plod around the block makes me almost feel sorry for him.

For the three days that follow, I fixate on Dick and the letter. Is this the day he'll call or email? Will he return the medical questionnaire and agree to DNA testing? Sprinkled among these questions are worries. Does he understand the magnitude of my request, his sister's breast cancer and the threat of it to me, Jenny, and our daughters? Is there anything else I should have said in the note?

Exactly one week after I posted the letter, the mailman rings the front doorbell. He's the same young man that brought my original birth record from the Illinois Department of Vital Statistics several summers ago, and the first letter from Shirley.

"Hello there. Certified letter. I need your Hancock." The name I scribble is a shaky version of my usual signature.

"Thanks very much." I stare at the return address—the one I've fantasized about driving past just to see Dick stroll out for the morning paper.

Inside the white cardboard mailer is an envelope. My chewed-up cuticles slide out a handwritten note:

I may or may not be your father. Enclosed is the medical history you requested. I will not comply with a DNA test. Do not contact me again for any reason.

It's signed Dr. Richard A. Thomlinson. Not Dick, not your birth dad, not your biological father, but a formal signature like one would see on an official document.

As I study the brief message, my heart lunges into a funky rhythm. It's helter-skelter like a kid chasing an errant ball. Frustration sends it bouncing, disappointment dips it dangerously low, and anger makes it rise to a risky height. What is this mixed message? He either is or isn't my birth dad. Why be evasive, and why send back a completed medical questionnaire if he isn't related to me? Perhaps he's trying to be helpful but unwilling to risk some kind of liability or responsibility.

Sinking to the bottom step of the front stairs, I read Dick's message over and over. It's as if my eyes are searching for something that my heart longs to find there. Besides the family health history, some of which I already know, is a concerning threat: *Do not contact me again for any reason.* It's as if he said, *Leave me alone and go back to the rock you crawled out from.*

Leaning over the cup on the eighteenth green, Jenny scoops up her golf ball. "What do you want to do now?"

My twin's expression is hard to read from beneath her dark glasses, but I know what she means. We're holing out at a charity golf outing. Since the early morning tee off, thunderstorms have skirted the course and brisk spring breezes buffeted our jackets and caps. Paired in a foursome with my youngest brother and his buddy, Jenny and I have sipped coffee between abysmal shots, and giggled over our lackluster efforts to help better the scramble score.

No matter. Sharing the golf cart with my twin this morning is less about golf and more about discussing our birth dad's letter, which landed in time to spoil the weekend. Just thinking about Dick's "may or may not be" message irritates me more than I let on. Without his DNA or an admission of being our birth father, we're in limbo—an all too familiar place. Reminding myself that we've dug out of similar dead ends several times before does nothing to lift my sagging mood.

We climb into the golf cart, and I look at Jenny. "I'm tired. I say we contact one of our new half siblings in the fall. Maybe use Linda to do that. All I know is I'd like to put this awful mess behind me until after Kassie's graduation from high school."

Jenny puts her arm around my shoulders. "I hear you," she says. "Whatever you want to do is fine. Dick may change his mind, like Shirley did."

Her optimism forces my smile. "He might. We'll give him the summer."

Shoving our clubs into the back of Jenny's car, we charge toward the warm, dry clubhouse. As we walk, voices roll around in my head. Taking the time to process all that's happened within such a short amount of time is exactly what Lisa and Linda would advise.

29

❧

Brother from Another Mother

My shoulders and back are tighter than a new pair of shoes, a result from either yesterday's bad golf, or the wrangling with my pillow between two and three in the morning. At the golf outing yesterday, Jenny and I settled on a strategy to deal with our birth dad's dismissal—we'd take the summer off before contacting our half siblings. As I think about this decision now, conflicting emotions shoot between my head and heart like fireworks. Grabbing my red IU ball cap and sunglasses, I slip out the side door without the dogs.

I'm not even to the end of the driveway when my new brother and sister pop into my head. Thanks to Sandy's research over the past two months, I'm up to date on their personal stats. While I haven't driven past their homes, I know how much gas I need to get there. I also know that each will have a birthday over the summer, and that I'm an aunt to two nieces and a nephew.

Once Sandy alerted me that Dick Thomlinson had two children from his first marriage, I hit the computer and pulled up my new brother's headshot off his corporate website. I'm convinced that Richie's grin mimics Jenny's and mine and that freckles sprinkle his nose and cheekbones, too. The photo is impressive—it makes Richie look smart, not clever in a conniving way, but intelligent with a considerate manner. It didn't take me long to decide that he looks like a nice guy, like a brother I might like to have.

From a hedge near the grammar school, I twist a sprig of lilacs free and waft the sweet scent past my nose. Schoolkids on bicycles hurtle toward me, and I step off the sidewalk onto the grass. As the boys chase past me, a blaze of yellow forsythia across the playground catches my eye. Beyond that, a copse of purple magnolia towers over the swing sets. All around me, life is erupting into uncontained growth, but I'm stuck in another adoption search funk with few options. My birth father doesn't want me in his life, but I have two siblings I'd very much like to get to know. When I contact them, will they shun me or welcome me with open arms?

The minute I step into my driveway, the collies bark madly as if catching me off with a secret lover. So frantic are they for my attention that we tangle up with one another at the side door. Adding to the calamity, the landline launches into its shrill tones as soon as we burst inside. I grab for the phone and try to calm the dogs.

"Hello, is this Julie?" The caller has a deep, professional voice and my first reaction is annoyance—lately, I've fielded too many auto-warranty calls.

My words are clipped. "Yes, it is."

I'm debating about hanging up, but the caller says, "This is your brother from another mother."

Every muscle in my body tenses. Staring at the antiquated phone, I curse its lack of caller ID. When I realize who it is on the phone, I'm too stunned to appreciate the notorious *Saturday Night Live* punch line.

"Excuse me?"

The caller chuckles at his own dry humor. "Sorry! I've been dying to use that line. This is Richie. After a conversation with my father this weekend, I guess I'm your brother!"

Richie laughs as if delighted by this incredible turn of events, but I'm not there yet. I'm locked in that dark place where my birth father demanded I hide.

Despite my silence, Richie presses on. "Perhaps you and I can settle this without letters and lawyers?"

"Uh, hold on, please. Let me get to a better phone. Sorry."

Needing more time to process what's happening, I charge toward the kitchen, the dogs at my heels. The voice in my head raves: *Your brother is on the phone. Your brother . . .* I put the dogs back outside and grab the cordless phone off the counter.

I stammer into the receiver, "Sorry, Richie."

A spurt of laughter blankets over my bumbling. "Sure. So I took a long walk this morning to decide if I should call you and what I would say. After Googling you this weekend, I figured Dad was wrong about you being a kook wanting to sue us for our DNA. My wife encouraged me to pick up the phone and talk this out with you."

Richie's so quick to lay this all out that I wonder if he's as nervous as I am. One of the things he said hits me hard—my birth dad portraying me to my new siblings as a nut job flicking out random lawsuits. A scalding flush heats up my cheeks. That guy!

Counting to three, I switch gears. "Richie, when you called, I was coming in from a long walk, too. I've been trying to decide what to do about the note your dad sent back to me."

As Richie and I talk, I tromp aimlessly around the house like a pensive teenager. I'm grappling with the realization that I'm actually speaking to the brother I've stalked online, and that this summer I won't be wallowing in self-pity or prepping for the next iteration of my adoption probe. I can't wait to text Jenny.

"I'm sure you can imagine how shocked Dad was to open your

letter. Your request for DNA testing has put him on the defensive. Anyway, I thought I'd call and talk to you about all of this, see if I can understand where this is going, what your intentions are."

Richie's pleasant, noncombative manner is endearing. "I'm so glad you did. This is why I contacted him. . . ."

Sliding into one of the sunroom chairs, I give Richie the short version of why I reached out to Dick Thomlinson. I talk about my health issues and my wish for my birth family's medical history and background.

As I explain all this to Richie, I tap out a text to Jenny: *You won't believe who I'm talking to! Richie Thomlinson!*

Richie fills me in about what happened once my birth father absorbed my letter. Over this past weekend, Dick called Richie and Cynthia and revealed his brief relationship with my birth mom— one that preceded Dick's marriage to their mother. During these unveilings, Dick confessed that he and my birth mom had quarreled about the unplanned pregnancy, the idea of a forced marriage, and their religious differences. A Protestant, he didn't appreciate her pressure to convert to Catholicism. In the end, they'd agreed marriage wasn't right. She left town, and Dick lost track of her. It's a relief to me that Dick's version of the facts matches what's in my notes from Catholic Charities.

Until my letter arrived last week, Dick Thomlinson had no idea what had become of my birth mom, or that she'd given birth to twin daughters and placed them for adoption. As I listen to Richie relate this, it infuriates me that Dick could be honest with Richie and Cynthia while evading and dismissing Jenny and me. I squash the urge to rant at Richie about his dad.

Jenny's text flies in: *really? what's he got to say?* I flip my cell over. Her questions will have to wait—different ones gnaw at me.

"Richie, did you read the letter I sent your dad?"

"Nope. He didn't share it with us."

All my willpower goes into straining irritation out of my voice. "Shall I send you a copy so there's no misunderstanding? I never mentioned suing any of you."

"Uh, yeah. That would definitely help."

My new brother doesn't defend or bash his dad—I respect this, and I also like that he asks reasonable questions and listens calmly without interrupting me. I think about the qualities I'd projected onto his company website photo: intelligent and considerate. Kind and sincere get added to the list.

Richie moves the conversation along. "You know what's crazy? My mom knew about all of this. Not that there were two of you, but that Dad had gotten a gal in trouble before he met her. It's astounding really. Mom can't keep a secret about what she's gifting for Christmas." Richie chuckles at this little jest, but then he's serious again. "Mom said she thought it was Dad's story to tell."

Richie's mom sounds like a decent person, and he strikes me as more like her than the father we share. Lifting my cell, I shoot a text to Jen: *we're talking about the letter, DNA, his mom he's nice* ☺ *still talking!!! xo*

I tune back into Richie. "When my stepmom married Dad, she wasn't crazy about him already having two kids. You can imagine what she thinks about two more showing up."

Other than offering an appreciative giggle at Richie's quip, I'm not sure how to respond. I hate being the visitor no one wants on their doorstep.

"Your dad—"

Richie interrupts me. "What do you call him?"

I giggle first, and then admit, "Mostly just 'Dick,' but to each other, Jenny and I call him 'the sperm donor.'"

Richie rewards me with a quick laugh. "Fair enough. Listen, you should know this. I have a daughter my wife and I adopted from China. I'm very sensitive to your need for information. We've been back to China with her, to the orphanage, hoping to learn more about her birth family."

With adoption a bond between us, I sink deeper into the sunroom chair. This moment with Richie is "otherworldly," similar to the scene in the Target parking lot and when I spoke with Shirley for the first time—it feels like it's happening to someone else. What makes it even more bizarre is that I'm straddling two worlds with different phones in my palms. In one hand, I'm conversing with a brother I don't know, and in the other, I'm texting with a sister who's been at my side since before we were born.

While Richie's call boggles my mind, it serves to intensify my inner conflict. Dick Thomlinson refused to acknowledge me as his daughter, and his sister died of breast cancer. I'm being pulled apart by joy and discovery and rejection and fear. Breast cancer has become my second shadow, one I definitely wish I could get rid of.

My brother cracks into my mood with another question. "When I was checking you out this past weekend on the internet, I saw that you own a lake house? Indiana or Michigan?"

"Indiana." Perhaps because Richie shared so much about his mother and stepmom, I rattle on. "My parents have owned a cottage in Michigan, though, since I was a teenager. Because of my dad's health and the cost of keeping it up, they sold it two years ago."

Silence. I keep talking. "It's in a small summer community near South Haven. You probably haven't heard of it."

Even through the phone lines, I sense Richie's intensity shift. I can almost see him sitting straighter in his Wacker Drive office chair. The tempo change sets me on my feet.

Before he asks, I know his question. "Where near South Haven?"

I pace the sunroom. It's as if I sense the threshold we're about to cross, a premonition that two worlds that were once separate are about to converge.

"Palisades Park."

The mere mention of Palisades sets my memory reel rolling: the root beer floats and greasy burgers, red licorice and Scrabble games, pinball at the Soda Bar, riptides and blown-up inner tubes, catching minnows in the Brandywine, stunning sunsets, sandy sheets and damp towels strung up on porch railings. Thirty years of memories and infinitely more snapshots pasted in the Ryan family album.

I half expect Richie to say, "You're right. No, I haven't heard of it," but he doesn't.

A deep infectious laugh, full of incredulity, engulfs our connection. "You're kidding, right?" When I don't answer, Richie fills the pause. "I'm on the owners' association there."

Only our breaths crackle on the line. Gripping the edge of the wicker sofa, I squeeze my eyelids and wait for the next question.

"Julie, who are your parents?"

"Jeanne and Jack Ryan."

"Oh . . . my . . . God . . . I know your parents! My wife is Audrey, Buzz Williams's daughter—the family that owns the cottage next to Jeanne and Jack's old place—you must know Audrey and her sisters?"

Richie spews all this lickety-split, and I'm a second off his pace, but then like a delayed hit, the truth finds its mark. My new brother is married to the girl next door—as in the summer cottage separated from my parents' place by a few clumps of dune grass.

"Audrey . . . She was the youngest, right? I don't remember her as clearly as I do her sister Patty. Because my husband and I had our own cottage in Indiana, I wasn't at my folks' place much. If I did stop up at Mom and Dad's, it was Patty who was staying with her family at your in-laws. She used to drop by to chat with my mom or to borrow an egg or something."

As I say her name again, Patty Williams's dark hair and dimples ease into my mind's eye.

I struggle to match the other Williams sisters with names and faces, and whether I'd ever met Richie on the boardwalk or on the beach. To think that my brother was right there, sliding past me but never crossing my path, makes a corner of my heart ache. Even if we had met, the circumstances of my adoption prevented us from piecing all this together. Richie's connection to Jenny and me was waiting for today, for this phone call.

Almost giddy, Richie layers on more coincidences. "Audrey and I got married at Palisades Park in a party tent behind the Soda Bar. My mom and aunt stayed with your parents at their cottage the weekend of our wedding."

My brother stops as if his lungs have run out of air. I wait.

"Julie, your parents were at our wedding."

The magnitude of these coincidences cramps my brain: my new brother married the girl next door. In Palisades Park. My parents were there. With my birth father. My folks mingled with Dick, probably raised a glass with him to toast to his son's health and happiness. Where was I?

"This is nuts. Hold on, I have to shoot Jenny a quick text."

As I type, Richie says, "I don't think I've ever met you, but I know Jenny and . . . Is her husband named Dan?"

"Yes, it's Dan." A spark of jealousy ignites, then fades. They met Richie first.

"I've met them on the beach several times." Richie pauses and laughs. "Hell, I know all your brothers and sisters. Crazy. Wait till I tell Audrey."

I giggle too. "My dad is going to love this. He and Buzz are still such good pals."

Richie clears his throat. "Julie, this changes everything."

I want to ask him what he means, but Richie is jazzed up. "Okay, we need to talk more. In person. Let's have lunch. How's Friday? Can you meet downtown? Early, like eleven thirty? I'm meeting Buzz at Union Station, then we're going to Palisades for the weekend. How's that for timing?"

My laugh blends with Richie's. "Yes. Friday lunch is good. I'll see if Jenny can join us. What about Cynthia?"

"I'll check with her. I'm sorry about my father. I'll keep talking to him, but he may never come around."

This last part stings, but just as Richie dashes my hopes, he raises me up. "Let's talk about the DNA test more on Friday. I need a few more days to think it through."

As suddenly as my new brother insinuated himself into my Tuesday, he's off. Our exchange has left me stiff and limp all at the same time. Richie caught me off guard with the sudden call, and then both of us were set on our heels with the cottage connection. Racking my brain, I hunt for the word that sums up our situation. Two lives living parallel existences in such close proximity that we'd often breathed the same lake air. Synchronicity!

The link with Richie is such a stunning, ridiculous surprise that before I realize it, my cheeks are damp. The what-ifs have overwhelmed me. What if Shirley had refused to give me Dick's name? What if I hadn't found Sandy, and what if she hadn't taken that second trip to the city's archives? What if Audrey hadn't urged Richie to reach out to me today, and what if they hadn't experienced adoption firsthand? If, if, and more ifs trickle in.

I wipe my cheeks. Richie's phone call is everything: confirmation, validation, and a connection to family. Without a doubt, I hit the jackpot with this new brother. Dick's rejection last week left me disappointed and angry, and today's call with Richie jolted me with adrenaline. The emotional roller coaster ride has left me feeling numb. Before I rehash the last forty minutes with Jenny, I need to find my equilibrium.

Outside the sunroom, bands of striated clouds speckle the spring sky. I watch them float into a new order, and then something else catches my eye in the yard. The lindens have finally leafed out, and below them saffron daffodils and purple muscari poke through the dark pachysandra. The contrast of colors is intoxicating. Somehow, I missed this display while out for my morning walk. I ponder how light filters through the clouds and trees, how it has the power to coax an explosion of hidden beauty, and then I'm struck by how satisfying it is to witness and receive life's bountiful surprises.

The grandfather clock chimes and echoes throughout the first floor. My cell phone is in my palm, but I don't lift it to my ear. I need to remind myself how far we've come. The breast biopsy was six years ago. Three years ago, I found Shirley. Until a few months ago I'd all but given up on finding my birth dad. This Friday, I have a lunch date with a brother I didn't know existed. I can't wait to meet him.

When I stand and stretch, my whole body smiles.

If the cottage in Palisades Park is the bridge linking my birth and adoptive families, then I have to believe that God has a sense of humor.

30

The Final Test

"Seriously. Who's late the first time they meet their new brother?"

Alone in the Buick, I curse myself as I weave around a clog of taxis and pedestrians in the Loop. The traffic was terrible coming into the city, and now the parking garage near the restaurant is full. There's too much riding on this lunch with Richie, and being late sets such a bad tone. My grip on the steering wheel eases once I find a place to park.

It's just the two of us for lunch, Richie and me. Yesterday, he texted: *Cynthia isn't going to join us*, and the one I sent in return said: *Jenny has to work.*

"You go," Jenny had said, a quick laugh lifting her voice. "I've already met Richie on the beach at Palisades." That pushed my jealousy button again.

I lock the car and text Richie: *Bad traffic and trouble parking. Going to be a few minutes late.* Sad emoji.

Today's lunch is more complicated than simply getting to know my new brother. As eager as I am to meet Richie, I'm equally as nervous about what I need to convey. A DNA test from one of the

Thomlinsons is essential. For two reasons. The name that Shirley gave me was incorrect—a fact Richie's unaware of because it didn't come up in Tuesday's conversation—and because of his Aunt Frances's terminal breast cancer. Even though Dick confirmed to Richie and Cynthia that Jenny and I are his daughters, the facts of our conception are circumstantial. Only a DNA test will solidify our biological link—it's a simple cheek swab that I can set up in a heartbeat.

As I race to the restaurant, I replay in my head the morning text exchange with Richie:

Richie: *11:30 still good for lunch?*
Me: A thumbs-up emoji. *Where?*
Richie: *There's a spot I've taken my dad before. That'd be appropriate.*
Me: *LOL maybe he can join us next time?*

Then the restaurant confirmation came in: Trattoria #10 on Dearborn.

Richie (an hour ago): *How will I recognize you?*
Me: *Orange print pants and a polo—a walking J. Crew ad.*
Richie: Laughing emoji
Me: *Don't worry, I know what you look like.*
Richie: *I bet you do.*

Fourteen minutes late for my debut, I check in with the hostess and mumble my brother's name, but then I see him. The white hair is unmistakable and so is his profile thanks to his work website. Already seated in the dining room, Richie has tucked his briefcase under the table, and his head bows over his phone. Perhaps, he's reading my text from a few minutes ago. He must sense my hurried steps, for as I approach, he stands. I'm struck by his height and his smile. It's as wide as mine and our teeth are blindingly similar. What an odd thing to share.

"Hi, Richie! Brother from another mother." I giggle like a nervous teen.

Smirking, he greets me, "Sister!" and then dwarfs me in a hug. "Let's sit."

Just like the day I met Shirley, there's no Kleenex, just belly butterflies and vibrant smiles.

"I'm so sorry to keep you waiting." He waves off my apology, and I say, "I didn't know you wore glasses. You look very professorial."

Richie smiles as he clears a smudge on a lens. "And indeed I am that. I teach an evening finance class at U of C."

When I quip back that my alma mater, Northwestern, often swaps places with University of Chicago as the number one B-School, it dawns on me that we're a family of teachers.

The waitress interrupts us impressing one another. "Can I get you a beverage before lunch?"

Before our cold drinks arrive, Richie's blue eyes study me. "I have to tell you. All of this has been quite a shock to me and Cynthia. Finding out you have not one, but two older sisters takes some getting used to. Of course, the connection to Palisades is incredible. All the Williams sisters are burning up the phone lines. Buzz says hello to Jeanne and Jack. He's beyond thrilled to be related to them by marriage."

Richie cleans his glasses again, and I twist my dinner napkin.

"Jeanne and Jack are happy, too. All along, Dad has been fine about me looking into my adoption, but Mom . . . not so much." I wave a hand in the air. "Knowing you and Audrey and the Williamses has changed all that. I haven't talked to Mom this much in months. I couldn't be more pleased . . . and relieved."

Richie's grin flashes. "You'll like this. My mom has taken to calling you and Jenny her stepdaughters."

My eyes bug out. "Really? That's awfully generous, since technically we aren't."

"That's Mom!" Richie chuckles and shakes his head.

"I'd love to meet her sometime."

I look down at my menu. My eyes fill. My adoption search has conditioned me to expect less, not more. I'm more familiar with people fending me off or squirreling me away than I am with being accepted and welcomed.

When I look up, Richie says, "Shall we order before the waitress comes back for the third time?"

Before our Caesar salads arrive, Richie quizzes me about my adoption search. I repeat what I told him three days ago about my breast biopsy and wanting my medical history. I elaborate on my failed search efforts and how we landed on the confidential intermediary program.

"Are you in touch with your birth mother?" Richie asks.

"Yes. I found her a few years ago. Like your dad, she didn't initially want contact, but she changed her mind." I offer him a weak smile.

"My father—excuse me, 'our' father—was quite surprised. He never knew your mother had twins, or what happened to her." Richie drains his club soda, and the corners of his mouth inch up. "It's good for me, by the way, that he and Shirley didn't get hitched up."

I chuckle at his dry humor. "Yes. Good for you and good for me. You're my only biological brother. Shirley never had any other children."

In between bites of salad and sips of iced tea, we discuss his Aunt Frances, her breast cancer, and the Chippewa Indian in our heritage. I share my amazement at receiving the genealogist's fax with Dick's college football photo, and his astounding likeness to my son, Danny.

Richie pushes his plate away and studies me. "Your research certainly has been thorough. With all of that, why do you need a DNA test?"

Grateful for this cue, I tell him. "The name Shirley gave me was Dick Thomson. Not Thomlinson. The intermediary I told you about spent a year tracking down every Dick Thomson that fit the bill. When the judge dismissed my case, I lucked into a genealogist who figured this all out."

"Why would your birth mom give you the wrong name?"

Prickling at Richie's insinuation that her error was deliberate, I say, "I don't know how much you know about birth mothers, but often they don't remember much of the details surrounding the trauma of placing their child for adoption. I assume that Shirley mangled Dick's last name because of that." I look over at Richie. "A DNA test will verify that Dick is indeed my birth dad, and that you and Cynthia are my siblings." Pushing away the salad I've barely touched, I go on. "If we're related, it will mean my doctor will order testing for the breast cancer gene."

I avoid Richie's gaze for fear I'll cry. With Dick's rejection, my request for DNA has landed on my new brother's shoulders. We both look up at the waitress as she sets the check down.

Richie drums his fingers on the bill. "I'm sorry about my dad. I think he thought you were after money or something, but that's not the case." He sighs. "I'm sorry that I said on Tuesday that Cynthia was uncertain about all this. She's softened. Mostly because my wife, Audrey, is proclaiming how wonderful the Ryan family is." We grin at one another, loving how Palisades is the thread that united us.

When Richie whips out his credit card, I protest. "Let a guy take a sister to lunch."

He looks up from signing the bill, and his mouth is fixed in that familiar smile, but his eyes are serious. My breath hitches.

"I'll be happy to do the DNA test. Set it up. Again, I'm sorry about my dad. He won't do it."

"That would be amazing. Thank you. Thank you." I squeeze his hand, and then bring my napkin to my eyes.

Richie looks at his watch and pushes out of his chair. "Sorry. I have to go meet Buzz at the train." Once more, his face is serious. "Let's meet up with Jenny. And Dan. And Steve. Let's figure out how to make that happen. Can you work out the details with Audrey?"

When I nod, he kisses my cheek. "I'm sorry that you had to find me this way. I hope we pass the DNA test. I'd be honored to have you and Jenny as sisters."

In return for Richie's repeated kindness, I offer him the only thing I have to give—my brightest smile. It's funny—when someone gives you a gift you were desperate to have, "thank you" doesn't seem to capture the supreme joy filling the empty spaces in your heart. In spite of my reluctant birth father, my new siblings have entered my life. Richie's willingness to undergo DNA testing will not only help hone my health risks, it will shove the stubborn, remaining pieces of my personal story into place.

Ten days later, I meet Richie in a gravel lot near a suburban strip mall. I park my Buick next to his Volvo, and then we check in for our lab appointment. Sitting in stiff office chairs, we gawk at one another as if surprised to find ourselves here. He's in khakis and a casual shirt, and I'm in a summer dress and flats. We trade shy glances and vacillate between grins and giggles.

"Can you believe we're doing this?" Richie booms to the room. I shake my head at him.

The lab technician arranges prepackaged sterile swabs for our DNA testing. One look at the swabs, which are larger than Q-tips, and I joke about gag reflexes.

"Exactly," Richie says, laughing.

"You're a good sport. I'm so grateful. I hope we pass." Holding up my crossed fingers, I give him a wistful smile.

"Oh, we will. I have no doubt."

As the technician places Richie's damp swab into the testing container, he grins. "Let's have lunch after this?"

"Sure. Lunch and DNA. They go together."

My sarcasm does little to ease the somersaults in my gut. The technician packages up our tests with the lab order and stacks it in an outgoing bin. Picking up my purse, I follow Richie to the door, but then I stop and turn back.

There it is over there. The truth. It's as near as my next breath.

"Richie's house should be right up there. On the next corner." Steve drives to where I point. "He said to park anywhere on the street."

"There's your sister's car." Steve pulls in behind Jenny's sedan, and I crane my neck up at the house.

In front of Richie's home, a woman with short, sandy hair wearing a stylish black dress and ballet flats exits the passenger side of a car. At the front door, she balances a foil-covered tray and struggles with the doorknob. Slightly built, she's about my height.

"That must be Cynthia," I say, my voice soft with wonder.

Steve's big smile reassures me. "Are you ready?"

I'm every bit as nervous to meet Cynthia today as I was to meet Richie. I reach for the salad, the one I promised Audrey I'd bring. Steve's fingers find my elbow as we trudge toward the attractive stone house. Audrey and Richie Thomlinson's home.

I shake my head in wonder. Today's summer supper would not have made the calendar if my DNA hadn't aligned with Richie's. When the lab report was emailed last week, I stared at it for a good minute before clicking on it.

"It's here," I'd yelled to Steve.

Scanning through the details, I zeroed in on the bottom line: 98 percent—nearly a perfect match! I'd closed my eyes and slumped in the desk chair—the waiting was over.

I'm a Thomlinson!

I didn't have to deliberate long on who to call next, because Richie's number lit up my cell. "Hello, Sistah!"

I'd giggled. "Hello, brother from another mother. Even with the margin of error, there isn't much doubt."

The pride I felt in not just passing the test, but knocking it out of the park, was enormous. It filled my chest, my world.

Before I could ask if this improved my chances of meeting Dick, Richie barreled on. "Sounds like we need to celebrate. Audrey wants to host all of you for dinner. You, Jenny and the hubbies. At our house. Cynthia and Ed will come, and Buzz, of course. Why don't you check with Jeanne and Jack, and I'll see if my mom is up for it, too. The more the merrier."

I'd called Jenny right after that. "We passed!"

She'd chuckled. "Was there ever any doubt? You worked hard to figure this all out, Jules. We were due a big break. I'm still grinning about the Palisades connection."

"Me, too." I fill her in on Richie's dinner idea. "Since Audrey's invited her dad, Richie says to ask Mom and Dad. What do you think?"

Silence. "Well . . . Jules. It's not how I envisioned meeting Cynthia or her husband for the first time, but if Buzz is going to be there, I guess we need to include Mom and Dad."

"That's what I thought, too."

As Steve and I approach the front door, Richie waves to us from the other side like a crazy teenager. His silly antics make my stomach hurt, shaking loose some of the angst I've been carrying around.

"Come in. Come in. Audrey's in the kitchen whipping up a feast." His blue eyes blaze at me. "With your new sister, Cynthia. Your old sister, Jenny, is in the living room with Dan, your parents, and Buzz. It's like old home week in there. Jack and Buzz are talking about boardwalks and lake levels and parking egress, and no one can hear each other because their hearing aids aren't turned up high enough. So it's really loud. My girls are wandering around here somewhere, too."

Richie yells up the stairs for my nieces, Maddie and Mia. Laughing at all the chaos, I relax. I feel right at home in Richie's house, for it reminds me of my home when our family comes together.

"I'm going to take the salad to the kitchen." My eyes brighten at Steve. "And meet Cynthia."

Steve whispers in my ear, "Here comes your mom."

My shoulders tense, but I paste a smile on my lips. "Hi, Mom. Are you and Dad having fun catching up with Buzz?"

Mom glows. "Yes. This is such a treat seeing Richie and Audrey and Buzz again. The last time I saw all of them was Labor Day, almost two years ago. Before we sold the cottage." She stifles a frown. "Can I help you with that dish?"

I tell her no, that I'll be right in to say hello to Dad and Buzz, and I turn toward the kitchen. I mean for her to return to the party, not follow me, but my mother says she'd like to come and meet Cynthia, too. My heart sinks. I'm going to meet my new sister for the first time, and my mom will be looking over my shoulder. That's not what I wanted.

Steve gives me a look. A glance that means more than "good luck" meeting your new sister. He's reminding me. For years, my mom has put herself squarely on the wrong side of my adoption search, and now she's making significant strides to fix that rift.

Stifling a huge sigh, I wander into the kitchen with my mother on my heels like one of the collies. Mom leans against the kitchen counter as Audrey introduces me to Cynthia. My mother lurks behind me like a shy younger sister, content to watch and not say a word. As if I have eyes in the back of my head, I see her comparing me to Cynthia. She's studying our profiles, our lips, our eyes, our hair, our figures, and I suppose she's wondering what it feels like to meet your sister for the first time. Surely, she can tell that this moment is like sending me to the moon and back. Mom would know this—she is my mother, after all.

"Cynthia, this is my mom."

I grab Mom's hand, pull her over to me, and slide my arm up around her shoulders.

"It's nice to meet you, Cynthia."

Mom looks at my new sister and then up at me. Love is in her eyes, and also etched into her gently lined face is pride. My mom escapes from under my arm and reaches for Cynthia's hand.

Mom's brown eyes glitter, as she takes Cynthia's hand in both of hers. "Welcome to the family."

Audrey shoos us off to the living room where appetizers and drinks and photo albums are being passed from Jenny and Dan to Buzz and Dad. Richie and Ed pass out drinks and cocktail napkins to Mom and me. The room is so loud with chatter that you'd think we'd been gathering like this for years.

Leaning over Dad's chair, I wrap my arms around his shoulders and kiss him. "Are you having fun?"

Dad grins up at me and pats my cheek like he used to do when I was a young girl saying my good-nights. I linger over him as he finishes his story.

"I was telling Buzz that when I met Richie, I never would have guessed that his new son-in-law was secretly my relative, too."

Buzz's blue eyes have the same delighted gleam as Dad's. "It's just astounding, Jack. Isn't it wonderful to have good news to share?" Buzz's throaty laugh fills the room.

When Audrey calls us in from the living room for dinner, she says, "Please everyone, sit wherever you'd like."

Jenny snickers as Richie puts Buzz and Dad next to him at the far end. "Oh, that's trouble. There's going to be nothing but jokes and ribbing coming from that end of the table." Everyone chuckles, but no one tries to bust up the trio.

Audrey takes the chair at the opposite end of the table from Richie and winks at him. As we mill around toward open seats, we ooh and aah at how lovely the table looks and how delicious the food smells. At the center of the table is a huge platter of salmon and scattered about are bowls of salads and steaming side dishes, candles and more candles. In all shapes and sizes, the candles flicker, competing with the stars emerging in the summer's night sky.

I scoot around to the other side of the table and settle into a chair next to Richie. Across from me, Jenny slides in between Cynthia and her husband, Ed, and when I look up, my mother is getting comfortable in the seat next to me. Over her shoulder, Steve and Dan pull out chairs near Audrey. Elbow to elbow, our cheerful faces glow. I study everyone. My family. New and old. Such a fabulous coming together, yet I can't help but notice who's missing—my birth parents, the two people who unknowingly launched this happenstance over fifty years ago.

Audrey taps her water glass with a spoon and nods at Buzz. "Daddy, would you please do us the honor of saying grace?"

Buzz's blue eyes question hers. "Shall we hold hands?"

Audrey beams at him. "If you'd like us to, then we will."

Richie reaches for my right hand, squeezes it for a second, and then my mother's warm palm slides into my other hand.

Audrey's dad clears his throat, and we bow our heads.

"Lord, we praise you for the magnificent food that you have bestowed upon us tonight, for the continued health of all of us gathered here, and for the love and friendship that joins all of us here as family. God bless you all!"

We cheer. "Hear, hear, Buzz! Well done."

When the plates of food begin traveling around the table, I

catch Jenny's eye. She winks and grins broader than I've ever seen her smile. I wink back and we hold each other's gaze. Our look acknowledges the incredible journey we undertook to get to this moment, a moment neither of us expected or could have predicted. Mom notices the looks flying between Jenny and me, and her hand caresses my back. As Cynthia passes a dish to Jenny, her eyes move from Jenny to me and then over to Richie. She opens her mouth as if to say something, but Richie grabs our attention with a clink of his glass.

"Yes, very nice job, Buzz. I have something to add. Bravo for DNA tests, which proved that Cynthia and I won the lottery and gained two new sisters! To the Ryan twins from Palisades. Raise your glasses, all!"

"To new siblings. To family," I say as I clink my glass with the others.

As I look around the table again, my face is bright. I count my blessings for all the efforts that culminated in this moment, and I give wings to the lingering hope in my heart: let my circle of family continue to widen.

Epilogue

◥◆◤

Before the celebratory dinner in Richie and Audrey's home, Jenny and I had met with our new brother and sister-in-law at a local bistro. With Richie sandwiched between Jenny and me, our spouses angled their cameras this way and that while curious diners looked on. Richie's under-the-breath comments forced giggly grins from Jenny and me. Audrey proclaimed the Thomlinson smile as our most obvious commonality, but a similar fair and freckly complexion poked out from under our necklines and shirtsleeves, too. Ecstatic to share our first meal as Thomlinson siblings, the evening culminated with us poring over Richie and Audrey's wedding album.

Audrey couldn't flip fast enough for me to the photos of my birth dad. Until that instant, the only images I'd seen of Dick Thomlinson were the faxed copies Sandy had unearthed from institutional archives. Witnessing my adoptive parents in the same frame with my birth father during the wedding at Palisades Park felt like a practical joke. The stunning sequence of events—Richie, my unknown half brother, marrying Audrey, the girl-from-the-cottage-next-door, while my adoptive parents and birth dad looked on together—was surreal. It had the feel of a fictional Hollywood plot rather than the hard facts of a true story.

After that mind-blowing summer evening when I first met my sister, Cynthia, Richie and Audrey hosted another important family meal. When I walked up to the Thomlinsons' front door, this time with a brunch dish in my hands, the same set of nerves and anticipation as before coursed through my body. Richie was again the official greeter, but now his mother stood next to him. She welcomed Jenny and me with a warm hug and light banter about her pleasure in having two new stepdaughters. Her easy acceptance and willingness to include us has been one of the most precious outcomes in our reunion with the Thomlinson family.

Cynthia and Ed have also hosted the Thomlinson siblings for numerous dinners in their home and in Chicago. I'm continually touched by their efforts to include my mother, Jeanne, and any of my kids who happen to be in town. A particular favorite event of mine is the annual holiday tea that Cynthia organizes—it's a festive and intimate way to kick off the Christmas season with my new family.

For several winters now, Steve and I have enjoyed skiing with Richie and Audrey and their girls in Montana, the site of my "aha moment"—the New Year's resolution that spurred hiring Sandy the genealogist. In addition to the many milestones we've already celebrated together—birthdays, engagements, and weddings—the Thomlinson and Ryan joint calendars continue to fill. Soon, Richie will add "minister" to his resume when he presides over the marriage of Jenny's son to a young woman whose parents Richie just happens to know from his high school days.

Once my adoptive mother, Jeanne, processed our link to the Williams family, her rigid attitude toward my adoption search softened. She stunned me with an offer to write Shirley a letter, a copy of which she willingly shared with me. In two handwritten paragraphs, Mom thanked Shirley for the gift of two cherished daughters. Shirley returned the note of gratitude with her own—she praised my parents for rearing such intelligent, accomplished, and moral people. While this was a one-and-done effort, the contact between my two mothers was more than I ever expected. My parents' friendship with the Williams family may have contributed to my mother's coming around, but I'd like to think that a deciding factor was the delight Mom observed in me on the afternoon I met Cynthia.

After gifting us with the birthday boxes on the first birthday we celebrated with her, Shirley began to expand the circle of "who knows." Jenny and I were thrilled with Shirley's invitation to meet her youngest brother and sister at their family dairy farm in Wisconsin. After a full day of touring the highlights of Shirley's life, we closed out the evening in the kitchen of the farmhouse. Over Folgers and gooey, chocolate desserts, Jenny and I were privy to more tales from Shirley's upbringing. It was warm in that kitchen, cozy and close. It felt familiar—as if Jenny and I had come home after having been away too long. It wasn't just that our aunt and uncle were welcoming. No, it was more than that—we felt like we belonged. The visit to the farm was not just an introduction to family, it was a homecoming. Jenny and I still speak reverently of that day.

Since the day at the farm, Shirley began the arduous process of informing her remaining siblings about her unwed pregnancy and our return into her life. Scattered throughout the country, there remain a handful of aunts and uncles I have yet to connect with. Recently, I linked up with two of my first cousins through one of the genetic genealogy sites. When they visited Chicago, Jenny and I joined them for breakfast. It was great fun, and a framed photo of the four of us nestles near my computer. Ironically, the café we chose was in full view of St. Vincent's, the orphanage from which Jenny and I began our life as the Ryan twins.

After we discovered that Richie's DNA matched with mine, I met with Dr. Stanley to discuss Dick Thomlinson's family health. Because of Aunt Frances's early bout with breast cancer and the incidence of the disease on Shirley's side, Dr. Stanley ordered further gene testing. For Jenny and me, the three weeks of waiting were interminable. We learned we do not carry the breast cancer gene, and our risk of developing it is slightly greater than the general population. Heartened by this upbeat prognosis, I no longer see that unwelcome and chilling second shadow—breast cancer.

At the end of that first summer of getting to know Richie and Cynthia, my most trusted confidante and mother-in-law, Mary Lou McGue, fell ill. She died shortly after Labor Day. Losing her was a deep loss. Not only had she cheered and cried with me during the many upticks and pitfalls of my adoption search, Mary Lou had been a consistent and revered figure in the lives of my four children, her only grandchildren. A writer herself, Mary Lou encouraged me to keep journals and notes throughout my adoption search. "You have to write this one day. It's too good a story not to put out there in the world." Her influence is imbedded in every chapter.

In the weeks that followed my mother-in-law's death, my reunion with Shirley hit a speed bump. Both Linda, my intermediary, and Lisa, the social worker at Catholic Charities, had warned me this was inevitable, but over the first years of getting acquainted, we'd been spared. Once Shirley learned that I'd found my birth father and two half siblings, she confessed to giving me the wrong last name for Dick. She informed me that she had lied to keep him from reentering her life, accused me of meddling in her private business, and was infuriated that I'd gone around her to find him. Devastated that Shirley could lie to me even though I'd apprised her of the importance of assembling my complete health history, I feared that our reunion had abruptly ended.

With our relationship in jeopardy, I had time to wonder what it was that happened so long ago that made Shirley assume such an adversarial position. Was it Dick's rejection of her? Had the traumas of the unwed pregnancy, giving birth to twins, and suffering the secret emptiness afterward left a permanent mark on her? Had my insistence on resurrecting the truths of my birth circumstances opened up those wounds again? Whatever it was that had transpired between my birth parents, Shirley was scarred. I know that she was well within her rights to keep me from prying into that. My disagreement with her is at the core of closed adoption: the "right to privacy" versus the "right to know." This battle continues to be waged in many states, and it affects families on both sides of the equation.

Since that fall day when Shirley and I faced off about my birth dad, we've learned to listen better to each other, and our desire to be present in each other's lives remains strong. Equally strong is my conviction that either individual therapy or group counseling is vital in order to heal from the trauma of adoption's many losses. Though my attendance is irregular now, I continue to benefit from Lisa's post-adoption support group at Catholic Charities. If both of my mothers could have sought expert advice as we climbed through the uncomfortable stages of my adoption search, perhaps some of the hurt and misunderstanding we experienced might have been avoided.

I'm still in touch with Linda, my intermediary and esteemed search angel. Shortly after my case closed with her office, Jenny and I were asked to join the board at the Midwest Adoption Center. We were the first clients to assume roles on the board. While no longer serving MAC in that manner, I continue to be a huge advocate for the work that MAC does—assisting adoptees and those in the foster care system to connect with their past. As for Sandy, the genealogist who unearthed the most difficult secret of all, she is also still involved in our lives. Having completed extensive research on both sides of my family tree, she is currently working on my husband's genealogy.

The weekend that followed my first phone conversation with Richie, Kassie graduated from high school. Four years later, at Kassie's college graduation, I received another call from Richie.

Dick Thomlinson had suffered a fatal heart attack. Despite all the pleadings and discussions with my birth dad, Richie was unable to convince him to talk or meet with Jenny and me. Dick's last comment to Richie on the topic was, "It's too complicated." While it's hurtful to be an unacknowledged offspring, as Linda pointed out, he was well within his rights to do so. Dick Thomlinson must have had his own memories and reasons, just as Shirley had hers. We will never know what went on between them, moments lost to history between two people who did everything they could to put it behind them.

While I regret that I never met my birth father, I was blessed with an amazing dad. Jack Ryan was kind and funny, honest and generous, intelligent and a devout Catholic. When you were in Dad's company, he made you feel as if you were the most important person in the room. The unwavering support he provided me during my adoption searches equaled my mother-in-law's efforts. Dad passed away in September 2017, the day after he and my mom celebrated their sixty-fourth wedding anniversary. At Dad's funeral, Jenny and I shared the podium for his eulogy. In the course of his long and fruitful life, he'd provided us with a wealth of hilarious and dear memories with which to celebrate him. In thinking about my father, I believe that Mom's words sum it up best: "He was a good man, and I miss him every day."

Richie and Audrey's family still own the Williams's cottage in Palisades Park, Michigan, but Audrey's dad, Buzz, died of old age in the fall of 2019. I like to think that Buzz and Jack are up there in heaven entertaining my god—the one with the sense of humor who connected Richie with me on a beautiful spring day in 2014—with their very best jokes and antics. Perhaps Buzz and Jack include Dick Thomlinson in their circle of fun. That wouldn't shock me. Nothing surprises me anymore.

As a result of my adoption search journey, made easier with

Jenny by my side, I have come to believe that all of us are connected in some mysterious way. If we wish, we have the gifts to unravel our past and make sense of our present existence. As we chisel away at the mystery, we find life frustrating and fascinating, disappointing and rewarding. And nothing short of astounding.

Thank you . . .

To my parents, my mom and dad, and my birth mother: each of you are "real" to me. One of you gave me life, and the other gave me *a* life.

To my immediate family for your love and support, especially in the days when there was nothing to do except listen, pray, and watch me sniffle and reach for a tissue: Steve, Colleen, Molly, Danny, Kassie, Jonathan, Sean, Jenny, Dan, Christie, Bob, Howie, Carmen, Patrick, Lisa, Elizabeth, John, and most especially, Mary Lou.

To my new family for welcoming me as you have: you know who you are!

To the team that unlocked the secrets and the people that have offered invaluable information, solace and cheers along the way: Linda Fiore, Sandy Thalmann, Lisa Holmes-Francis, Ray, "the History Cop," Nancy Golden at the Midwest Adoption Center, and my fellow adoptees and the birth parents who share with me regularly at the Catholic Charities post-adoption support group. And to Judge Aurelia Pucinski for humanizing the intermediary process.

To Catholic Charities for maintaining an adoption policy that kept twin girls together in 1959.

To the people who influenced how this book took form: Linda Joy Myers and Brooke Warner—Write Your Memoir in Six Months,

Sara Connell, Samantha Strom, and the staff at She Writes Press. An especially big thanks to my writing coach and mentor, Linda Joy Myers. Without her diligent and able stewardship, this manuscript might still be lingering in half-finished form. Much gratitude to my publicity team led by Marissa DeCuir at BooksForward.

To my friends who listened and laughed and cajoled as this incredible story unfurled: Sue, Diane P., Michelle, Nancy, Georgia, Cynthia, Mary Jo, Kate, Carol, Kathy, Donna, Anne, JoAnne, Judy, Joni, Diane C., Peggy, Siobhan, Patty, Sheila, Cathy, Elizabeth, Karen, Amy, Ann, Linda S., Linda R., Diane K., Dick and Teri, Linda and Jim, and my inspirational furry friends, Emmett and Nellie. Thanks for your active support.

To my writing teachers at University of Chicago–The Writer's Studio, Creative Nonfiction, and Gotham Writer's Workshop for impacting my most recent writing journey. Heartfelt appreciation goes to my early writing teachers, Ken Kane and Tim White, who taught me to read with discernment and write more than the page would hold.

About the Author

Credit: Mary Lou Johnson Photography

Julie Ryan McGue was born in Chicago, Illinois. She is a domestic adoptee and an identical twin. She received her BA from Indiana University in Psychology in 1981. She earned an MM in Marketing from the Kellogg Graduate School of Business, Northwestern University in 1984. *Twice a Daughter: A Search for Identity, Family, and Belonging* is her first book.

Married for over thirty-five years, Julie and her husband split their time between Northwest Indiana and Sarasota, Florida. She is the mother of four adult children. Her grandsons call her Lulu.

Julie is currently working on a collection of personal essays and a novel about a search angel who handles adoption and foster care search and reunion.

AUTHOR WEBSITE AND SOCIAL MEDIA HANDLES:
Author website: www.juliemcgueauthor.com
Facebook: www.facebook.com/juliemcguewrites
Twitter: @juliermcgue
Instagram: @juliemcgue
LinkedIn: www.linkedin.com/in/julie-mcgue-a246b841

271

SELECTED TITLES FROM SHE WRITES PRESS

She Writes Press is an independent publishing company
founded to serve women writers everywhere.
Visit us at www.shewritespress.com.

The Beauty of What Remains: Family Lost, Family Found by Susan Johnson Hadler. $16.95, 978-1-63152-007-5. Susan Johnson Hadler goes on a quest to find out who the missing people in her family were—and what happened to them—and succeeds in reuniting a family shattered for four generations.

The Butterfly Groove: A Mother's Mystery, A Daughter's Journey by Jessica Barraco. $16.95, 978-1-63152-800-2. In an attempt to solve the mystery of her deceased mother's life, Jessica Barraco retraces the older woman's steps nearly forty years earlier—and finds herself along the way.

Don't Call Me Mother: A Daughter's Journey from Abandonment to Forgiveness by Linda Joy Myers. $16.95, 978-1-93831-402-5. Linda Joy Myers's story of how she transcended the prisons of her childhood by seeking—and offering—forgiveness for her family's sins.

A Different Kind of Same: A Memoir by Kelley Clink. $16.95, 978-1-63152-999-3. Several years before Kelley Clink's brother hanged himself, she attempted suicide by overdose. In the aftermath of his death, she traces the evolution of both their illnesses, and wonders: If he couldn't make it, what hope is there for her?

Motherlines: Letters of Love, Longing, and Liberation by Patricia Reis. $16.95, 978-1-63152-121-8. In her midlife search for meaning, and longing for maternal connection, Patricia Reis encounters uncommon women who inspire her journey and discovers an unlikely confidante in her aunt, a free-spirited Franciscan nun.

Patchwork: A Memoir of Love and Loss by Mary Jo Doig. $16.95, 978-1-63152-449-3. Part mystery and part inspirational memoir, *Patchwork* chronicles the riveting healing journey of one woman who, following the death of a relative, has a flashback that opens a dark passageway back to her childhood and the horrific secrets that have long been buried deep inside her psyche.